Collins

QUIZ NIGHT

HarperCollins Publishers
Westerhill Road
Bishopbriggs
Glasgow
G64 2QT

First Edition 2012

Reprint 10 9 8 7 6 5 4 3 2 1 0

© HarperCollins Publishers 2012

ISBN 978-0-00-747998-6

Collins® is a registered trademark of
HarperCollins Publishers Limited

www.collinslanguage.com

A catalogue record for this book is
available from the British Library

Typeset by Davidson Publishing
Solutions, Glasgow

Printed in Great Britain by Clays Ltd,
St Ives plc

Acknowledgements
We would like to thank those authors
and publishers who kindly gave
permission for copyright material
to be used in the Collins Corpus.
We would also like to thank Times
Newspapers Ltd for providing
valuable data.

Entered words that we have reason to
believe constitute trademarks have
been designated as such. However,
neither the presence nor absence of
such designation should be regarded
as affecting the legal status of any
trademark.

HarperCollins does not warrant
that www.collinsdictionary.com,
www.collinslanguage.com or any
other website mentioned in this title
will be provided uninterrupted, that
any website will be error free, that
defects will be corrected, or that the
website or the server that makes it
available are free of viruses or bugs.
For full terms and conditions please
refer to the site terms provided on the
website.

AUTHOR
Chris Bradshaw

EDITOR
Gerry Breslin
Freddy Chick

FOR THE PUBLISHER
Lucy Cooper
Julianna Dunn
Kerry Ferguson
Elaine Higgleton

Introduction

What draws us so strongly to quizzes? What is the secret to quizzical attraction? No one can say for sure. All we know is that when the time comes, it can be pretty hard to resist getting a quiz going.

When we look through the annals of 'quizstory' we can see how often quizzes have cropped up. There was Alfred at the Battle of Hastings, who was distracted by one of his Dukes asking him a multiple choice question just as the arrow hit. Then there was Hannibal who only marched his elephants across the Alps so that he could retrospectively win a pub quiz where the tie-breaker question had been 'Has anyone ever marched elephants across the Alps?'. Mao Zedong cheered up the gang on the Long March with the longest continuous string of general knowledge questions in history. The point is that when the mood is right, there's just no stopping the urge to start popping questions.

Collins Quiz Night is here to satisfy your quizzing needs, whenever and wherever they happen to arise. It would be great to have with you if you were stuck in a lift, or during a long wait at the doctor's, or perhaps at a campsite. If they don't sound likely situations to you, then it is perfect for an evening in with family and friends.

The quizzes

Half of the quizzes are themed. All the classics are covered: animal quizzes, movie quizzes, written word, sport, soap opera and history quizzes. Astronomy and space are covered. So too is food and drink, and the human body. Everything you could want really. The other half of the quizzes are pot luck rounds, because you can never have enough of these.

The quizzes are grouped together according to how tricky they are. First come the easy ones, then medium and finally the difficult quizzes.

Easy
The easy questions should not have you scratching your head for very long. If they do, you need to wonder if there's anything inside it. A few of them are trickier than others and might even be labelled as 'challenging' by some judges. These have been included to add the frisson of mental sweat to an easy round.

Medium
These are the heartland of a great quiz. To the quiz fanatic they'll be a delightful amuse-bouche before the main course of the difficult questions. To the rest of us they'll be a veritable feast of brain-teasers, mind-bogglers and head-scratchers.

Difficult
These questions are tricky. Tricky, tricky, tricky. Tricky as the fifth entry in an alphabetical list of skateboard stunts: trick E. Anyone who gets all of these questions right you should immediately suspect of cheating. Ask to see their smartphone's browser history and be ready for a nasty showdown. You might not want to throw too many of this level into your quiz, but they are great for spicing things up or as tie-breaker questions.

The answers
The answers to each quiz are printed at the end of the following quiz. For example, the answers to Quiz 1-Art and Architecture appear at the bottom of Quiz 2-Pot Luck. The exception to this rule is the last quiz in every level. The answers to these quizzes appear at the end of the very first quiz in the level.

Running a quiz
Collins Quiz Night is only half-finished. (Wait! Don't demand a

refund yet, read on!) People don't go to the theatre to sit and read a script. Likewise, the quizzes in this book need someone to read them out. That's you.

If you're just quizzing your family during a car journey, or your mates of an afternoon, then there's probably no need to put in lots of preparation. If you're planning on using this book to run a more organized and formal quiz however, there are a few things you need to get right before you start:

❖ Rehearse: don't just pick this book up and read out the questions cold. Go through all the quizzes you're going to use by yourself beforehand. Note down all the questions (notes look better in a quiz environment than reading from a book) and answers. Although every effort has been made to ensure that all the answers in *Collins Quiz Night* are correct, despite our best endeavours, mistakes may still appear. If you see an answer you are not sure is right, or if you think there is more than one possible answer, then check.

❖ Paper and writing implements: do yourself a favour and prepare enough sheets of paper for everyone to write on. The aim of the game here is to stop the mad impulse certain people feel to 'help'. They will spend ten minutes running around looking for 'scrap' paper, probably ripping up your latest novel in the process. The same problem applies to pens. Ideally, have enough for everyone. Remember, though, that over half of them will be lost forever once you've given them out.

❖ Prizes: everyone likes a prize. No matter how small, it's best to have one on offer.

Good luck! We hope you enjoy *Collins Quiz Night*.

Contents

Easy Quizzes

Medium Quizzes

Difficult Quizzes

EASY QUIZZES

Quiz 1: Art and Architecture

EASY

1. Which graffiti artist is famous for his stencilled images?

2. Which sculptor created The Angel of the North?

3. Architect, designer and painter Charles Rennie Mackintosh is most commonly associated with which British city?

4. Who designed St Paul's Cathedral in London?

5. What famous London building would you find at 30 St Mary Axe?

6. Who painted the Mona Lisa?

7. Which painter was famous for his matchstick-like men and women?

8. Which Norwegian artist painted The Scream?

9. In which British city would you find the Liver Building?

10. Which sculptors works include The Kiss and The Thinker?

11. Andy Warhol was a leading figure in which art movement?

12. Which actress starred in the 2002 biopic about Mexican painter Frida Kahlo?

13. In what sort of building would you find a nave, chancel and altar?

14. Cantilever, swing and suspension are examples of what type of construction?

15. A Bigger Picture was a 2012 exhibition at the National Gallery featuring the works of which Yorkshire-born painter?

16. Whose unmade bed was shortlisted for the 1999 Turner Prize?

17. Who painted the ceiling of the Cistine Chapel?

18. Which British artist is famous for preserving animals in formaldehyde?

19. A skilled European painter who worked before the 19th century is said to be an old
    a) master
    b) craftsman
    c) artisan

20. In 1911, Vincenzo Perrugia stole which famous painting?
    a) Sunflowers
    b) The Mona Lisa
    c) The Laughing Cavalier

Answers to Quiz 68: Pot Luck

1.	Screwdriver	11.	Ukulele
2.	Mermaid	12.	The Star Spangled Banner
3.	Midas	13.	Spain
4.	Katrina	14.	Coventry
5.	4th July	15.	Outdoors (in the air)
6.	Jim Davidson	16.	Kosher
7.	Rugby World Cup	17.	Palindrome
8.	Watergate	18.	Chicago
9.	Oxford	19.	Hung parliament
10.	Eat it	20.	Big Bang

Quiz 2: Pot Luck

1. In computing, what are JPEGs, GIFs and TIFs?

2. The Booker Prize is awarded in which field of the arts?

3. In June 1963, Valentina Tereshkova became the first woman to do what?

4. What is measured using the Beaufort scale?

5. Sarajevo is the capital city of which country?

6. Alec Guinness and Ewan McGregor have both played which character on film?

7. In Dad's Army, what was Captain Mainwaring's first name?

8. What colour are the cheapest squares in the board game Monopoly?

9. A golden jubilee is celebrated after how many years?

10. Someone born on 1st October would have what star sign?

11. In which TV quiz show would you hear the phrase 'I've started so I'll finish'?

12. Which country singer was known as The Man In Black?

13. Polytheism is the belief that there is more than one what?

14. Marshall Mathers III is the real name of which rapper?

15. What does a philatelist collect?

16. Conchiglie, fusili and penne are types of what food?

17. Somebody admitting to a humiliating mistake is said to eat what sort of pie?

18. Rhodesia was the former name of which African country?

19. What is a stevedore more commonly known as?
    a) miner
    b) docker
    c) driver

20. Before joining the euro, what was the currency of Spain?
    a) drachma
    b) escudo
    c) peseta

Answers to Quiz 1: Art and Architecture

1. Banksy
2. Anthony Gormley
3. Glasgow
4. Sir Christopher Wren
5. The Gherkin
6. Leonardo da Vinci
7. LS Lowry
8. Edvard Munch
9. Liverpool
10. Rodin

11. Pop Art
12. Salma Hayek
13. A church
14. Bridges
15. David Hockney
16. Tracey Emin
17. Michelangelo
18. Damien Hirst
19. Master
20. The Mona Lisa

Quiz 3: Astronomy and Space

1. Which planet is closest to the sun?

2. Who was the first man in space?

3. What is the largest planet in the solar system?

4. What was the name of the US Space Shuttle that exploded 72 seconds after take off in Jan 1986?

5. On 18 March 1965 Alexey Leonov was the first person to do what in space?

6. What constellation is also known as The Hunter?

7. Keck I & II, Kepler and Hobby-Eberly are examples of what type of instrument?

8. What was the name of the first artificial satellite to enter the earth's orbit?

9. Who was the first Briton to go into space?

10. What planet was downgraded to a dwarf planet in 2006?

11. Also the name of a popular Spanish beer, what is the outermost layer of the sun called?

12. Which Greek god gave his name to the American manned space programme?

13. Who was the first man to walk on the moon?

14. What does the acronym NASA stand for?

15. Which planet is named after the messenger of the gods?

16. What are astronauts called in Russia?

EASY

17. What is the constellation Crux Australis more commonly known as?

18. What is the only planet not named after a Greek or Roman god?

19. The GPS system is operated by which organisation?
a) The UN
b) the US Department of Defense
c) The Foreign Office

20. Which of the following planets does not have rings?
a) Mars
b) Neptune
c) Saturn

Answers to Quiz 2: Pot Luck

1. Images
2. Literature
3. Go into space
4. Wind
5. Bosnia and Herzegovina
6. Obi Wan Kenobi
7. George
8. Brown
9. 50
10. Libra
11. Mastermind
12. Johnny Cash
13. God
14. Eminem
15. Stamps
16. Pasta
17. Humble pie
18. Zimbabwe
19. Docker
20. Peseta

Quiz 4: Pot Luck

1. Land of our Fathers is the national anthem of which country?

2. Which came first, the stone age or the bronze age?

3. Web addresses ending .nl are from which country?

4. The Sugar Hut is a nightclub in which reality TV show?

5. What word represents G in the International Radio Alphabet?

6. Prague is the capital city of which country?

7. The poisonous death cap is a variety of which vegetable?

8. Which newspaper launched a Sunday edition in February 2012?

9. In which Scottish city would you find the Royal Mile?

10. What herb is the central ingredient of the sauce pesto?

11. Which English king abdicated in 1936?

12. 'Don't go in the water' is the tagline to which classic film?

13. What was the policy of racial segregation in South Africa from 1948 until 1992?

14. What instrument is used to measure atmospheric pressure?

15. X Factor judge Kelly Rowland was a member of which group?

16. The Dalai Lama is the spiritual leader of which religion?

17. Wild Wood was a best-selling album by which male singer?

18. Which US state is known as the Golden State?

19. On a film set, what is the name of the mobile platform that enables a camera to move during a shot?
    a) colly
    b) dolly
    c) molly

20. What sort of town did The Specials sing about in 1981?
    a) Ghost Town
    b) Party Town
    c) Glory Town

EASY

Answers to Quiz 3: Astronomy and Space

1. Mercury
2. Yuri Gagarin
3. Jupiter
4. Challenger
5. A space walk
6. Orion
7. Telescopes
8. Sputnik I
9. Helen Sharman
10. Pluto
11. Corona
12. Apollo
13. Neil Armstrong
14. National Aeronautics and Space Administration
15. Mercury
16. Cosmonauts
17. Southern Cross
18. Earth
19. The US Department of Defense
20. Mars

Quiz 5: Fashion

1. Manolo Blahnik is a famous designer of what article of clothing?

2. A burqa is worn by women of which religion?

3. The presenters of which BBC TV programme included Jeff Banks, Caryn Franklin and Brenda Emmanus?

4. Which London Street is famous for its tailors?

5. Which fashion designer invented the mini skirt?

6. Ralph Lifshitz is the real name of which fashion designer?

7. What do Australians call flip flops?

8. On a clothes care label, what does a circle inside a square mean?

9. A kimono is a traditional costume in which country?

10. Who invented denim jeans?

11. What type of dancer would usually wear a tutu?
    a) ballet dancer
    b) flamenco dancer
    c) ballroom dancer

12. Often worn by comedian Tommy Cooper, what name is given to a red, rimless felt hat with a tassel?

13. In America they call them suspenders but what are they known as in Britain?

14. Which British fashion designer was sacked by Dior in 2011 after being found guilty of making anti-Semitic comments?

15. A coiffeur is another name for what?

16. In fashion, what do the initials DKNY stand for?

17. Fashion designer Issey Miyake is from which Asian country?

18. Which British designer committed suicide in April 2010?

19. A ruff is usually worn around what part of the body?
    a) waist
    b) neck
    c) ankle

20. What is the first name of fashion designer Versace?
    a) Davina
    b) Donatella
    c) Dominga

Answers to Quiz 4: Pot Luck

1. Wales
2. Stone Age
3. Netherlands
4. The Only Way Is Essex
5. Golf
6. Czech Republic
7. Mushroom
8. The Sun
9. Edinburgh
10. Basil
11. Edward VIII
12. Jaws
13. Apartheid
14. Barometer
15. Destiny's Child
16. Buddhism
17. Paul Weller
18. California
19. Dolly
20. Ghost Town

Quiz 6: Pot Luck

1. Salt Lake City is the capital of which US state?

2. Who was the idiot in the TV series An Idiot Abroad?

3. The Koran is the holy book of which religion?

4. Which countries make up Benelux?

5. What national daily newspaper is published on pink paper?

6. In the song The 12 Days of Christmas, how many maids were a-milking?

7. A fawn is the young of what animal?

8. Which country has won the Eurovision Song Contest the most times?

9. According to the proverb, what is paved with good intentions?

10. The tango originated in which South American country?

11. Ding Dong the Witch is Dead is a song from which film musical?

12. How many strings are there on a violin?

13. What name is given to the number that is above the line in a fraction?

14. Gallophobia is the fear of things associated with which country?

15. Bishop of Rome and Primate of Italy are other names for which religious leader?

16. What was Coldplay's debut album?

17. Who played Frodo Baggins in The Lord of the Rings films?

18. In American currency, how much is a dime worth?

19. What are the two ends of a magnet called?
    a) shoals
    b) poles
    c) roles

20. Which composer wrote The Planets suite?
    a) Britten
    b) Holst
    c) Vaughan Williams

Answers to Quiz 5: Fashion

1. Shoes
2. Islam
3. The Clothes Show
4. Savile Row
5. Mary Quant
6. Ralph Lauren
7. Thongs
8. Suitable for tumble drying
9. Japan
10. Levi Strauss
11. Ballet dancer
12. Fez
13. Braces
14. John Galliano
15. Hairdresser
16. Donna Karan New York
17. Japan
18. Alexander McQueen
19. Neck
20. Donatella

Quiz 7: Food and Drink

1. Meat, vegetables and potato leftovers combined and reheated is bubble and what?

2. Chapati, naan and roti are all types of what?

3. What is the main ingredient in guacamole?

4. What beans are added to tomato sauce to make baked beans?

5. Maris Piper and King Edward are varieties of which vegetable?

6. Which part of Germany gives its name to a famous gateau?

7. Mozzarella cheese was originally made using the milk from which animal?

8. Tabasco sauce takes its name from a region in which country?

9. What fruit is the main ingredient in cider?

10. What vegetable is also known as ladies' fingers?

11. Feta cheese comes from which country?

12. What is Welsh Rarebit more commonly known as?

13. Sushi is a type of cuisine from which country?

14. Venison is the meat of which animal?

15. Pilau, basmati and long grain are varieties of what?

16. Kedgeree is usually eaten at what time of the day?

17. What meat is traditionally used when cooking a Wellington?

18. Distilled juniper berries are used to make which spirit?

19. What is kulfi? a) fruit b) vegetable c) ice cream

20. Cullen skink is a traditional soup from which country?
    a) Ireland
    b) Scotland
    c) Wales

EASY

Answers to Quiz 6: Pot Luck

1. Utah
2. Karl Pilkington
3. Islam
4. Belgium, Netherlands and Luxembourg
5. Financial Times
6. Eight
7. Deer
8. Ireland
9. The road to hell
10. Argentina
11. The Wizard of Oz
12. Four
13. Numerator
14. France
15. The Pope
16. Parachutes
17. Elijah Wood
18. 10 cents
19. Poles
20. Gustav Holst

Quiz 8: Pot Luck

1. What does a florist deal in?

2. Kabul is the capital city of which country?

3. What is missing from a Manx cat?

4. A stetson is a type of what?

5. What does a cooper make?

6. What sign of the zodiac is represented by twins?

7. Excluding Greenland, what is the biggest island in Europe?

8. What was the name of the department store in the TV comedy Are You Being Served?

9. Guinevere was the wife of which legendary king?

10. A polygraph is another name for what?

11. Justin Timberlake was a member of which boy band?

12. What is the name of the pub in TV soap Emmerdale?

13. Which family lives at 742 Evergreen Terrace?

14. What is the name of Postman Pat's cat?

15. Ted Bovis, Spike Dixon and Jeffrey Fairbrother were characters in which TV sitcom?

16. What spirit takes its name from the German word for snap?

17. Which branch of the military is known as the senior service?

18. Teriyaki is a style of cooking from which country?

19. In what year was the Great Fire of London?
    a) 1566
    b) 1666
    c) 1766

20. Where is the Black Country?
    a) England
    b) Germany
    c) Wales

EASY

Answers to Quiz 7: Food and Drink

1. Squeak
2. Bread
3. Avocado
4. Haricot beans
5. Potato
6. Black Forest
7. Buffalo
8. Mexico
9. Apples
10. Okra

11. Greece
12. Cheese on toast
13. Japan
14. Deer
15. Rice
16. Breakfast
17. Beef
18. Gin
19. Ice cream
20. Scotland

Quiz 9: Geography

1. What is the largest continent on earth?

2. What was the Indian city of Mumbai formerly known as?

3. Ibiza, Majorca, Menorca, Formentera and Cabrera collectively make up which Spanish island group?

4. What is the highest mountain in the world?

5. The most westerly point of mainland Europe is in which country?

6. The River Nile lies on which continent?

7. Which Scottish loch is said to be home to a mysterious monster?

8. The Rocky Mountains are located in which two countries?

9. Nippon is another name for which Asian country?

10. The city of Nottingham lies on which river?

11. What is the largest canyon in the world?

12. The Isle of Man lies in which body of water?

13. Which of the Channel Islands is the largest?

14. What is the highest mountain in Great Britain?

15. Helsinki is the capital city of which country?

16. Stoke-on-Trent is in which English county?

17. Mont Blanc is the highest mountain in which range?

18. The Urals are in which country?

19. Which of the following is a river in Dorset?
    a) Diddle
    b) Piddle
    c) Widdle

20. A Kentish man is one born on which side of the
    Medway River?
    a) west
    b) east

Answers to Quiz 8: Pot Luck

1. Flowers	11. N Sync
2. Afghanistan	12. The Woolpack
3. Tail	13. The Simpsons
4. Hat	14. Jess
5. Barrels	15. Hi-De-Hi
6. Gemini	16. Schnapps
7. Great Britain	17. Royal Navy
8. Grace Brothers	18. Japan
9. King Arthur	19. 1666
10. Lie detector	20. England

Quiz 10: Pot Luck

1. On what form of transport would you find a plimsoll line?

2. According to the rhyme, what does seeing two magpies signify?

3. On what date do Americans celebrate Independence Day?

4. Jimmy Choo is famous for designing what type of clothing?

5. Caledonia was the Roman name for which country?

6. What is the currency of Denmark?

7. The assassination of which person sparked the First World War?

8. Sinology is the study of things from what country?

9. Which river flows easterly into the North Sea at Tilbury?

10. Teams from which two countries traditionally compete for the Ashes?

11. The Maghreb is a region of which continent?

12. Anthony Benedetto is the real name of which legendary crooner?

13. Bel Paese is a cheese from which country?

14. Holly Golightly enjoyed what at Tiffany's?

15. The Leicestershire town of Melton Mowbray is famous for what type of pie?

16. Who invented the ball point pen?

17. Lima is the capital city of which South American country?

18. What occupation do Trevor Sorbie, Charles Worthington and John Frieda share?

19. What is Leyton Orient's home ground?
    a) Brisbane Road
    b) Adelaide Road
    c) Melbourne Road

20. A mercer traditionally deals in what?
    a) textiles
    b) food
    c) metal

Answers to Quiz 9: Geography

1. Asia
2. Bombay
3. Balearics
4. Mount Everest
5. Portugal
6. Africa
7. Loch Ness
8. The USA and Canada
9. Japan
10. Trent
11. The Grand Canyon
12. The Irish Sea
13. Jersey
14. Ben Nevis
15. Finland
16. Staffordshire
17. The Alps
18. Russia
19. Piddle
20. West

Quiz 11: History

EASY

1. In what year did the Battle of Hastings take place?

2. Which war was fought by the houses of York and Lancaster?

3. Which American civil rights leader made the 'I have a dream' speech?

4. Which US president resigned from office in 1974?

5. The Entente Cordiale was a series of agreements between Britain and which country?

6. The Battle of the Somme was fought in which war?

7. Which French general described England as 'a nation of shopkeepers'?

8. Which king of England was known as the Unready?

9. Who did David Cameron succeed as British prime minister?

10. The folk hero William Tell was from which country?

11. Which English king was nicknamed Lionheart?

12. Which prime minister said, 'Most of our people have never had it so good'?

13. Who was British prime minister during the Falklands War?

14. Who was Queen Victoria's husband?

15. Which general led parliamentary forces to victory over the monarchists in the English Civil War?

16. Who led the plot to blow up Parliament in 1605?

17. Which Admiral said, 'England expects that every man will do his duty'?

18. Which 19th century Prime Minister gave his name to a type of tea?

19. The Peterloo Massacre took place in which city?
    a) Birmingham
    b) Liverpool
    c) Manchester

20. Who were the opponents of the Cavaliers in the English Civil War?
    a) roundheads
    b) squareheads
    c) coneheads

Answers to Quiz 10: Pot Luck

1. Ship
2. Joy
3. 4th July
4. Shoes
5. Scotland
6. Krone
7. Archduke Franz Ferdinand
8. China
9. Thames
10. England and Australia
11. Africa
12. Tony Bennett
13. Italy
14. Breakfast
15. Pork pie
16. Laszlo Biro
17. Peru
18. Hairdresser
19. Brisbane Road
20. Textiles

Quiz 12: Pot Luck

1. Niall Horan, Zayn Malik, Liam Payne, Harry Styles and Louis Tomlinson are members of which boy band?

2. Which comedian raised over £1m for Sport Relief by swimming the length of the River Thames?

3. Lupine describes something as having qualities like what animal?

4. Huey, Dewey and Louie are the nephews of which Disney character?

5. What was name of the cruise ship that ran aground off the Italian coast in January 2012?

6. In what year was the Act of Union between England and Scotland signed?

7. In what unit of measurement is gold traditionally weighed?

8. Opium is extracted from the juice of which plant?

9. After China and India, what is the third most populous country in the world?

10. What word connects animals such as monkeys and apes and a type of bishop?

11. Which actor's autobiography was called Re-minder?

12. What is the highest female singing voice?

13. Which naturalist sailed on a ship called The Beagle?

14. What is the largest democracy in the world?

15. Who co-starred alongside Steve Coogan in BBC comedy The Trip?

EASY

16. The Bangles and Atomic Kitten both topped the charts with what song?

17. The 1989 film Great Balls of Fire was based on the life of which rock 'n' roll legend?

18. Who is the eldest of Queen Elizabeth's children?

19. On which side of a ship is starboard?
    a) front
    b) left
    c) right

20. The River Cottage is the home of which chef?
    a) Hugh Fearnley-Whittingstall
    b) Jamie Oliver
    c) Rick Stein

Answers to Quiz 11: History

1. 1066
2. The War of the Roses
3. Martin Luther King
4. Richard Nixon
5. France
6. World War One
7. Napoleon
8. Aethelred
9. Gordon Brown
10. Switzerland
11. Richard I
12. Harold Macmillan
13. Margaret Thatcher
14. Prince Albert
15. Oliver Cromwell
16. Guy Fawkes
17. Admiral Horatio Nelson
18. Earl Grey
19. Manchester
20. Roundheads

Quiz 13: TV Comedies

EASY

1. What is the character Geraldine Grainger more commonly known as?

2. Who played Edina in Absolutely Fabulous?

3. Norman Stanley Fletcher was the main character in which classic sitcom?

4. Who did Rob Brydon play in Gavin and Stacey?

5. What is the name of the family in Outnumbered?

6. Frasier was a spin-off from what bar-based sitcom?

7. Who played Granville in Open All Hours?

8. Sheldon, Penny, Leonard, Howard and Raj are characters in which American sitcom?

9. Which three priests lived on Craggy Island?

10. Which curmudgeonly comedian starred in Lead Balloon?

11. What was the name of the coffee shop in Friends?

12. Who played Blackadder in the TV series of the same name?

13. Which wartime comedy was set in Walmington-on-Sea?

14. What British sitcom was set in a Peckham barber shop?

15. Which bespectacled comedian hosts Chatty Man?

16. The Office was set in which Berkshire town?

17. Who is the female presenter on The Ten O'Clock Show?

18. Home Truths, This is My..., and Ring of Truth are rounds in which comedy panel show?

19. In My Family, what is Ben's occupation?
    a) Dentist
    b) Doctor
    c) Driver

20. Complete the sitcom title: Mrs Brown's...?
    a) Boys
    b) Girls
    c) Friends

Answers to Quiz 12: Pot Luck

1. One Direction
2. David Walliams
3. Wolf
4. Donald Duck
5. Costa Concordia
6. 1707
7. Troy ounce
8. Poppy
9. USA
10. Primate
11. Dennis Waterman
12. Soprano
13. Charles Darwin
14. India
15. Rob Brydon
16. Eternal Flame
17. Jerry Lee Lewis
18. Prince Charles
19. Right
20. Hugh Fearnley-Whittingstall

Quiz 14: Pot Luck

1. Caviar comes from the eggs of which fish?

2. Which football team play their home games at Molineux?

3. What does the acronym BAFTA stand for?

4. In the board game Monopoly, what colour are Trafalgar Square, Fleet St and Strand?

5. What sign of the zodiac is represented by a water carrier?

6. Stringer Bell, Jimmy McNulty and Omar Little are characters in which American TV show?

7. What is measured in decibels?

8. Scurvy is caused by a deficiency of which vitamin?

9. Kuala Lumpur is the capital city of which Asian country?

10. In Romeo and Juliet, who were the enemies of the Capulets?

11. A Novocastrian comes from which British city?

12. A hexagon has how many sides?

13. The River Isis flows through which English city?

14. What day precedes Good Friday?

15. What animal is used to describe a false lead or a misleading clue?

16. Long running radio serial The Archers is set in which village?

17. Who created the fictional detective Inspector Kurt Wallander?

18. Ananas is another name for which fruit?

19. How many deadly sins are there?

20. A gift of wood is usually given to celebrate which wedding anniversary?
    a) 3
    b) 5
    c) 7

21. In University Challenge, how many points is a starter question worth?
    a) 5
    b) 10
    c) 15

Answers to Quiz 13: TV Comedies

1. The Vicar of Dibley
2. Jennifer Saunders
3. Porridge
4. Uncle Bryn
5. The Brockmans
6. Cheers
7. David Jason
8. The Big Bang Theory
9. Fathers Ted, Dougal and Jack
10. Jack Dee
11. Central Perk
12. Rowan Atkinson
13. Dad's Army
14. Desmond's
15. Alan Carr
16. Slough
17. Lauren Laverne
18. Would I Lie To You?
19. Dentist
20. Boys

Quiz 15: Movies

1. Who played Gandalf in The Lord of the Rings trilogy?

2. What are Autobots and Decepticons?

3. Ingrid Bergman and Humphrey Bogart starred in which wartime classic?

4. What silent, black and white film won the BAFTA for Best Film in 2012?

5. Sacha Baron Cohen played a fictitious journalist from Kazakhstan in which 2006 film?

6. Who played George Smiley in the 2011 film version of Tinker, Tailor, Soldier, Spy?

7. What iconic movie landmark, standing 45ft tall and 350ft long, was erected in 1923 at a cost of $21,000?

8. What is the name of the boys' gang in Grease?

9. Which actor has Scotland Forever tattooed on his arm?

10. In Star Wars, what is the name of Han Solo's ship?

11. Who directed Raiders of the Lost Ark, Jaws and ET?

12. Who played King George V in The King's Speech?

13. Michael Keaton, George Clooney and Christian Bale have all played which caped crusader?

14. Tom Cruise played Maverick in which 80s classic?

15. Who played Sir Sidney Ruff-Diamond in Carry On Up The Khyber?

16. The Damned United was based on the life of which football manager?

17. What movie trilogy was based on a novel by Mario Puzo?

18. Which director's films included North By Northwest, Vertigo and Psycho?

19. What was the name of the 2011 film starring Ryan Gosling?
    a) Cycle
    b) Drive
    c) Fly

20. Complete the title of the Woody Allen film: Midnight In...?
    a) London
    b) Paris
    c) Rome

EASY

Answers to Quiz 14: Pot Luck

1. Sturgeon roe
2. Wolverhampton Wanderers
3. British Academy of Film and Television Arts
4. Red
5. Aquarius
6. The Wire
7. Noise
8. Vitamin C
9. Malaysia
10. Montagues
11. Newcastle
12. Six
13. Oxford
14. Maundy Thursday
15. Red herring
16. Ambridge
17. Henning Mankell
18. Pineapple
19. Seven
20. 5
21. 10

Quiz 16: Pot Luck

EASY

1. Tyke is a slang term for someone from which county?

2. The musical We Will Rock You is based on the music of which band?

3. Bratislava is the capital city of which country?

4. An email address ending in .ie is for people from which country?

5. Canines, molars, premolars and incisors are types of what?

6. Rossini wrote an opera about which Swiss hero?

7. Active, dormant and extinct are classifications of which geographical feature?

8. What illness is nicknamed the kissing disease?

9. In ballet, what term describes rapid spinning on the toe of one foot?

10. The wine-producing region of Rioja is in which country?

11. The clarinet is a member of which musical family?

12. What helicopter shares a name with a warm dry wind that blows in the Rocky Mountains?

13. How many years did Rip Van Winkle sleep for?

14. The Tet Offensive was a military operation in which conflict?

15. Hydrophobia is the fear of what?

16. What is the largest desert in the world?

17. A car registration sticker bearing the initials DK is from which country?

18. Which Northern Irish golfer won the 2011 US Open by an amazing 8 shots?

19. Oscar Wilde wrote the Ballad of which Gaol?
    a) Swindon
    b) Oxford
    c) Reading

20. What type of oranges are usually used to make marmalade?
    a) Malaga
    b) Madrid
    c) Seville

EASY

Answers to Quiz 15: Movies

1. Sir Ian McKellen
2. Transformers
3. Casablanca
4. The Artist
5. Borat
6. Gary Oldman
7. The Hollywood sign
8. The T Birds
9. Sean Connery
10. The Millennium Falcon
11. Steven Spielberg
12. Colin Firth
13. Batman
14. Top Gun
15. Sid James
16. Brian Clough
17. The Godfather
18. Alfred Hitchcock
19. Drive
20. Paris

Quiz 17: James Bond

1. Who was the first actor to play James Bond in a feature film?

2. How does Bond like his Martini?

3. In which film did 007 get married?

4. What rank does James Bond hold?

5. Which actress played Pussy Galore in Goldfinger?

6. Who is Bond's boss?

7. The character James Bond was created by which author?

8. Which actor's one and only appearance as 007 was in On Her Majesty's Secret Service?

9. Complete the title: The Man With The Golden...?

10. Who sang the theme tune to Goldfinger, Diamonds Are Forever and Moonraker?

11. Timothy Dalton played 007 in The Living Daylights and what other Bond film?

12. Which Oscar-winning actress played Jinx Johnson in Die Another Day?

13. Richard Kiel played which Bond baddie?

14. Which actor first played Bond in Live and Let Die?

15. What is the name of Bond's counterpart from the CIA?

16. Which Welshman sang the theme to Thunderball?

17. Daniel Craig made his debut as Bond in which film?

EASY

18. Which Bond villain appeared in From Russia With Love, Thunderball, You Only Live Twice, On Her Majesty's Secret Service, Diamonds Are Forever and For Your Eyes Only?

19. James Bond works for which organisation?
    a) MI5
    b) MI6
    c) Special Branch

20. Which actor has played Bond in the most films?
    a) Sean Connery
    b) Roger Moore
    c) Pierce Brosnan

Answers to Quiz 16: Pot Luck

1. Yorkshire
2. Queen
3. Slovakia
4. Republic of Ireland
5. Teeth
6. William Tell
7. Volcano
8. Glandular fever
9. Pirouette
10. Spain
11. Woodwind
12. Chinook
13. 20
14. The Vietnam War
15. Water
16. Sahara Desert
17. Denmark
18. Rory McIlroy
19. Reading
20. Seville

Quiz 18: Pot Luck

1. In Internet dating, what does GSOH stand for?

2. Thor was the Norse god of what?

3. The Motown record label originated in which American city?

4. Damascus is the capital city of which Middle Eastern country?

5. On a London Underground map, what colour is the District Line?

6. Complete the title of the 2012 film: Salmon Fishing in the...?

7. A silver jubilee is celebrated after how many years?

8. Ceylon is the former name of which Asian country?

9. A yarmulke is worn by practitioners of what religion?

10. Nucky Thompson is the main character in which prohibition era TV drama?

11. What type of dish is gazpacho?

12. What name is given to someone who stuffs animals?

13. What sign of the zodiac is represented by a fish?

14. The wine claret comes from which region of France?

15. Which cartoon character's catchphrase was 'Er, what's up doc?'?

16. Where would you find the Sea of Tranquility?

17. What is the name of the person who keeps the accounts on a ship or plane?

18. Proverbially, what shouldn't you look in the mouth?

19. In which ocean would you find the Falkland Islands?

20. In the TV sitcom Frasier, what was the name of Niles'
    unseen wife
    a) Lilith
    b) Rebecca
    c) Maris?

Answers to Quiz 17: James Bond

1. Sean Connery
2. Shaken, not stirred
3. On Her Majesty's Secret Service
4. Naval Commander
5. Honor Blackman
6. M
7. Ian Fleming
8. George Lazenby
9. Gun
10. Shirley Bassey
11. Licence To Kill
12. Halle Berry
13. Jaws
14. Roger Moore
15. Felix Leiter
16. Tom Jones
17. Casino Royale
18. Ernst Stavro Blofeld
19. MI6
20. Roger Moore

Quiz 19: Religion

1. The pope is the leader of which religion?

2. Who is the most senior cleric in the Church of England?

3. What is the Muslim month of fasting called?

4. In the Bible, Jesus turned water into what?

5. An imam is a prayer leader in which religion?

6. What is the first book of the Old Testament?

7. Shinto is a major religion of which Asian country?

8. What Christian religion was founded by John Wesley in 1738?

9. Brahma is one of the three central deities in which religion?

10. The Watchtower is the journal of which religion?

11. Who was the first human child born in the Bible?

12. In the Bible, how many gospels are there?

13. Yom Kippur and Rosh Hashanah are holy days in which religion?

14. The Church of England was formed after which monarch broke away from the Catholic Church?

15. What are members of the Society of Friends known as?

16. In the Bible, Judas betrayed Jesus for how many pieces of silver?

17. What are the four cardinal virtues?

18. What is the holiest city in Islam?

19. Which of the following is not the name of a pope?
    a) Innocent
    b) Sylvester
    c) Bartholomew

20. Which saint is believed to have been the first pope?
    a) St Paul
    b) St Peter
    c) St Pius

Answers to Quiz 18: Pot Luck

1. Good sense of humour
2. Thunder
3. Detroit
4. Syria
5. Green
6. Yemen
7. 25
8. Sri Lanka
9. Judaism
10. Boardwalk Empire
11. A cold soup
12. Taxidermist
13. Pisces
14. Bordeaux
15. Bugs Bunny
16. On the Moon
17. Purser
18. A gift horse
19. Atlantic
20. Maris

Quiz 20: Pot Luck

EASY

1. Between 1957 and 1960, which country had a 'Great Leap Forward'?

2. Sternum is another name for which bone?

3. Harry Beck created which iconic piece of London design?

4. The last edition of which Sunday newspaper was published on 10 July 2011?

5. Barn, horned and long eared are types of what bird?

6. The flute is in which family of musical instruments?

7. With what song did Abba win Eurovision?

8. Mossad is the intelligence service of which country?

9. Balthazar and Caspar were two of the Biblical three wise men. Who was the third?

10. Hypertension is another name for what?

11. What is the Oxford Committee for Famine Relief better known as?

12. What is the young of a kangaroo called?

13. According to the proverb, what cannot be made without breaking eggs?

14. Little Rock is the capital of which American state?

15. The Audacity of Hope was written by which US President?

16. Who was the Roman god of wine?

17. How many red balls are on the table at the start of a frame of snooker?

EASY

18. Which car manufacturer takes its name from the German for 'people's car'?

19. In The Muppet Show, what nationality was the chef?
    a) Danish
    b) Finnish
    c) Swedish

20. The musical instruction allegro means to play in what manner?
    a) quickly
    b) gently
    c) slowly

Answers to Quiz 19: Religion

1. Roman Catholicism
2. Archbishop of Canterbury
3. Ramadan
4. Wine
5. Islam
6. Genesis
7. Japan
8. Methodism
9. Hinduism
10. Jehovah's Witnesses
11. Cain
12. 4
13. Judaism
14. Henry VIII
15. Quakers
16. 30
17. Prudence, Justice, Temperance and Fortitude
18. Mecca
19. Bartholomew
20. St Peter

Quiz 21: Transport

EASY

1. In which English city would you find railway stations called New Street, Moor Street and Snow Hill?

2. At 408 miles long, where is the largest underground railway in the world?

3. What unit describes a speed of one nautical mile per hour?

4. What colour is Thomas the Tank Engine?

5. What is the name of the anonymous test driver on TV's Top Gear?

6. SNCF is the national railway of which country?

7. Concorde was co-produced by which two countries?

8. What was the name of 2011 thriller starring Jake Gyllenhaal set on a Chicago commuter train?

9. Liverpool Airport is named after which Beatle?

10. In motoring, what do the initials MoT stand for?

11. The Titanic set sail from which port on its maiden voyage?

12. What does supersonic mean?

13. The Spirit of Ecstasy hood ornament adorns what make of car?

14. Aer Lingus is an airline from which country?

15. Eurostar trains from London depart from which station?

16. What is the kitchen on a ship called?

17. Which major British airport was formerly known as Ringway?

EASY

18. What time did Gladys Knight and the Pips get a train to Georgia in their 1976 hit?

19. Who built the first steam locomotive?
    a) Richard Trescothick
    b) Richard Trevithick
    c) Richard Trewick

20. What is the back end of a ship called?
    a) bow
    b) starboard
    c) stern

Answers to Quiz 20: Pot Luck

1. China
2. Breastbone
3. London Underground map
4. The News of the World
5. Owl
6. Woodwind
7. Waterloo
8. Israel
9. Melchior
10. High blood pressure
11. Oxfam
12. Joey
13. An omelette
14. Arkansas
15. Barack Obama
16. Bacchus
17. 15
18. Volkswagen
19. Swedish
20. Quickly

Quiz 22: Pot Luck

1. Which footballer launched his own range of underwear in February 2012?

2. Which Sex and the City actress was born in Liverpool?

3. What is the longest river solely in England?

4. The Everglades are in which American state?

5. In what decade was the Korean War?

6. Zucchini is another word for which vegetable?

7. Mothra, Megalon and Biollante have all battled against which movie monster?

8. Which artist has had the most UK number one hit singles?

9. Bernard Woolley and Sir Humphrey Appleby were characters in which political comedy?

10. A craniometer is used to measure what part of the body?

11. Gary Lightbody is the lead singer with which band?

12. In which part of London do the Wombles live?

13. The Charge of the Light Brigade took place in which war?

14. Haggis is a dish associated with which country?

15. Which countries make up Great Britain?

16. In darts, how much do you get for hitting the bullseye?

17. In January 2011, Chelsea spent £50m on which Spanish footballer?

18. Which EastEnder won Dancing On Ice in 2011?

19. Cryptography is the study of what?
    a) codes
    b) graveyards
    c) vampires

20. What beer was banned from the House of Commons in February 2012?
    a) Luscious Ale
    b) Top Totty
    c) Saucy Sup

Answers to Quiz 21: Transport

1. Birmingham
2. London
3. Knot
4. Blue
5. The Stig
6. France
7. Britain and France
8. Source Code
9. John Lennon
10. Ministry of Transport
11. Southampton
12. Faster than the speed of sound
13. Rolls Royce
14. Ireland
15. St Pancras
16. Galley
17. Manchester
18. Midnight
19. Richard Trevithick
20. Stern

Quiz 23: Pop Music

EASY

1. What was the name of the Christmas number 1 single by the Military Wives?

2. Which Poker Faced artist's debut album was called The Fame?

3. Which reality TV star's second album was called The Gift?

4. Who went Bonkers alongside Armand van Helden in May 2009?

5. Who recorded hit albums called 19 and 21?

6. What was Robbie Williams' first UK number one single?

7. Don't Cha was a 2005 hit for which girl group?

8. Which member of Girls Aloud had a hit with Messy Little Raindrops?

9. Mika had a 2007 number one hit singing about which actress?

10. Viva La Vida or Death And All His Friends was by which band?

11. Who topped the charts in 2011 with a song called Price Tag?

12. Who Kissed A Girl (and liked it) in 2008?

13. Kevin Rowland was the lead singer with which group?

14. What was the name of Bob Marley's backing band?

15. According to a 2000 hit by Ronan Keating, Life Is A what?

16. Whitney Houston's chart topping I Will Always Love You was recorded for which film?

17. Arctic Monkeys, Pulp and the Human League are from which city?

18. Which Spice Girl famously wore a Union Jack dress?

19. In 2004, what did the Kaiser Chiefs predict?
    a) A Victory
    b) A Fortune
    c) A Riot

20. What sort of day did U2 enjoy in 2000?
    a) Beautiful
    b) Brilliant
    c) Fantastic

Answers to Quiz 22: Pot Luck

1. David Beckham
2. Kim Cattrall
3. Thames
4. Florida
5. 1950s
6. Courgette
7. Godzilla
8. Elvis Presley
9. Yes, Minister (and Yes, Prime Minister)
10. The skull
11. Snow Patrol
12. Wimbledon
13. Crimean War
14. Scotland
15. England, Scotland and Wales
16. 50
17. Fernando Torres
18. Sam Attwater
19. Codes
20. Top Totty

Quiz 24: Pot Luck

1. Londinium was the Roman name for which city?

2. Which Norwegian was the first man to reach the South Pole?

3. Chop suey is a dish common in which cuisine?

4. Yam Yam is slang for someone from which part of England?

5. The Battle of Britain was an aerial conflict in which war?

6. Java, Kenyan and Colombian are varieties of what drink?

7. Manila is the capital city of which country?

8. What is the Hebrew name for God?

9. What sign of the zodiac is represented by a ram?

10. Which X Factor runner-up went one better on Dancing On Ice?

11. EastEnders actress Laila Morse, aka Big Mo, is the sister of which Oscar-nominated actor?

12. Mistral, sirocco and etesian are types of what?

13. Which British singer won six awards at the 2012 Grammys?

14. Louis Reard was the creator of which classic beachwear?

15. Murrayfield is the home ground of which international rugby team?

16. Robert Alan Zimmerman is the real name of which musician?

17. The tart or pudding is synonymous with which Derbyshire town?

18. What is the smallest continent on earth?

19. A Member of Parliament who isn't a minister or shadow minister is
    a) a backbencher
    b) a crossbencher
    c) a frontbencher

20. Which of the following chess pieces cannot move diagonally?
    a) rook
    b) king
    c) bishop

Answers to Quiz 23: Pop Music

1. Wherever You Are
2. Lady Gaga
3. Susan Boyle
4. Dizzee Rascal
5. Adele
6. Millennium
7. The Pussycat Dolls
8. Cheryl Cole
9. Grace Kelly
10. Coldplay
11. Jessie J
12. Katy Perry
13. Dexy's Midnight Runners
14. The Wailers
15. Rollercoaster
16. The Bodyguard
17. Sheffield
18. Geri Halliwell
19. A Riot
20. Beautiful

Quiz 25: US Politics

EASY

1. In what month of the year do US presidential elections take place?

2. The donkey is the symbol of which US political party?

3. Which US President was killed by John Wilkes Booth?

4. Which US President appears on a $1 bill?

5. Which US political party is also known as the GOP?

6. The Great Society is associated with which US President?

7. What is President Obama's middle name?

8. Which US President was nicknamed the Comeback Kid?

9. What major speech is given by the US President every January?

10. Which US President wrote a book called Decision Points?

11. Who did Barack Obama beat to win the 2008 US Presidential election?

12. Who is the only US President to resign from office?

13. What is the name of the US President's official plane?

14. Who was the oldest President of the United States?

15. What is Barack Obama's wife called?

16. Anthony Hopkins and Frank Langella have both played which US President on film?

17. Camelot was the nickname of whose presidency?

EASY

18. What is the official residence of the President of the USA?

19. US presidential elections take place every
    a) 3 years
    b) 4 years
    c) 5 years?

20. What term was given to the advisers of President Andrew Jackson?
    a) drawing room cabinet
    b) kitchen cabinet
    c) dining room cabinet

Answers to Quiz 24: Pot Luck

1. London
2. Roald Amundsen
3. Chinese
4. The Black Country
5. World War Two
6. Coffee
7. The Philippines
8. Yahweh
9. Aries
10. Ray Quinn
11. Gary Oldman
12. Wind
13. Adele
14. Bikini
15. Scotland
16. Bob Dylan
17. Bakewell
18. Australia
19. Backbencher
20. Rook

Quiz 26: Pot Luck

EASY

1. Cirrus, nimbus and cumulus are types of what?

2. What is the only station on the Underground with London in its name?

3. Firenze is another name for which Italian city?

4. Sea parrot is another name for which bird?

5. The Soldier's Song is the national anthem of which country?

6. Which English county cricket team are nicknamed The Bears?

7. The Rio Grande river forms the boundary between Mexico and which US state?

8. What disease, found mostly in men, prevents blood from clotting?

9. Which came first, the iron age or the bronze age?

10. What is boat race cockney rhyming slang for?

11. Who was the Roman god of war?

12. Hibernia was the Roman name for which country?

13. Which Russian author wrote The Idiot and Crime and Punishment?

14. What name is given to a group of eight musicians?

15. What was the currency of The Netherlands before it joined the euro?

16. Which country duo had a 1983 hit with Islands in the Stream?

17. Who were Scooby Doo's two female companions?

18. What month comes in like a lion but goes out like a lamb?

19. Scandinavian popsters A-Ha are from which country?
    a) Denmark
    b) Norway
    c) Sweden

20. What is Lindisfarne also known as?
    a) Remote Island
    b) Holy Island
    c) Craggy Island

Answers to Quiz 25: US Politics

1. November
2. Democratic
3. Abraham Lincoln
4. George Washington
5. The Republican Party
6. Lyndon B Johnson
7. Hussein
8. Bill Clinton
9. The State of the Union
10. George W Bush
11. John McCain
12. Richard Nixon
13. Air Force One
14. Ronald Reagan
15. Michelle
16. Richard Nixon
17. John F Kennedy
18. The White House
19. 4 years
20. Kitchen cabinet

Quiz 27: Initials and Acronyms

EASY

1. What do the initials BBC stand for?

2. If somebody has gone AWOL what are they?

3. The NUT and NASUWT represent people working in what profession?

4. What does the acronym NATO stand for?

5. In publishing what do the initials ISBN stand for?

6. The SDLP and DUP are political parties in which part of the United Kingdom?

7. In law and order, what crime do the initials GBH represent?

8. The RSPB is a charity that protects which type of animal?

9. In politics, what do the initials MEP stand for?

10. What do the initials CCTV stand for?

11. Associated Dairies was the original name of which UK supermarket chain?

12. In athletics what does DNF mean?

13. In politics, which type of voting system is represented by the initials STV?

14. What do the initials YMCA stand for?

15. RTE is the national broadcaster in which country?

16. If somebody has received an ASBO what have they been given?

17. In motoring what do the initials AA stand for?

Answers – page 57

18. Cash machines are also known as ATMs but what does ATM stand for?

19. The UNHCR is the United Nations Commission for
    a) Religion
    b) Refugees
    c) Relics

20. RIBA stands for the Royal Institute of British
    a) Artisans
    b) Architects
    c) Actors

EASY

Answers to Quiz 26: Pot Luck

1. Clouds
2. London Bridge
3. Florence
4. Puffin
5. Republic of Ireland
6. Warwickshire
7. Texas
8. Haemophilia
9. Bronze Age
10. Face
11. Mars
12. Ireland
13. Fyodor Dostoevsky
14. Octet
15. Guilder
16. Kenny Rogers and Dolly Parton
17. Velma and Daphne
18. March
19. Norway
20. Holy Island

Quiz 28: Pot Luck

1. According to the proverb, what can't be made out of a sow's ear?

2. Voodoo originated from which Caribbean country?

3. Which archbishop was murdered in Canterbury Cathedral?

4. What word describes the point from the centre of a circle to the perimeter?

5. Nashville is the capital of which US state?

6. Which creepy family live at 1313 Mockingbird Lane?

7. Strictly Come Dancing professionals Vincent and Flavia were world champions at which dance?

8. In 1963, Gene Pitney was 24 hours from where?

9. Osama Bin Laden was killed at a compound in which Pakistani town?

10. In the Bible, which prophet baptised Jesus?

11. From what London station does the Hogwarts Express leave from in the Harry Potter books?

12. What Italian cooking term literally means 'to the tooth'?

13. The War of the Roses happened in which century?

14. What were names of the two gangs in West Side Story?

15. Which US state is known as the Sunshine State?

16. Jack Nicholson won his first Best Actor Oscar in 1975 for his performance in which film?

17. Cerys Matthews was the lead singer with which group?

18. Which British prime minister is associated with the policy of appeasement with Hitler?

19. Something that is acting with fox-like qualities is
    a) bovine
    b) porcine
    c) vulpine

20. What voting system is used in UK general elections?
    a) First past the post
    b) First to the vote
    c) First past the line

EASY

Answers to Quiz 27: Initials and Acronyms

1. British Broadcasting Corporation
2. Absent Without Official Leave
3. Teaching
4. North Atlantic Treaty Organisation
5. International Standard Book Number
6. Northern Ireland
7. Grievous Bodily Harm
8. Birds
9. Member of the European Parliament
10. Closed Circuit Television
11. ASDA
12. Did Not Finish
13. Single Transferable Vote
14. Young Men's Christian Association
15. Republic of Ireland
16. Anti Social Behaviour Order
17. Automobile Association
18. Automated Teller Machine
19. Refugees
20. Architects

Quiz 29: Natural World

1. What is the tallest animal in the world?

2. How many tentacles does an octopus have?

3. Most birds have how many toes?

4. What is a young swan called?

5. What is the fastest running bird in the world?

6. At which Pole would you find polar bears?

7. Hereford, Ayrshire and Aberdeen Angus are breeds of which animal?

8. What is the biggest land mammal by weight?

9. What animal lives in a drey?

10. What is the only bird that can swim but cannot fly?

11. What is a female fox called?

12. Angora, Manx and Siamese are breeds of which animal?

13. Canis familiaris is the Latin name for which animal?

14. An elver is the young of which animal?

15. What animal is the symbol for the World Wide Fund for Nature?

16. The kangaroo is the national symbol of which country?

17. What type of bird can be bearded, blue, crested, great, long-tailed, march, penduline and willow?

18. What is the crane fly more commonly known as?

19. What is the fastest land mammal?
    a) cheetah
    b) lion
    c) tiger

20. Where do ants live?
    a) colonies
    b) dominions
    c) commonwealths

Answers to Quiz 28: Pot Luck

1. A silk purse
2. Haiti
3. Thomas à Becket
4. Radius
5. Tennessee
6. The Munsters
7. Argentine Tango
8. Tulsa
9. Abbottabad
10. John the Baptist
11. King's Cross
12. Al dente
13. 15th
14. The Jets and The Sharks
15. Florida
16. One Flew Over The Cuckoo's Nest
17. Catatonia
18. Neville Chamberlain
19. Vulpine
20. First past the post

Quiz 30: Pot Luck

1. What is the name of the central family in TV drama Downton Abbey?

2. The ampere is used to measure what?

3. Bridgetown is the capital city of which Caribbean country?

4. Gene Wilder and Johnny Depp have both played which character from a famous children's film?

5. What is the most expensive square in the board game Monopoly?

6. What is the name of the pub in TV soap EastEnders?

7. What type of gift is traditionally associated with a 40th wedding anniversary?

8. Which English monarch was known as The Virgin Queen?

9. Origami is the Japanese art of what?

10. Curtis Jackson is the real name of which rapper?

11. What is wrapped around oysters in the dish Angels on Horseback?

12. What is the largest lake in England?

13. What sign of the zodiac is represented by a bull?

14. Tortillas, tacos and fajitas are common in which country's cuisine?

15. In what Olympic sport do teams have to move backwards to win?

16. Who played The Prisoner in the 1960s TV series of the same name?

EASY

17. Who is Emilio Estevez's famous father?

18. Who wrote Lady Chatterley's Lover?

19. What is the name of the protective leather trousers worn
by American cowboys?
a) chaps
b) guys
c) lads

20. What is the name for the courtyard in a castle?
a) bailey
b) daley
c) rayleigh

Answers to Quiz 29: Natural World

1. Giraffe
2. 8
3. Four
4. Cygnet
5. Ostrich
6. North Pole
7. Cattle
8. African elephant
9. Squirrel
10. Penguin
11. Vixen
12. Cat
13. Dog
14. Eel
15. Panda
16. Australia
17. Tit
18. Daddy Long Legs
(or yellowjacket)
19. Cheetah
20. Colonies

Quiz 31: Dogs

1.   What did a dog called Pickles famously discover in 1966?

2.   In Oliver Twist, who owned a dog called Bullseye?

3.   Which British politician has owned dogs called Ruby, Teddy, Offa, Lucy and most recently Sadie?

4.   What was the name of the dog in The Magic Roundabout?

5.   Which dictator owned a dog called Blondi?

6.   A dog called Nipper appears on the logo of which company?

7.   What is the name of Tintin's dog?

8.   A fox terrier called Laika was the first dog to do what?

9.   In cartoon strip Peanuts, what breed of dog is Snoopy?

10. What was the dog called in the Famous Five stories?

11. What was the name of Dorothy's dog in The Wizard of Oz?

12. Who directed the film Reservoir Dogs?

13. Bouncer the dog appeared in which TV soap?

14. In EastEnders what breed of dog was Roly?

15. What is Dennis the Menace's dog called?

16. What is the name of the three-headed dog that guarded the Philosopher's Stone in the Harry Potter books?

17. In the Wacky Races, Muttley was the canine companion of which villainous driver?

18. What was name of the dog in TV comedy Frasier?

19. What breed was Winston Churchill's dog, Rufus?
    a) Bulldog
    b) German Shepherd
    c) Poodle

20. Which Blue Peter presenter owned a dog called Goldie?
    a) Peter Purves
    b) John Noakes
    c) Simon Groom

Answers to Quiz 30: Pot Luck

1. Crawley
2. Electrical current
3. Barbados
4. Willy Wonka
5. Mayfair
6. The Queen Vic
7. Ruby
8. Elizabeth I
9. Paper folding
10. 50 Cent
11. Bacon
12. Lake Windermere
13. Taurus
14. Mexico
15. Rowing
16. Patrick McGoohan
17. Martin Sheen
18. DH Lawrence
19. Chaps
20. Bailey

Quiz 32: Pot Luck

EASY

1. Santiago is the capital city of which South American country?

2. Something cooked au beurre is cooked in which ingredient?

3. Americans call them pants but what are they called in Britain?

4. What type of curtain was said to divide East and West Europe during the Cold War?

5. Someone born on St George's Day would have what star sign?

6. Hosni Mubarak was the former president of which country?

7. Vine Street and Bow Street are two of the orange properties on a Monopoly board but what is the third?

8. Francis Scott Key wrote the words to which country's national anthem?

9. The yen is the currency of which country?

10. Cha is the Chinese word for which drink?

11. If a cockney invited you to a rub-a-dub-dub, where would you go?

12. The Tasman Sea is situated between which two countries?

13. Which comedian plays Chummy Brown in BBC drama Call The Midwife?

14. Bourbon comes from which state in America?

15. What are Opera, Chrome and Safari?

16. The Hawaiian Islands lie in which ocean?

EASY

17. Which Russian city was formerly known as Petrograd and Leningrad?

18. Which 16th French astrologer is famous for his prophecies?

19. Which river flows through Newcastle?
    a) Tees
    b) Tyne
    c) Wear

20. A biryani is a dish common in which type of cuisine?
    a) Chinese
    b) Indian
    c) Italian

Answers to Quiz 31: Dogs

1. The World Cup
2. Bill Sikes
3. David Blunkett
4. Dougal
5. Adolf Hitler
6. HMV (His Master's Voice)
7. Snowy
8. Go into space
9. Beagle
10. Timmy
11. Toto
12. Quentin Tarantino
13. Neighbours
14. Poodle
15. Gnasher
16. Fluffy
17. Dick Dastardly
18. Eddie
19. Poodle
20. Simon Groom

Quiz 33: Connections

1. Who was leader of the Monster Raving Loony Party from 1983 until 1999?

2. In the British Army, what rank comes after corporal?

3. According to Cyndi Lauper's 1984 hit who just want to have fun?

4. What famous mountain pass links Pakistan with Afghanistan?

5. Bactrian and Dromedary are types of what animal?

6. In Aussie Rules Football, what is awarded when the ball passes through the centre and outer posts?

7. What is the capital of the US state of Ohio?

8. Which artist painted The Hay Wain?

9. Tom O'Connor, Norman Pace and Greg Davies all had what occupation before finding fame as comedians?

10. Who served as US Vice President under George W Bush?

11. Which country won the cricket World Twenty 20 in 2010?

12. Which Brazilian-born actress was a regular sidekick of comedian Kenny Everett?

13. What is commonly said to be the world's second oldest profession?

14. What 1980 film starred Al Pacino as a detective searching for a serial killer who preyed on gay men?

15. What was the name of Minnie Riperton's only UK top 40 hit?

16. What is the English equivalent of the Spanish name Enrique?

17. What role was reintroduced into British hospitals in 2002 after a 30-year absence?

18. In the band the Village People, Randy Jones wore what costume? A) Cowboy b) Sailor c) Biker

19. Complete the Gregory Isaacs song covered by Simply Red in 1997: Night...?
A) Shade
b) mare
c) Nurse

20. What links the answers to the above questions?

EASY

Answers to Quiz 32: Pot Luck

1. Chile
2. Butter
3. Trousers
4. Iron Curtain
5. Taurus
6. Egypt
7. Marlborough Street
8. USA
9. Japan
10. Tea
11. The Pub

12. Australia and New Zealand
13. Miranda Hart
14. Kentucky
15. Internet web browsers
16. Pacific
17. St Petersburg
18. Nostradamus
19. Tyne
20. Indian

Quiz 34: Pot Luck

EASY

1. What name describes someone who doesn't believe in God?

2. Which group takes its name from the lead character in the Back To The Future films?

3. Anaplasty is the medical name for what type of surgery?

4. What is the only rock eaten by humans?

5. Dermatology is the medical study of what?

6. Sayonara means goodbye in which language?

7. Arachnophobia afflicts people afraid of what type of animal?

8. Which country singer had an Achy Breaky Heart in 1992?

9. Memoirs of an Unfit Mother was the title of which TV presenter's autobiography?

10. Which comedian hosts a chat show called Opinionated?

11. What is the text of an opera called?

12. Which dance troupe beat Susan Boyle in the final of Britain's Got Talent?

13. Which Irish county is also the name of a five-line nonsense poem?

14. Which fictional boxer is associated with the song Eye of the Tiger?

15. The Globe Theatre specialises in works by which playwright?

16. The musical Taboo was based on the life of which singer?

17. Which group won the Eurovision Song Contest with Making Your Mind Up?

18. Who was the Roman god of love?

19. What would you do with a balalaika?
    a) play it
    b) eat it
    c) wear it

20. Blackwall, Dartford and Rotherhithe are examples of what type of structure?
    a) bridges
    b) tunnels
    c) viaducts

Answers to Quiz 33: Connections

1. Screaming Lord Sutch
2. Sergeant
3. Girls
4. Khyber
5. Camel
6. A behind
7. Columbus
8. John Constable
9. Teacher
10. Dick Cheney
11. England
12. Cleo Rocos
13. Spying
14. Cruising
15. Loving You
16. Henry
17. Matron
18. Cowboy
19. Nurse
20. They all feature in the titles of Carry On Films

Quiz 35: Brothers and Sisters

EASY

1. Who starred alongside Arnold Schwarzenegger in the 1988 film Twins?

2. Which brothers founded the Guinness Book of Records?

3. Which Old Testament figure was sold into slavery by his 11 brothers?

4. Marilyn Monroe, Easy Terms and Shoes Upon The Table are songs from which long-running West End show?

5. Leonard, Arthur, Julius Henry, Milton and Herbert Manfred were the real first names of which brothers?

6. Brothers in Arms was a number one-selling album for which group?

7. Who played Sister Mary Clarence in the 1992 comedy Sister Act?

8. In Star Wars, who is Luke Skywalker's twin sister?

9. Who wrote and directed the films Dumb and Dumber, There's Something About Mary and The Heartbreak Kid?

10. What nationality are boxing's Klitschko brothers?

11. In The Simpsons, what are Ned Flanders' two sons called?

12. Automatic, Jump (For My Love) and I'm So Excited were hits for which sisters?

13. What was the last novel written by Fyodor Dostoevsky?

14. In the TV sitcom Frasier, what is the name of the psychiatrist's younger brother?

15. Which of the Minogue sisters appeared in Aussie TV soap Home and Away?

EASY

16. Who is the dictator of Oceania in George Orwell's novel 1984?

17. Which sisters topped the charts in 1987 with Respectable?

18. Which video game series is based on a pair of Italian-American plumbers?

19. What word describes the act of killing one's brother?
    a) patricide
    b) batricide
    c) fratricide

20. Which of the Gallagher brothers is older?
    a) Noel
    b) Liam

Answers to Quiz 34: Pot Luck

1. Atheist
2. McFly
3. Plastic surgery
4. Salt
5. The skin
6. Japanese
7. Spider
8. Billy Ray Cyrus
9. Anne Robinson
10. Frank Skinner
11. Libretto
12. Diversity
13. Limerick
14. Rocky
15. Shakespeare
16. Boy George
17. Bucks Fizz
18. Cupid
19. Play it
20. Tunnels

Quiz 36: Pot Luck

1. What is traditionally eaten on Shrove Tuesday?

2. Which film won the Oscar for Best Picture in 2011?

3. What part of the eye is responsible for controlling the size and diameter of the pupil?

4. According to the proverb, what does nature abhor?

5. What is the only digit that has the same number of letters as its value?

6. How many bones are there in an adult human body?

7. In cockney rhyming slang, what drink is Rosy Lee?

8. Stretching 4,500 miles, what is the longest mountain range in the world?

9. Anglia was the Roman name for which country?

10. Erich Weiss was the real name of which illusionist?

11. Blanche Du Bois is the central character in which play by Tennessee Williams?

12. Riyadh is the capital city of which country?

13. In 1980, the SAS rescued a group of hostages being held at the London embassy of which country?

14. A loiner is a slang term for someone from which English city?

15. Before joining the euro, what was the currency of Greece?

16. The Warren Commission was established to investigate the assassination of which politician?

EASY

17. What does the Latin term carpe diem mean?

18. Where does a funambulist like to walk?

19. Regicide is the killing of what sort of person?
    a) brother
    b) father
    c) king

20. What would you do with a croque monsieur?
    a) eat it
    b) play it
    c) wear it

Answers to Quiz 35: Brothers and Sisters

1. Danny DeVito
2. Ross and Norris McWhirter
3. Joseph
4. Blood Brothers
5. The Marx Brothers
6. Dire Straits
7. Whoopi Goldberg
8. Princess Leia Organa
9. The Farrelly Brothers
10. Ukrainian
11. Rod and Todd
12. The Pointer Sisters
13. The Brothers Karamazov
14. Niles
15. Dannii Minogue
16. Big Brother
17. Mel and Kim
18. Mario Brothers
19. Fratricide
20. Noel

Quiz 37: Written Word

1. Who wrote the novel One Day?

2. Stephanie Meyer wrote which quartet of vampire-inspired books?

3. Philip Pirrip is the central character in which novel by Charles Dickens?

4. A Tiny Bit Of Marvellous is a novel by which actress and comedian?

5. Oberon, Titania, Puck and Bottom appear in which of Shakespeare's plays?

6. Discworld features in the books written by which author?

7. Which Julian won the Booker Prize in 2011?

8. Who wrote The Girl With The Dragon Tattoo?

9. Detective Jack Reacher features in the novels of which author?

10. In the novel by Jules Verne, Phileas Fogg had how many days to get Around the World?

11. Which poet wrote The Love Song of J. Alfred Prufrock?

12. Ooh! What a Pair is the autobiography of which diminutive TV duo?

13. Nick Carraway is the narrator in which classic American novel?

14. Which reclusive author wrote The Catcher in the Rye?

15. Which magazine shares its name with a novel by WM Thackeray?

16. George Smiley appears in the novels of which spy writer?

17. Complete the title of the play: The Importance of Being...?

18. Badger, Mole, Toad and Water Rat are characters in which book?

19. Where is The Lord of the Rings trilogy set?
    a) Lower Earth
    b) Middle Earth
    c) Upper Earth

20. Who was the first Mr Man?
    a) Mr Strong
    b) Mr Happy
    c) Mr Tickle

Answers to Quiz 36: Pot Luck

1. Pancakes
2. The King's Speech
3. Iris
4. A vacuum
5. Four
6. 206
7. Tea
8. The Andes
9. England
10. Harry Houdini
11. A Streetcar Named Desire
12. Saudi Arabia
13. Iran
14. Leeds
15. Drachma
16. John F Kennedy
17. Seize the day
18. On a tightrope
19. King
20. Eat it

Quiz 38: Pot Luck

EASY

1. Timpani, bass and side are examples of what type of instrument?

2. Haymarket and Waverley are railway stations in which British city?

3. What is the highest rank in the British Army?

4. Denver is the capital of which US state?

5. Who founded the Boy Scout movement?

6. The zloty is the currency of which European country?

7. What is the second book of the Old Testament?

8. What is Joseph Ratzinger better known as?

9. According to the proverb, what is the mother of invention?

10. 2, 3, 5, 7, 11, 13 and 17 are examples of what type of number?

11. The hymn Abide With Me is traditionally sung at which sporting event?

12. What major conflict began on 25 June 1950?

13. Who wrote the Mr Men books?

14. The Roman city of Pompeii was destroyed after the eruption of which volcano?

15. In the Bible, who wrote the four Gospels?

16. What is the currency of India?

17. What is the fear of enclosed spaces more commonly known as?

18. Where does the Northern Ireland Assembly sit?

Answers – page 79

19. What is Bruce Springsteen's nickname?
    a) The Boss
    b) The Chief
    c) The Guvnor

20. What is the Rubella more commonly known as?
    a) Danish measles
    b) Belgian measles
    c) German measles

EASY

Answers to Quiz 37: Written Word

1. David Nicholls
2. Twilight
3. Great Expectations
4. Dawn French
5. A Midsummer Night's Dream
6. Terry Pratchett
7. Julian Barnes
8. Stieg Larsson
9. Lee Child
10. 80
11. TS Eliot
12. Ant and Dec
13. The Great Gatsby
14. JD Salinger
15. Vanity Fair
16. John Le Carré
17. Earnest
18. The Wind in the Willows
19. Middle Earth
20. Mr Tickle

Quiz 39: Children's TV

EASY

1. What are Bella, Fizz, Jake, Milo, Judy and Max better known as?

2. What was the name of Scooby-Doo's canine nephew?

3. In what town would you find characters called Sportacus, Stephanie and Robbie Rotten?

4. Professor Yaffle and Madeleine were characters in which children's TV programme?

5. Which children's TV show opened with the lines 'Here is a box, a musical box. Wound up and ready to play'?

6. Wilson, Brewster, Koko, Hoot, Toot and Piper are locomotives in which fictional town?

7. Which children's TV show featured Perkin, Posie and Pootle?

8. 'Can we fix it?' is the catchphrase of which animated handyman?

9. What was the name of the pink hippo in children's TV show Rainbow?

10. Where would you find Iggle Piggle, Upsy Daisy and Makka Pakka?

11. Who lived at 52 Festive Road?

12. Cut-throat Jake was the arch enemy of which fictional pirate?

13. Which Carry On star provided the voices in Willo the Wisp?

14. What are the first names of the Chuckle Brothers?

15. Complete the title of the Children's BBC programme: Sorry, I've Got No...?

EASY

16. Which unlikely superhero lived at 29 Acacia Road?

17. In Thunderbirds, who was Lady Penelope's driver?

18. Baron Silas Greenback was the arch nemesis of which animated superhero?

19. What is the name of the popular Children's BBC character?
    a) Mr Mumble
    b) Mr Rumble
    c) Mr Tumble

20. What was the name of Morph's slightly more aggressive sidekick?
    a) Chaz
    b) Chip
    c) Chuck

Answers to Quiz 38: Pot Luck

1. Drum
2. Edinburgh
3. Field Marshall
4. Colorado
5. Robert Baden-Powell
6. Poland
7. Exodus
8. Pope Benedict II
9. Necessity
10. Prime numbers
11. The FA Cup Final
12. Korean War
13. Roger Hargreaves
14. Vesuvius
15. Matthew, Mark, Luke and John
16. Rupee
17. Claustrophobia
18. Stormont
19. The Boss
20. German measles

Quiz 40: Pot Luck

1. What is the capital city of South Korea?

2. In spring 2001, Dennis Tito became the first tourist to travel where?

3. The BBBC is a governing body for which sport?

4. What is measured by the Celsius scale?

5. According to George Bernard Shaw, what is wasted on the young?

6. The Halle Orchestra is based in which city?

7. The Magellan Straits link which two oceans?

8. What tissue cord attaches a muscle to a bone?

9. Steveland Judkins is the real name of which soul singer?

10. A car registration sticker bearing the initials AUS is from which country?

11. In 1968, which British politician made the Rivers of Blood speech?

12. The beers Foster's, XXXX and Swan are from which country?

13. What English city did the Romans call Deva?

14. Pollo is the Italian word for what food?

15. The name of which district of London, famous for its Hindu temple, means Nose-shaped Hill?

16. Which river flows through New York City?

17. Bogota is the capital city of which country?

18. The song As Times Goes By is commonly associated with which classic wartime film?

19. In what decade did the American Civil War take place?
    a) 1840s
    b) 1850s
    c) 1860s

20. In what type of restaurant would you eat a calzone?
    a) Chinese
    b) Indian
    c) Italian

Answers to Quiz 39: Children's TV

1. The Tweenies
2. Scrappy-Doo
3. Lazytown
4. Bagpuss
5. Camberwick Green
6. Chuggington
7. The Flumps
8. Bob The Builder
9. George
10. In The Night Garden
11. Mr Benn
12. Captain Pugwash
13. Kenneth Williams
14. Barry and Paul
15. Head
16. Bananaman
17. Parker
18. Danger Mouse
19. Mr Tumble
20. Chaz

Quiz 41: Days of the Week

1. What is the last day before the start of Lent?

2. Which football club's name includes a day of the week?

3. According to a 1974 Elton John song, Saturday Night Is Alright for what?

4. In 1968, The Small Faces enjoyed what type of Sunday afternoon?

5. According to the folk rhyme, which child is fair of face?

6. In 1979, which group had a number one hit with Sunday Girl?

7. Elections in the UK usually take place on what day of the week?

8. In the Christian church, what day occurs 46 days before Easter Sunday?

9. According to Morrissey, Everyday Is Like?

10. Which day of the week is named after the Norse God of Thunder?

11. In America, Thanksgiving Day is celebrated on which day of the week?

12. What day of the week didn't the Boomtown Rats like?

13. On which day of the week is the newspaper The Observer published?

14. If This Is Love was the debut hit for which all-girl group?

15. On what day of the week are elections held in Australia and New Zealand?

16. Who was Robinson Crusoe's island companion?

17. In Ireland, Gaelic football and hurling matches are usually played on which day of the week?

18. What is the Sunday before Easter commonly known as?

19. Sunday trading was allowed in England and Wales from which year?
    a) 1990
    b) 1994
    c) 1998

20. What is the official day of rest in Israel?
    a) Friday
    b) Saturday
    c) Sunday

Answers to Quiz 40: Pot Luck

1. Seoul
2. Space
3. Boxing
4. Temperature
5. Youth
6. Manchester
7. Atlantic and Pacific
8. Tendon
9. Stevie Wonder
10. Australia
11. Enoch Powell
12. Australia
13. Chester
14. Chicken
15. Neasden
16. Hudson
17. Colombia
18. Casablanca
19. 1860s
20. Italian

Quiz 42: Pot Luck

1. Edson Arantes do Nascimento is the real name of which legendary footballer?

2. Who wrote the opera Madame Butterfly?

3. What is the capital of the US state of Georgia?

4. 'This summer four boys become men' is the tagline to which 2011 British film comedy?

5. Who did Ed Miliband succeed as leader of the Labour Party?

6. The prancing horse is the logo of which car manufacturer?

7. Which Scottish band took their name from a character in The Goonies?

8. What was the name of the then Queen Mother's horse that fell while leading the 1956 Grand National?

9. Which Hollywood A-lister's real name is Thomas Mapother?

10. What does a toxicologist study?

11. What is cartoon character Norville Rogers more commonly known as?

12. The book Eat! Consume! Die! was written by which controversial Scottish comedian?

13. A lactometer is used to measure the density of what liquid?

14. Who was Livin' La Vida Loca in 1999?

15. Complete the sitcom title: Roger and Val Have...?

16. 2011 movie The Rum Diary is based on a novel by which author?

17. In the Bible, who demanded the head of John the Baptist on a plate?

18. Which American actress played Emma Morley in the 2011 film version of One Day?

19. The weight of diamonds is measured in what unit?
    a) carat
    b) point
    c) Troy ounce

20. What is the nickname of the US state of Texas?
    a) Lone Star State
    b) Two Star State
    c) Tri Star State

Answers to Quiz 41: Days of the Week

1. Shrove Tuesday
2. Sheffield Wednesday
3. Fighting
4. Lazy
5. Monday's
6. Blondie
7. Thursday
8. Ash Wednesday
9. Sunday
10. Thursday
11. Thursday
12. Monday
13. Sunday
14. The Saturdays
15. Saturday
16. Man Friday
17. Sunday
18. Palm Sunday
19. 1994
20. Saturday

Quiz 43: Occupations

EASY

1. A bibliophile is someone who loves what?

2. What name is given to the person in charge of finance in educational establishments?

3. What is the technical name for someone who draws maps?

4. A campanologist is a person who does what?

5. What does a cobbler make and mend?

6. What does a draper traditionally sell?

7. What name is given to a doctor who specialises in childbirth?

8. A haberdasher sells goods relating to which type of craft?

9. What does a fletcher traditionally make?

10. What is the traditional name for a barrel maker?

11. What does a vintner sell?

12. Where do roughnecks work?

13. On which form of transport would you find a coxswain?

14. A groom usually looks after what animal?

15. What does a milliner make?

16. An ophthalmologist is a medical practitioner who specialises in which part of the body?

17. What does a costermonger traditionally sell?

18. In a hospital, what does a radiographer do?

19. What does a chandler traditionally make?
    a) rings
    b) candles
    c) cheese

20. With which material does a tanner usually work?
    a) cotton
    b) leather
    c) denim

EASY

Answers to Quiz 42: Pot Luck

1. Pele
2. Puccini
3. Atlanta
4. The Inbetweeners
5. Gordon Brown
6. Ferrari
7. The Fratellis
8. Devon Loch
9. Tom Cruise
10. Poisons
11. Shaggy
12. Frankie Boyle
13. Milk
14. Ricky Martin
15. Just Got In
16. Hunter S Thompson
17. Salome
18. Anne Hathaway
19. Carat
20. Lone Star State

Quiz 44: Pot Luck

1. What two elements combine to make water?

2. Which newsreader won the first series of Strictly Come Dancing?

3. How many years are in a millennium?

4. The first series of Downton Abbey was set in the run-up to which conflict?

5. Whose first number one single was Into The Groove?

6. Who won Best Actress Oscars for both Boys Don't Cry and Million Dollar Baby?

7. Eva Braun was the mistress of which dictator?

8. What was the name of the chest that housed the Ten Commandments?

9. What do the stars on the US flag represent?

10. The battles of El Alamein were fought in which war?

11. What is measured using a sextant?

12. A trimester is a period of how many months?

13. Who was the original host of Masterchef?

14. Who composed the music to Star Wars, ET and Raiders of the Lost Ark?

15. The Bayeux Tapestry depicts which battle?

16. What is the first event in the decathlon?

17. Which cartoon family lived at 39 Stone Canyon Way, Bedrock?

18. Which singer had 13 hits simultaneously in the UK Top 40 in July 2009?

19. Where in Britain would you find the Black Mountains?
    a) England
    b) Scotland
    c) Wales

20. When would you normally eat antipasti?
    a) before a main meal
    b) after a main meal

Answers to Quiz 43: Occupations

1.	Books	11.	Wine
2.	Bursar	12.	On an oil rig
3.	Cartographer	13.	On a boat
4.	Bell ringing	14.	Horse
5.	Shoes	15.	Hats
6.	Cloth	16.	Eyes
7.	Obstetrician	17.	Fruit and vegetables
8.	Sewing	18.	Takes X-rays
9.	Arrow	19.	Candles
10.	Cooper	20.	Leather

Quiz 45: Real Names

1. Reginald Dwight is the real name of which bestselling singer-songwriter?

2. Archibald Leach was the real name of which legendary Hollywood icon?

3. Which famous film director was born Allen Konigsberg?

4. What is actor Maurice Micklewhite more commonly known as?

5. Patrick Ogokwu is the real name of which British rapper?

6. Samuel Langhorne Clemens was the real name of which American man of letters?

7. Norma Jean Baker was the real name of which Hollywood icon?

8. David Cornwell is the real name of which thriller writer?

9. Which Indian-born crooner took his stage name from a German composer?

10. Dylan Mills is the real name of which British hip hop star?

11. Which Beatle's real name is Richard Starkey?

12. Which member of the Royal Family's real name is Marie von Reibnitz?

13. What is Paul Hewson more commonly known as?

14. George Hartree was the real name of which star of the Carry On films?

15. Michael Pennington is the real name of which rotund British comedian?

16. Hiram J Hackenbacker was the real name of which character in the puppet TV show Thunderbirds?

17. Chris Collins is the real name of which Brummie comedian?

18. Ilyena Lydia Mironoff is the real name of which British Oscar-winning actress?

19. Lev Bronstein was the real name of which Russian revolutionary?
    a) Lenin
    b) Stalin
    c) Trotsky

20. What is Marvin Lee Aday more commonly known as?
    a) Lemmy
    b) Meatloaf
    c) Sting

Answers to Quiz 44: Pot Luck

1. Hydrogen and oxygen
2. Natasha Kaplinsky
3. 1,000
4. World War One
5. Madonna
6. Hilary Swank
7. Adolf Hitler
8. The Ark of the Covenant
9. The 50 states
10. World War Two
11. Latitude
12. Three
13. Loyd Grossman
14. John Williams
15. Battle of Hastings
16. 100 metres
17. The Flintstones
18. Michael Jackson
19. Wales
20. Before a main meal

Quiz 46: Pot Luck

1. Colombo is the capital city of which country?

2. In South Africa, what are the South Western Townships better known as?

3. What is the art of clipping hedges more commonly known as?

4. Arctic King, cos and Tom Thumb are varieties of which vegetable?

5. A hectare is a unit that measures what?

6. Cosmology is the study of what?

7. Which UK city has the dialling code 0191?

8. Which figure from Greek mythology died after flying too close to the sun?

9. What are the Northern Lights also known as?

10. What colour are the stars on the Australian flag?

11. In Internet chat abbreviations what does ROFL mean?

12. What does a lepidopterist collect?

13. What sign of the zodiac is represented by a lion?

14. Which spirit literally means 'water of life'?

15. What is the national sport of Japan?

16. Vladimir Ilich Ulyanov is the real name of which Russian revolutionary?

17. Which American fashion designer also directed the film A Single Man?

18. What is the capital of the US state of Hawaii?

19. What would you do with a baklava?
    a) play it
    b) eat it
    c) wear it

20. What type of gift is traditionally associated with a tenth wedding anniversary?
    a) leather
    b) tin
    c) crystal

EASY

Answers to Quiz 45: Real Names

1. Elton John
2. Cary Grant
3. Woody Allen
4. Michael Caine
5. Tinie Tempah
6. Mark Twain
7. Marilyn Monroe
8. John Le Carré
9. Engelbert Humperdinck
10. Dizzee Rascal
11. Ringo Starr
12. Princess Michael of Kent
13. Bono
14. Charles Hawtrey
15. Johnny Vegas
16. Brains
17. Frank Skinner
18. Helen Mirren
19. Trotsky
20. Meat Loaf

Quiz 47: Reality TV

1. Which member of Girls Aloud was a judge on the US X Factor?

2. Contestants on Strictly Come Dancing compete for which trophy?

3. Will Young was the winner of which reality TV show?

4. Who won The X Factor in 2011?

5. Who presents Strictly Come Dancing alongside Bruce Forsyth?

6. The X Factor's Tulisa Contostavlos is a member of which group?

7. Which star of The Only Way Is Essex was runner up in I'm A Celebrity...Get Me Out of Here?

8. Who was the first winner of TV talent show The Voice?

9. The wife of which rock star was on the original judging panel on The X Factor?

10. Which duo present I'm A Celebrity...Get Me Out of Here!

11. Which member of Take That won Celebrity Big Brother?

12. Strictly's Jason Donovan and Holly Vallance both appeared in which Aussie soap?

13. How Do You Solve A Problem Like Maria was a talent show to find an actress for which musical?

14. Which Loose Woman won Celebrity Big Brother in 2012?

15. The stars of The X Factor reached number one in 2011 with a cover of which Rose Royce song?

16. Who replaced Margaret Mountford as an assistant on The Apprentice?

17. Which radio DJ sat in for Claudia Winkleman on 2011's Strictly Come Dancing: It Takes Two?

18. Amy Childs, Lauren Pope, Sam Faiers and Nanny Pat appeared in which reality TV show?

19. Dancer and choreographer Louie Spence found fame on which TV show?
a) Pineapple Dance Studios
b) Pomegranate Dance Studios
c) Watermelon Dance Studios

20. Which of the following has not won The X Factor?
a) Matt Cardle
b) Joe McElderry
c) Olly Murs

Answers to Quiz 46: Pot Luck

1. Sri Lanka
2. Soweto
3. Topiary
4. Lettuce
5. Area
6. The universe
7. Newcastle-upon-Tyne
8. Icarus
9. Aurora Borealis
10. White
11. Rolling On Floor Laughing
12. Butterflies and moths
13. Leo
14. Whisky
15. Sumo wrestling
16. Lenin
17. Tom Ford
18. Honolulu
19. Eat it
20. Tin

Quiz 48: Pot Luck

1. What Greek word translates into English as 'I have found it'?

2. How many minutes does a rugby union match last?

3. What was Abba's first UK number one hit?

4. What is the fourth largest country in the world by population?

5. Nicolas Cage is the nephew of which Oscar-winning film director?

6. Albany is the capital of which US state?

7. In an opera, what word describes a song for a single voice?

8. What does an anemometer measure?

9. Augustus Gloop, Veruca Salt and Mike Teavee are characters in which children's film?

10. In 1909, Louis Bleriot became the first person to fly across what body of water?

11. Which child actress gave her name to a non-alcoholic cocktail?

12. Three members of the band Duran Duran shared what surname?

13. The car manufacturer Hyundai is based in which country?

14. Who were the first winners of football's World Cup?

15. What does the D stand for in Franklin D Roosevelt?

16. Zeta, iota and kappa are letters in which alphabet?

17. Which English king was executed in 1649?

Answers – page 99

18. Which British comedy has the tagline 'A romantic comedy. With zombies'?

19. The Garden State is the nickname of which US state?

20. What is the largest penguin?
    a) Lord Penguin
    b) King Penguin
    c) Emperor Penguin

21. What is a female ferret called?
    a) Jane
    b) Jill
    c) Jackie

Answers to Quiz 47: Reality TV

1. Cheryl Cole
2. Glitterball Trophy
3. Pop Idol
4. Little Mix
5. Tess Daly
6. N-Dubz
7. Mark Wright
8. Leanne Mitchell
9. Ozzy Osbourne (Sharon)
10. Ant and Dec
11. Mark Owen
12. Neighbours
13. The Sound of Music
14. Denise Welch
15. Wishing On A Star
16. Karren Brady
17. Zoe Ball
18. The Only Way Is Essex
19. Pineapple Dance Studios
20. Olly Murs

Quiz 49: TV Gameshows

1.   Who hosts ITV dating show Take Me Out?

2.   Which TV duo have invited audiences to Push The Button, enjoy a Saturday Night Take Away and take part in a Gameshow Marathon?

3.   'It's a good guess but it's not right' was often said on which show?

4.   Who succeeded Magnus Magnusson as the host of Mastermind?

5.   In which quiz show will you find rounds called Intros, Identity Parade and Next Lines?

6.   Nicky Campbell, Bradley Walsh, John Leslie and Paul Hendy hosted which show?

7.   On Fool Us, budding illusionists have to fool which pair of magicians?

8.   What is the top prize on Deal or No Deal?

9.   On Who Wants To Be A Millionaire, how many questions must a contestant successfully answer to win the jackpot?

10. Who was the original host of Countdown?

11. On Pointless, who is Alexander Armstrong's Pointless friend?

12. Brendan Sheerin is the name of the tour guide on which travelling gameshow?

13. What was the name of the booby prize in 3-2-1?

14. Who hosts The Million Pound Drop?

15. In which long-running quiz show did contestants have the option 'question or nominate'?

16. Which magician hosted Odd One Out, Wipeout and Every Second Counts?

17. True or false. Jade Goody single-handedly beat TV's Eggheads?

18. Which stand-up comedian hosts The Big Fat Quiz of the Year?

19. What sort of Factor did contestants need in the long running game shows?
    a) Argon Factor
    b) Krypton Factor
    c) Neon Factor

20. Which of the following isn't one of TV's Eggheads?
    a) Daphne Fowler
    b) Kate Hall
    c) Judith Keppel

Answers to Quiz 48: Pot Luck

1. Eureka
2. 80
3. Waterloo
4. Indonesia
5. Francis Ford Coppola
6. New York
7. Aria
8. Wind speed
9. Willy Wonka and the Chocolate Factory
10. The English Channel
11. Shirley Temple
12. Taylor
13. Korea
14. Uruguay
15. Delano
16. Greek
17. Charles I
18. Shaun of the Dead
19. New Jersey
20. Emperor Penguin
21. Jill

Quiz 50: Pot Luck

1. Which actor played TV gangster Tony Soprano?

2. What is the holy book in Islam?

3. Amaretti biscuits are flavoured using what type of nut?

4. Who were the four horsemen of the apocalypse?

5. Which former editor of the News of the World resigned as David Cameron's director of communications?

6. What sacrament initiates a person into the Christian church?

7. What is chorizo?

8. Which group finished runner-up to Alexandra Burke in 2008's X Factor?

9. What is the fifth letter of the Greek alphabet?

10. Who was director of the FBI from 1924 until 1972?

11. Police drama Scott & Bailey is set in which city?

12. The Boer War was fought in which country?

13. Gumbo is a dish associated with which state of America?

14. Which Buckinghamshire country house was the home to Britain's Government Code & Cypher School in World War II?

15. Valletta is the capital city of which country?

16. What herb is usually used with onion in Christmas stuffing?

17. In the folk tale, the Pied Piper was from which German town?

18. Richard Harris and Michael Gambon both played which character in the Harry Potter films?

EASY

19. 'If anything can go wrong, it will' is whose law?
    a) Byrne's Law
    b) Begley's Law
    c) Murphy's Law

20. What shape is the pasta farfalle?
    a) shell
    b) butterfly
    c) ribbon

Answers to Quiz 49: TV Gameshows

1. Paddy McGuinness
2. Ant and Dec
3. Catchphrase
4. John Humphrys
5. Never Mind The Buzzcocks
6. Wheel of Fortune
7. Penn and Teller
8. £250,000
9. 15
10. Richard Whiteley
11. Richard Osman
12. Coach Trip
13. Dusty Bin
14. Davina McCall
15. Fifteen to One
16. Paul Daniels
17. False (but she did take them to sudden death)
18. Jimmy Carr
19. Krypton Factor
20. Kate Hall

Quiz 51: Sport

EASY

1. Goodison Park is the home ground of which football team?

2. In athletics, over what distance is the steeplechase usually run?

3. What game is traditionally played at Trent Bridge?

4. How many laps are there in a speedway race?

5. How many riders are there in a speedway race?

6. What nationality is Formula One champion Sebastian Vettel

7. In rugby league, the Bulls play in which city?

8. In what year did England win the Rugby World Cup?

9. Which county cricket team play their home games at Chester-le-Street?

10. In what sport would someone perform a triple axel?

11. Clean and jerk and snatch are elements of which Olympic sport?

12. Simon Whitlock, Gary Anderson and Steve Beaton are well known practitioners of which sport?

13. Which team did Chelsea meet in the final of the 2012 Champions League?

14. How many English classic horse races are there?

15. The Grand National is run at which course?

16. In what month does the Cheltenham Festival usually take place?

17. Which two teams compete for golf's Ryder Cup?

18. Mark Spitz won seven Olympic gold medals in which sport?

19. Which former Olympic champion was in charge of running the 2012 London Games?
    a) Seb Coe
    b) Steve Cram
    c) Steve Ovett

20. Which Scottish football club went into administration in February 2012?
    a) Celtic
    b) Rangers
    c) Aberdeen

Answers to Quiz 50: Pot Luck

1. James Gandolfini
2. The Koran
3. Almond
4. War, famine, pestilence and death
5. Andy Coulson
6. Baptism
7. A spicy sausage
8. JLS
9. Epsilon
10. J Edgar Hoover
11. Manchester
12. South Africa
13. Louisiana
14. Bletchley Park
15. Malta
16. Sage
17. Hamelin
18. Dumbledore
19. Murphy's Law
20. Butterfly

Quiz 52: Pot Luck

1. What is the capital city of Turkey?

2. What is the highest mountain in Wales?

3. What type of gift is traditionally given to someone celebrating their 30th wedding anniversary?

4. What American city is nicknamed the City of Angels?

5. Which central American country was formerly known as British Honduras?

6. Which straits link the Atlantic Ocean with the Mediterranean Sea?

7. Igneous, sedimentary and metamorphic are types of what?

8. A car with a sticker featuring the initials SK is from which country?

9. Frances Gumm was the real name of which actress and singer?

10. Which sea is classed as the largest lake in the world?

11. The lev is the currency which European country?

12. Somebody born on St Patrick's Day would have what star sign?

13. Juan Peron was the president of which South American country?

14. Which fortified wine was originally only made in Jerez and San Lucar in Spain?

15. Which path stretches from Edale in Derbyshire to Kirk Yetholm in the Scottish Borders?

16. Sauerkraut is made by pickling what type of vegetable?

17. Ashton Gate is the home of which football club?

18. The Appenines are a mountain range in which country?

19. In Texas Hold'em poker which is the best of the three following hands
    a) trips
    b) a flush
    c) a straight

20. What is the longest river in the world?
    a) Amazon
    b) Nile
    c) Yellow

Answers to Quiz 51: Sport

1. Everton
2. 3,000m
3. Cricket
4. Four
5. Four
6. German
7. Bradford
8. 2003
9. Durham
10. Ice skating
11. Weight lifting
12. Darts
13. Bayern Munich
14. Five
15. Aintree
16. March
17. Europe and the USA
18. Swimming
19. Seb Coe
20. Rangers

Quiz 53: Britain

1. What is the highest mountain in England?

2. Which county is famous for its pasties?

3. What is the most northerly inhabited town in mainland Britain?

4. Which Welsh town is famous for its bookshops?

5. What is the third largest city in Scotland?

6. What was the name of the Roman fortification that separated England from Scotland?

7. The UK has a land border with which country?

8. The Ceremony of the Keys takes place at which London landmark?

9. Which London suburb is home to the All England Lawn Tennis Club?

10. Parkway and Temple Meads are railway stations in which city?

11. What is the Old Lady of Threadneedle Street more commonly known as?

12. Which county is known as The Garden of England?

13. Where is the oldest cathedral in England?

14. What is the largest castle in England?

15. What colour is the Bakerloo Line on a London Underground map?

16. Which Scottish port is famous for its haddock 'smokies'?

17. The M60 motorway works its way around which English city?

18. Tintagel Castle is associated with which mythical king?

19. In which English city would you find the Alhambra Theatre?
    a) Bradford
    b) Leeds
    c) Sheffield

20. Which river flows through the city of Liverpool?
    a) Mersey
    b) Trent
    c) Tyne

EASY

Answers to Quiz 52: Pot Luck

1. Ankara
2. Mount Snowdon
3. Pearl
4. Los Angeles
5. Belize
6. Straits of Gibraltar
7. Rock
8. Slovakia
9. Judy Garland
10. The Caspian Sea
11. Bulgaria
12. Pisces
13. Argentina
14. Sherry
15. Pennine Way
16. Cabbage
17. Bristol City
18. Italy
19. Flush
20. The Nile

Quiz 54: Pot Luck

1. An outgoing US president who will be replaced the following January is said to be a lame what?

2. A kibbutz is a community typically found in which country?

3. What is the medical name for the voice box?

4. The Stasi was the name of the secret police in which country?

5. Aris is cockney slang for what object?

6. Which Russian playwright wrote The Cherry Orchard?

7. Jarvis Cocker was the lead singer with which group?

8. In what year did the Berlin Wall fall?

9. Nicosia is the capital city of which country?

10. Folic acid is another name for what vitamin?

11. Doghouse and bull fiddle are alternative names for what musical instrument?

12. Hi hat, ride, splash and crash are types of what instrument?

13. Spamalot was a musical inspired by which comedy team?

14. What style of music literally means new trend in Portuguese?

15. Hypotension is another name for what?

16. Which group is named after three of the four ancient elements?

17. Helios was the Greek god of what?

Answers – page 111

18. Which British comedian starred in the film Forgetting Sarah Marshall?

19. Pathology is the study of what?
    a) paths
    b) diseases
    c) maps

20. Ginsberg, Kerouac and Ferlinghetti are known as?
    a) Beat Poets
    b) Fleet Poets
    c) Street Poets

EASY

Answers to Quiz 53: Britain

1. Scafell Pike
2. Cornwall
3. John O'Groats
4. Hay-on-Wye
5. Aberdeen
6. Hadrian's Wall
7. Republic of Ireland
8. The Tower of London
9. Wimbledon
10. Bristol
11. The Bank of England
12. Kent
13. Canterbury
14. Windsor Castle
15. Brown
16. Arbroath
17. Manchester
18. King Arthur
19. Bradford
20. Mersey

Quiz 55: London

1. Which famous address has the postcode SW1A 2AA?

2. What colour shares a name with a central London park?

3. The Crown Jewels are housed in which building?

4. The Houses of Parliament are also known as the Palace of where?

5. Real cockneys are born within earshot of the bells of which church?

6. Who, in 2000, became London's first elected mayor?

7. Who lives at Lambeth Palace?

8. What is the HQ of the Metropolitan Police called?

9. What £5 levy was introduced in central London on 17 February 2003?

10. In London what are Guy's and St Thomas's?

11. What is the shortest line on the London Underground?

12. What in London are the Groucho, Athenaeum, White's and the Garrick?

13. Which London palace is home to a famous maze?

14. Which pedestrian bridge links St Paul's Cathedral with Tate Modern?

15. The names of only two London Underground stations are four letters long. What are they?

16. What is sold at Billingsgate Market?

17. In which London building would you find Poets' Corner?

18. A statue of which 'boy who never grew up' stands in Kensington Gardens?

19. The Great Fire of London started in which Lane?
    a) Pie Lane
    b) Pudding Lane
    c) Tart Lane

20. Portobello Road, Petticoat Lane and Camden are homes to what?
    a) hospitals
    b) markets
    c) prisons

Answers to Quiz 54: Pot Luck

1. Duck
2. Israel
3. Larynx
4. East Germany
5. Bottle
6. Anton Chekhov
7. Pulp
8. 1989
9. Cyprus
10. B
11. Double bass
12. Cymbals
13. Monty Python's Flying Circus
14. Bossa Nova
15. Low blood pressure
16. Earth, Wind and Fire
17. The sun
18. Russell Brand
19. Diseases
20. Beat Poets

Quiz 56: Pot Luck

1. By The Sleepy Lagoon is the theme music to which radio programme?

2. Who wrote The Communist Manifesto?

3. Who was the original host of The X Factor?

4. Which band took their name from a leisure centre in Swindon?

5. What form of transport was the Titfield Thunderbolt?

6. Which county in England is the only one to have two coastlines?

7. Which English king tried to turn back the tide?

8. Who did David Cameron succeed as leader of the Conservative Party?

9. Jacob Marley was the partner of which literary character?

10. Which Alfred Hitchcock film is also the title of a number one single by U2?

11. Which Aardman animation had the tagline 'Escape or Die Frying'?

12. The Menai Straits separate the Welsh mainland from which island?

13. What fish is traditionally used in the dish kedgeree?

14. Which Sky Sports regular briefly hosted TV quiz Countdown?

15. Karl Marx, Lucian Freud and Douglas Adams are buried at which London cemetery?

EASY

16. Which religious movement was founded in 1950 by science-fiction writer L. Ron Hubbard?

17. The Knesset is the parliament of which country?

18. Downton Abbey is set in which English county?

19. What is the shop Poundland known as in Europe?
    a) Eurland
    b) Dealz
    c) Eurostretcher

20. On a film set, what is a boom?
    a) explosion
    b) microphone
    c) camera

Answers to Quiz 55: London

1. 10 Downing Street
2. Green Park
3. The Tower of London
4. Westminster
5. St Mary le Bow
6. Ken Livingstone
7. The Archbishop of Canterbury
8. New Scotland Yard
9. Congestion Charge
10. Hospitals
11. Waterloo and City
12. Clubs
13. Hampton Court
14. Millennium Bridge
15. Bank and Oval
16. Fish
17. Westminster Abbey
18. Peter Pan
19. Pudding Lane
20. Markets

Quiz 57: Royalty

1. Who is the youngest of the Queen's children?

2. Which royal won the Sports Personality of the Year award in 2006?

3. What breed of dog is associated with the Royal Family?

4. What parade marks the Queen's Official Birthday?

5. Who is the elder of Prince Andrew's two daughters?

6. Prince William is the Duke of where?

7. What is the name of the Queen's private home in Aberdeenshire?

8. What is the Duchess of Cambridge's real name?

9. The Royal Family hold accounts at which bank?

10. The funeral of which royal had the codename Tay Bridge?

11. In what English county is Sandringham House?

12. Who is the first female in the line of succession to the British throne?

13. In what month is the Queen's Official Birthday celebrated?

14. What football team does Prince William support?

15. In what year did Diana, Princess of Wales die?

16. In 1974, which British royal survived a kidnapping attempt?

17. What is the official residence of the Prince of Wales?

18. Prince Philip was born on which Greek island?

19. The Queen is not the head of state of which of these countries?
    a) Canada
    b) India
    c) New Zealand

20. When is the Queen's birthday?
    a) 21st February
    b) 21st March
    c) 21st April

Answers to Quiz 56: Pot Luck

1. Desert Island Discs
2. Karl Marx and Friedrich Engels
3. Kate Thornton
4. Oasis
5. Train
6. Devon
7. Canute
8. Michael Howard
9. Ebeneezer Scrooge
10. Vertigo
11. Chicken Run
12. Anglesey
13. Smoked haddock
14. Jeff Stelling
15. Highgate
16. Scientology
17. Israel
18. Yorkshire
19. Dealz
20. Microphone

Quiz 58: Pot Luck

1. According to the proverb, the proof of the pudding is in the what?

2. Samuel Pepys, Anne Frank and Alan Clark are noted writers of what style of book?

3. What famous American road runs from Chicago to Los Angeles?

4. Which Oscar-winning screenwriter wrote Downton Abbey?

5. What is the largest US state by area?

6. Which US president instituted the New Deal?

7. What is the last book of the New Testament?

8. What was the name of the movement that campaigned for votes for women in the late 19th and early 20th century?

9. Which car manufacturer's slogan is Vorsprung durch Technik?

10. Lord Nelson died during which battle?

11. Who said, 'I can resist everything but temptation'?

12. The acronym POTUS describes which political leader?

13. What meat is used to make pastrami?

14. In which city is the HQ of the UN Security Council?

15. Farmer Barleymow, PC Copper and Aunt Flo were characters in which children's animation?

16. Some Might Say was the first number one single for which group?

EASY

17. Which Motown band almost ended up being called The Commodes?

18. Who replaced Terry Wogan in the Eurovision commentary box in 2009?

19. In which part of England will you find a wetland area called the Broads?
    a) North West
    b) East Anglia
    c) West Country

20. What is the holy day in Islam?
    a) Friday
    b) Saturday
    c) Sunday

Answers to Quiz 57: Royalty

1. Edward
2. Zara Phillips
3. Corgi
4. Trooping The Colour
5. Beatrice
6. Cambridge
7. Balmoral Castle
8. Kate Middleton
9. Coutts & Co.
10. The Queen Mother
11. Norfolk
12. Princess Beatrice
13. June
14. Aston Villa
15. 1997
16. Princess Anne
17. Clarence House
18. Corfu
19. India
20. 21st April

Quiz 59: 1980s Pop

1. Which synth popsters recorded the album Speak and Spell?

2. Siobhan Fahey, Keren Woodward and Sara Dallin were members of which group?

3. Whose debut single was Goody Two Shoes?

4. What sort of day did Haircut 100 enjoy in 1982?

5. Holly Johnson was the lead singer with which band?

6. What is singer Graham McPherson better known as?

7. What are the names of the Pet Shop Boys?

8. Abba had their last UK number one in 1980. What was it?

9. Which European capital gave Ultravox the title of their 1981 hit?

10. Falco reached number 1 in the UK and America in 1986 with a song about which composer?

11. What music TV show first aired on Bonfire Night 1982?

12. Who were the hosts of The Hit Man and Her?

13. Which Scottish group enjoyed a Happy Birthday in 1981?

14. What mysterious location was the title of a 1981 Barry Manilow song?

15. Which group went Through The Barricades in 1986?

16. What sort of girls did the Pet Shop Boys sing about in 1985?

17. Who, in 1985, became the first Western pop group to play in Communist China?

18. The Goss twins were members of which group?

19. Which band opened the Wembley Live Aid concert?
    a) The Who
    b) Spandau Ballet
    c) Status Quo

20. Who had a hit in 1988 with Shake Your Love?
    a) Debbie Gibson
    b) Martika
    c) Tiffany

EASY

Answers to Quiz 58: Pot Luck

1. The eating
2. Diaries
3. Route 66
4. Julian Fellowes
5. Alaska
6. Franklin D Roosevelt
7. Revelation
8. Suffragette
9. Audi
10. Trafalgar
11. Oscar Wilde
12. President Of The United States
13. Beef
14. New York
15. Bod
16. Oasis
17. The Commodores
18. Graham Norton
19. East Anglia
20. Friday

Quiz 60: Pot Luck

EASY

1. Tirana is the capital city of which country?

2. Peter Sellers and Steve Martin have both starred in films as which fictional detective?

3. Someone born on 10th August would have what star sign?

4. In Internet chat abbreviations what does TTYL mean?

5. What is sashimi?

6. In which American state is the Grand Canyon?

7. The musical Our House is based on which band's music?

8. The River Taff flows through which British capital?

9. Wine is the fermented juice of which fruit?

10. In what year was the Battle of Agincourt?

11. What is the largest ocean in the world?

12. Which actor played Harry in the Harry Potter films?

13. Which Scottish city is known as The Athens of the North?

14. Windscale is the former name of which nuclear plant?

15. The French aperitifs Pastis and Pernod are both flavoured using what?

16. Siam is the former name of which Asian country?

17. What is the currency of China?

18. Krakatoa, Mount St Helens and Eyjafjallajokull are examples of what?

Answers – page 123

19. Checkers is the American word for which game?
    a) backgammon
    b) chess
    c) draughts

20. The press is also known as the fourth what?
    a) arm
    b) estate
    c) column

EASY

Answers to Quiz 59: 1980s Pop

1. Depeche Mode
2. Bananarama
3. Adam Ant
4. Fantastic Day
5. Frankie Goes To Hollywood
6. Suggs
7. Neil Tennant and Chris Lowe
8. Super Trouper
9. Vienna
10. (Amadeus) Mozart
11. The Tube
12. Pete Waterman and Michaela Strachan
13. Altered Images
14. Bermuda Triangle
15. Spandau Ballet
16. West End Girls
17. Wham!
18. Bros
19. Status Quo
20. Debbie Gibson

Quiz 61: Pop Music 2000 and Beyond

EASY

1. Which TV talent show winner had the biggest-selling single of the noughties?

2. Rockferry was the title of an album by which Welsh singer?

3. Which former soldier had the biggest-selling album of the noughties?

4. Who recorded an album called White Ladder?

5. Who Let The Dogs Out in 2000?

6. Laurie Blue are the middle names of which British singer?

7. According to Shakira's 2006 hit single what don't lie?

8. What was Amy Winehouse's only top ten single?

9. Thom Yorke is the lead singer with which group?

10. Which female singer won the 2011 Mercury Music Prize with Let England Shake?

11. Which Manchester group recorded the album Build A Rocket Boys?

12. Who had a 2009 hit with Boom Boom Pow?

13. Just Enough Education To Perform is an album by which Welsh rockers?

14. Which X factor star sang the 2010 Christmas Number One, When We Collide?

15. I Bet You Look Good on the Dancefloor was a hit for which group?

16. Which ginger-haired singer won two awards at the 2012 Brits?

Answers – page 125

17. What is Mike Skinner more commonly known as?

18. Mr Brightside was a hit for which band?

19. Who went In For The Kill in 2009?
    a) Lady Gaga
    b) La Roux
    c) Madonna

20. What was the name of Take That's 2010 number one album?
    a) Progress
    b) Reaction
    c) Future

Answers to Quiz 60: Pot Luck

1. Albania
2. Inspector Clouseau
3. Leo
4. Talk To You Later
5. Japanese raw fish
6. Arizona
7. Madness
8. Cardiff
9. Grape
10. 1415
11. Pacific Ocean
12. Daniel Radcliffe
13. Edinburgh
14. Sellafield
15. Aniseed
16. Thailand
17. Yuan
18. Volcanoes
19. Draughts
20. Estate

Quiz 62: Pot Luck

EASY

1. According to the proverb, what is the thief of time?

2. What is the largest lake in Africa?

3. Which 1970s boy band got their name after sticking a pin in a map of the USA?

4. Nairobi is the capital city of which country?

5. What is the name of Ipswich Town's home ground?

6. What branch of medicine is concerned with childbirth?

7. Someone born on Christmas Day would have what star sign?

8. What is the only London Underground station that is just one syllable long?

9. The city of Dublin lies on which river?

10. What bands of fibrous tissue connect bones?

11. What type of pasta takes its name from the Italian for 'little worms'?

12. What is the anatomical name for the chest?

13. Myanmar is another name for which Asian country?

14. The Battle of Naseby was fought in which war?

15. What famous US footpath stretches 2,000 miles between Georgia and Maine?

16. Who wrote the words to the hymn Jerusalem?

17. How many keys are on a standard piano?

EASY

18. Worcester Beacon is the highest point in which range of English hills?

19. The Pacific Ocean makes up approximately what percentage of the earth's water?
    a) 36%
    b) 46%
    c) 56%

20. The food tripe comes from which part of an animal?
    a) stomach lining
    b) breast
    c) thigh

Answers to Quiz 61: Pop Music 2000 and Beyond

1. Will Young with Evergreen
2. Duffy
3. James Blunt
4. David Gray
5. The Baha Men
6. Adele
7. Hips Don't Lie
8. Rehab
9. Radiohead
10. PJ Harvey
11. Elbow
12. Black Eyed Peas
13. The Stereophonics
14. Matt Cardle
15. Arctic Monkeys
16. Ed Sheeran
17. The Streets
18. The Killers
19. La Roux
20. Progress

Quiz 63: Europe

1. La Marseillaise is the national anthem of which country?

2. Edam cheese comes from which country?

3. Which Scandinavian country shares a border with Germany?

4. Which city is known as The Eternal City?

5. Which European country is also known as the Confederation of Helvetia?

6. Belgrade is the capital city of which country?

7. The most southerly point of Europe is in which country?

8. A car from which country would have the registration initials PL?

9. The Loire is the longest river in which country?

10. A web address ending .be comes from which country?

11. Which mountains form a natural border between Spain and France?

12. The Deutschlandlied is the national anthem of which country?

13. What was the currency of Portugal before it joined the euro?

14. Tenerife, Las Palmas, Lanzarote and Fuerteventura are part of which group of islands?

15. The Autostrada is the national motorway network of which country?

16. King Juan Carlos is the monarch of which country?

Answers – page 129

EASY

17. What is the capital city of Finland?

18. In what country would you ride an underground train on the U Bahn?

19. According to the proverb all roads lead to where?
    a) Athens
    b) Paris
    c) Rome

20. In what year did the French Revolution take place?
    a) 1689
    b) 1776
    c) 1789

Answers to Quiz 62: Pot Luck

1. Procrastination
2. Lake Victoria
3. The Bay City Rollers
4. Kenya
5. Portman Road
6. Obstetrics
7. Capricorn
8. Bank
9. Liffey
10. Ligaments
11. Vermicelli
12. Thorax
13. Burma
14. The English Civil War
15. The Appalachian Trail
16. William Blake
17. 88
18. The Malverns
19. 46%
20. Stomach lining

Quiz 64: Pot Luck

1. What is the Muslim name for God?

2. What word describes an angle that is more than 90 degrees but less than 180 degrees?

3. Which composer wrote the scores to the James Bond films Dr No, Thunderball, Goldfinger (and many more)?

4. In which European country was the first motorway built?

5. Who hosted Play Your Cards Right?

6. What is the main ingredient in guacamole?

7. Nina, Pinta and Santa Maria were the three ships on which explorer's 1492 voyage to America?

8. Wing Commander Guy Gibson was in charge of which daring World War II raid?

9. What do the initials POV stand for on a film shoot?

10. In which European city can you travel on a railway system called the DART?

11. Former Strictly Come Dancing winner and judge Alesha Dixon was a member of which band?

12. Barack Obama was born in which American state?

13. In the Old Testament, who was cast into the lion's den by Nebuchadnezzar?

14. Which Tudor galleon was sunk in 1545 but raised from the Solent in 1982?

15. Which number one-selling group needed A Little Time in 1990?

16. Austin is the capital of which US state?

Answers – page 131

17. What was the virus H1N1 more commonly known as?

18. Which football team is nicknamed The Canaries?

19. What was the name of the hard rock supergroup that included members of Guns 'n' Roses, Stone Temple Pilots and Wasted Youth?

20. What marked the first border between Wales and England?
    a) Giant's Causeway
    b) Hadrian's Wall
    c) Offa's Dyke

21. In 1961, Cuban exiles tried to invade and overthrow Fidel Castro at the
    a) Bay of Dogs
    b) Bay of Pigs
    c) Bay of Snakes

Answers to Quiz 63: Europe

1. France	11. Pyrenees
2. Netherlands	12. Germany
3. Denmark	13. Escudo
4. Rome	14. Canary Islands
5. Switzerland	15. Italy
6. Serbia	16. Spain
7. Spain	17. Helsinki
8. Poland	18. Germany
9. France	19. Rome
10. Belgium	20. 1789

Quiz 65: Doctors

1. Which Irish philanthropist opened his first children's home in 1870?

2. Which BBC film critic is sometimes known as the Good Doctor?

3. Who was US Secretary of State under Richard Nixon?

4. Julius was the first name of which Bond villain?

5. Who is the arch-nemesis of animated hero Inspector Gadget?

6. Which doctor performed the first heart transplant?

7. Who is Britain's most prolific mass murderer?

8. Dr Julius Hibbert appears in which TV show?

9. Which former Defence Secretary was a medical doctor?

10. Which rapper recorded an album called The Chronic?

11. Who was the first man to run a four-minute mile?

12. Which group reached number one in the charts in 1986 with Spirit in the Sky?

13. Who presents ITV comedy TV Burp?

14. Which member of the Monty Python comedy team studied medicine at Cambridge?

15. Dr Gaius Baltar was a character in which science fiction drama?

16. Which doctor could talk to the animals?

17. Brian Cox, Sir Anthony Hopkins and Gaspard Ulliel have all played which fictional doctor?

18. Who wrote The Strange Case of Dr Jekyll and Mr Hyde?

19. Dr Karl Kennedy appears in which TV soap?
    a) Coronation Street
    b) Home and Away
    c) Neighbours

20. Which Brazilian delayed his football career in order to complete his medical studies?
    a) Falcao
    b) Socrates
    c) Zico

Answers to Quiz 64: Pot Luck

1. Allah
2. Obtuse
3. John Barry
4. Germany
5. Bruce Forsyth
6. Avocado
7. Christopher Columbus
8. The Dambusters
9. Point of view
10. Dublin
11. Mis-teeq
12. Hawaii
13. Daniel
14. Mary Rose
15. The Beautiful South
16. Texas
17. Swine flu
18. Norwich City
19. Velvet Revolver
20. Offa's Dyke
21. Bay of Pigs

Quiz 66: Pot Luck

1. The Hawthorns is the home ground of which football club?

2. Which Irish duo finished eighth in the 2011 Eurovision Song Contest with the song Lipstick?

3. What is the capital city of Switzerland?

4. Sharon Gless and Tyne Daly played which detective duo?

5. A web address ending .ch comes from which country?

6. How often does golf's Ryder Cup take place?

7. A car with the registration initials GBZ is from which British Overseas Territory?

8. Which Soviet leader introduced policies of Glasnost and Perestroika?

9. How many humps does a dromedary camel have?

10. Which playwright was briefly married to Marilyn Monroe?

11. A tincture is a medicinal extract containing what substance?

12. According to the proverb, what can't be cured must be what?

13. Which 1970s disco band were named after an Aboriginal TV detective?

14. Which Docklands Light Railway station shares its name with a female pop group?

15. In 1966, The Daily Worker changed its name to what?

16. Rubeola is the medical name for which disease?

17. In Greek mythology, who was god of the sea?

Answers – page 135

18. What musical instrument was invented by Adolphe Sax?

19. What type of sandwiches does Paddington Bear like?
    a) Jam
    b) Lemon curd
    c) Marmalade

20. What is the most common name for a pope?
    a) John
    b) Paul
    c) Pius

Answers to Quiz 65: Doctors

1. Dr Thomas Barnardo
2. Mark Kermode
3. Dr Henry Kissinger
4. Dr No
5. Dr Claw
6. Dr Christiaan Barnard
7. Dr Harold Shipman
8. The Simpsons
9. Dr Liam Fox
10. Dr Dre
11. Dr Roger Bannister
12. Dr and the Medics
13. Dr Harry Hill
14. Graham Chapman
15. Battlestar Galactica
16. Dr Doolittle
17. Dr Hannibal Lecter
18. Robert Louis Stevenson
19. Neighbours
20. Socrates

Quiz 67: Money

1. Which composer appeared on the £20 note between 1999 and 2010?

2. In slang, how much money is a monkey?

3. What animal is used to describe a rising stock market?

4. The DAX is the stock exchange of which country?

5. Which Swedish pop group had a 1976 top ten hit with Money, Money, Money?

6. What is the central bank of America called?

7. 'Well it's one for the money, two for the show' is the opening line to which Elvis Presley song?

8. What is a product sold at below cost price to entice people to buy other products?

9. In finance, what do the initials FTSE stand for?

10. Which Scottish economist appears on the back of a £20 note?

11. The Nikkei is the stock exchange of which country?

12. Who said, 'The love of money is the root of all evil'?

13. What name describes a company with a reputation for quality, reliability and the ability to operate profitably in good times and bad?

14. Who is the most famous customer of the bank Coutts & Co.?

15. Which thoroughfare gives its name to New York's main financial district?

16. Which comedian created the character Loadsamoney?

EASY

17. What was the currency of Italy before it joined the euro?

18. Money's Too Tight To mention was a 1985 hit for which British group?

19. The transformation of the London Stock Exchange in 1986 was known as?
    a) Big Bucks
    b) Big Crash
    c) Big Bang

20. What was the name of the financial crisis of 1720?
    a) East Sea Bubble
    b) North Sea Bubble
    c) South Sea Bubble

Answers to Quiz 66: Pot Luck

1. West Bromwich Albion
2. Jedward
3. Berne
4. Cagney and Lacey
5. Switzerland
6. Every 2 years
7. Gibraltar
8. Mikhail Gorbachev
9. 1
10. Arthur Miller
11. Alcohol
12. Endured
13. Boney M
14. All Saints
15. The Morning Star
16. Measles
17. Poseidon
18. Saxophone
19. Marmalade
20. John

Quiz 68: Pot Luck

EASY

1. Which item found in a tool kit is also the name of a cocktail containing gin and orange juice?

2. What is the name of the mythical sea creature that is half woman, half fish?

3. In Greek mythology, which king turned everything he touched into gold?

4. What was the name of the hurricane that devastated New Orleans in 2005?

5. On what significant date did US Presidents John Adams, Thomas Jefferson and James Monroe die?

6. Which comedian hosted snooker-themed gameshow Big Break?

7. The Webb-Ellis Trophy is awarded to the winners of which sporting competition?

8. What scandal forced US president Richard Nixon out of office?

9. Detective drama Lewis is set in which English city?

10. What would you do with a Bedfordshire Clanger?

11. George Formby was associated with what musical instrument?

12. 'Oh, say can you see by the dawn's early light' is the opening line to what song?

13. Tapas is a common style of food in which country?

14. Lady Godiva rode naked through the streets of which city?

15. If someone is dining al fresco where are they eating?

16. What word describes food cooked in accordance with Jewish law?

17. What name is given to a word or phrase that reads the same backwards and forwards?

18. Named after an American city, which musical was named Best Picture at the 2002 Oscars?

19. What name is given to a parliament where no one party has an overall majority?
    a) hung parliament
    b) drawn parliament
    c) quartered parliament

20. What is said to have been the cause of the universe?
    a) Big Bang
    b) Crazy Crash
    c) Large Leap

Answers to Quiz 67: Money

1. Sir Edward Elgar	11. Japan
2. £500	12. St Paul
3. Bull	13. Blue Chip
4. Germany	14. The Queen
5. Abba	15. Wall Street
6. Federal Reserve	16. Harry Enfield
7. Blue Suede Shoes	17. Lira
8. Loss leader	18. Simply Red
9. Financial Times Stock Exchange	19. Big Bang
10. Adam Smith	20. South Sea Bubble

MEDIUM QUIZZES

Quiz 69: Art and Architecture

1. Which architect designed the Church of the Holy Family in Barcelona?

2. The Clifton Suspension Bridge was designed by which engineer?

3. The Hermitage Museum is in which Russian city?

4. Walter Gropius founded which school of architecture?

5. The Guggenheim Museum in New York was designed by which architect?

6. Which outspoken Chinese artist was imprisoned for 81 days in 2011 on tax avoidance charges?

7. Sir Edwin Lutyens designed which Asian capital city?

8. The Turner Contemporary gallery is in which Kent town?

9. What would you expect to find in a mastaba?

10. Which famous financial institution was designed by Sir John Soane?

11. In which country would you find the Burj Khalifa, the tallest building in the world?

12. What do the initials LS in LS Lowry stand for?

13. What was the architect Charles Edouard Jeanneret better known as?

14. Which abstract expressionist painter is mentioned in the song Going Down by the Stone Roses?

15. Which British architect designed London City Hall, the Millennium Bridge and Berlin's Reichstag?

16. The Whispering Gallery is in which London building?

17. St Chad's and St Philip's are cathedrals in which British city?

18. Which order of architecture is said to have proportions based on those of a woman's body?

19. Diane Arbus was a notable figure in which artistic discipline?
    a) Painting
    b) Photography
    c) Sculpture

20. A bronze artwork by which British sculptor was stolen from Dulwich Park in late 2011?
    a) Anthony Gormley
    b) Barbara Hepworth
    c) William Pye

MEDIUM

Answers to Quiz 134: Pot Luck

1. Boxing Day
2. Michael Gambon
3. Halal
4. Polyvinylchloride
5. 5 cents
6. CS Lewis
7. Candle in the Wind 97 by Elton John
8. Peter Davison
9. Labour
10. From Me To You
11. Abel
12. Pro bono
13. Pyrrhic Victory
14. Hosni Mubarak
15. California
16. In their forties
17. O, A, B, AB
18. Alice Cooper
19. Mr Bubbly
20. Stockholm

Quiz 70: Pot Luck

1. What does it mean when an MP applies for the stewardship of the Chiltern Hundreds?

2. In computing what does the acronym JPEG stand for?

3. In which county would you find Leeds Castle?

4. The 2012 film The Hunger Games is based on a novel by which American author?

5. Dhaka is the capital city of which country?

6. William Henry Pratt was the real name of which horror actor?

7. The Potomac River flows through which capital city?

8. What is the smallest English city to have a cathedral?

9. Which US Senator is best remembered for his anti-Communist witch hunts?

10. In Ireland, someone with the initials TD after their name is a member of which body?

11. What is the name of the nightclub in TV drama The Sopranos?

12. Which monarch was the proposed victim in the Babington Plot?

13. Which composer wrote the opera Aida?

14. Where is an epitaph usually written?

15. What was the ancient Egyptian form of writing in which pictures of people were used to represent words or sounds?

16. Roy of the Rovers played football for which club?

17. How many of Henry VIII's wives were beheaded?

18. Panama hats originated in which country?

19. At its shortest point, how far apart are England and France?
    a) 21 miles
    b) 25 miles
    c) 31 miles

20. In the cult TV show of the same name, what number was The Prisoner
    a) 4
    b) 6
    c) 8

Answers to Quiz 69: Art and Architecture

1. Antonio Gaudi
2. Isambard Kingdom Brunel
3. St Petersburg
4. Bauhaus
5. Frank Lloyd Wright
6. Ai Weiwei
7. New Delhi
8. Margate
9. Dead bodies – A mastaba is an ancient Egyptian tomb
10. Bank of England
11. United Arab Emirates
12. Laurence Stephen
13. Le Corbusier
14. Jackson Pollock
15. Norman Foster
16. St Paul's Cathedral
17. Birmingham
18. Ionic
19. Photography
20. Barbara Hepworth

Quiz 71: Astronomy and Space

1. Cape Canaveral is found in which American state?

2. What unit describes a distance of 3.26 light years?

3. What is the lowest part of the earth's atmosphere?

4. The Great Red Spot is found on which planet of the solar system?

5. Excluding the sun, what is the brightest star in the night sky?

6. How many known constellations are there in the night sky?

7. The volcano Olympus Mons is on which planet?

8. Which two gases make up approximately 98% of the sun?

9. What celestial event occurs when the moon is between the earth and the sun?

10. Which astronomer was the first to prove that comets travel in orbits?

11. Who was the first American to go into space?

12. Which astronomer showed that the sun rather than the earth was at the centre of the universe?

13. What celestial feature takes its name from the Greek word for milk?

14. What constellation is also known as Aquila?

15. What is the largest constellation in the night sky?

16. The asteroid belt is largely found between the orbits of which two planets?

17. Sir Francis Graham-Smith, Sir Arnold Wolfendale and Martin Rees are the three most recent holders of which post?

18. The 27 moons of Uranus are named after characters from the works of which two authors?

19. Approximately how many times bigger is the sun than the earth?
    a) 10
    b) 100
    c) 1000

20. Titan, Janus and Phoebe are moons that orbit which planet?
    a) Jupiter
    b) Saturn
    c) Uranus

Answers to Quiz 70: Pot Luck

1. He or she wants to resign
2. Joint Photographic Experts Group
3. Kent
4. Suzanne Collins
5. Bangladesh
6. Boris Karloff
7. Washington DC
8. Wells
9. Joseph McCarthy
10. Parliament
11. Bada Bing
12. Elizabeth I
13. Verdi
14. On a gravestone
15. Hieroglyphs
16. Melchester Rovers
17. Two
18. Ecuador
19. 21 miles
20. 6

MEDIUM

Quiz 72: Pot Luck

1. Tallinn is the capital city of which country?

2. Nirvana's Kurt Cobain, Rolling Stone Brian Jones and Amy Winehouse all died at what age?

3. The MPLA and UNITA were involved in a civil war in which African country?

4. What is the largest US state by population?

5. What is measured in joules?

6. In aviation what does the acronym QANTAS stand for?

7. Who was the last British sovereign to lead an army into battle?

8. The Grand Union Canal links which two English cities?

9. The musical My Fair Lady was based on which play by George Bernard Shaw?

10. The Miss World contest, the Eurovision Song Contest and Blue Peter all first appeared in which decade?

11. Triskaidekaphobia is the fear of what?

12. She Who Must Be Obeyed was the unseen wife of which TV character?

13. Which Hollywood legend directed the first ever episode of detective show Columbo?

14. Which Friends star, in an advert for Tampax, was the first person to say period on US TV?

15. Who was the first presenter of A Question of Sport?

16. What name describes a novel in which real people feature under assumed names?

17. A fromologist is someone who loves what type of food?

18. Which high-profile politician has been MP for Glasgow Kelvin, Bethnal Green and Bow, and most recently Bradford West?

19. How many characters of information are in a gigabyte?
    a) 1 million
    b) 1 billion
    c) 1 trillion

20. What is the Spanish soldier Rodrigo Diaz de Vivar better known as?
    a) El Cid
    b) Spartacus
    c) El Greco

MEDIUM

Answers to Quiz 71: Astronomy and Space

1. Florida
2. Parsec
3. Troposphere
4. Jupiter
5. Sirius (Dog star)
6. 88
7. Mars
8. Hydrogen and helium
9. Solar eclipse
10. Edmond Halley
11. Alan Shepard
12. Nicolaus Copernicus
13. Galaxy
14. The Eagle
15. Hydra
16. Mars and Jupiter
17. Astronomer Royal
18. William Shakespeare and Alexander Pope
19. 100
20. Saturn

Quiz 73: Food and Drink

1. What Japanese alcoholic drink is made using fermented rice?

2. What is a bratwurst?

3. What type of bread takes its name from the Italian word for slipper?

4. Capsicum annuum is the Latin name for which vegetable?

5. Which Cumbrian town gives its name to a type of mint cake?

6. Emmental cheese comes from which country?

7. What type of fish is a kipper?

8. In UHT milk, what does UHT stand for?

9. Raisins are the dried version of which fruit?

10. Which drink's name is derived from the Dutch for burnt wine?

11. Marmande, oxheart and pomodorino are varieties of which food?

12. What is a ramekin?

13. Ghee is an Indian type of what?

14. What is the main ingredient in the dish Bombay duck?

15. Bacon is wrapped around what to make the dish Devils on Horseback?

16. What is the main ingredient in the Russian soup borscht?

17. The wines Hock and Moselle comes from which country?

18. Pig's blood, fat and oatmeal are the ingredients in what type of pudding?

19. What is soya bean curd more commonly known as?
    a) spam
    b) tofu
    c) quorn

20. A blini is a a stuffed pancake most commonly found in which country?
    a) France
    b) Germany
    c) Russia

Answers to Quiz 72: Pot Luck

1. Estonia
2. 27
3. Angola
4. California
5. Energy
6. Queensland And Northern Territory Aerial Service
7. George II
8. London and Birmingham
9. Pygmalion
10. 1950s
11. The number 13
12. Rumpole of the Bailey
13. Steven Spielberg
14. Courtney Cox
15. David Vine
16. Roman a clef
17. Cheese
18. George Galloway
19. 1 billion
20. El Cid

Quiz 74: Pot Luck

1. What is the Gravelly Hill Interchange more commonly known as?

2. When describing an alcoholic drink what does the acronym VSOP stand for?

3. The Tales of Hoffman is an opera by which composer?

4. Which group, formed in the 1970s, took their name from a British cinema chain?

5. What award winning playwright was born Tomáš Straüssler?

6. Which four US states have the prefix New?

7. Which 18th century French philosopher wrote The Social Contract?

8. What is the name of the wide, water-filled ditch that surrounds a castle?

9. What type of vehicles were Airwolf and Blue Thunder?

10. The knot is a unit of measurement of what?

11. Martin Luther King and Robert Kennedy were both assassinated in which year?

12. Jakarta is the capital city of which country?

13. Which suffragette threw herself under the King's horse in the 1913 Epsom Derby?

14. Former UN General Secretary Kofi Annan is from which country?

15. Who did George W Bush beat in the 2004 US Presidential election?

16. The Mappa Mundi is housed in which English Cathedral?

17. Blue Mountain and Caturra are varieties of what type of drink?

18. You'll Never Walk Alone is a song from which Rodgers and Hammerstein musical?

19. The first Eurovision Song Contest took place in which year?
    a) 1954
    b) 1955
    c) 1956

20. When entering the House of Lords Margaret Thatcher became Baroness of
    a) Grantham
    b) Hendon
    c) Kesteven

MEDIUM

Answers to Quiz 73: Food and Drink

1. Sake
2. A German sausage
3. Ciabatta
4. Pepper
5. Kendal
6. Switzerland
7. Herring
8. Ultra High Temperature
9. Grapes
10. Brandy (brandewijn)
11. Tomato
12. A small casserole dish
13. Butter
14. Fish
15. Prunes
16. Beetroot
17. Germany
18. Black pudding
19. Tofu
20. Russia

Quiz 75: Geography

1. What is the second highest mountain in the world?

2. What is the German area of Bayern more commonly known as in English?

3. Which American city is known as the Mile High City?

4. Which Scottish mountain range separates the Lowlands from the Highlands?

5. The River Po is the longest river in which country?

6. What is the largest lake in mainland Britain?

7. Table Mountain overlooks which African city?

8. Quito is the capital city of which South American country?

9. The Bay of Biscay borders which two countries?

10. In what country would you find Sugar Loaf Mountain?

11. What is the former name of the Vietnamese capital Ho Chi Minh City?

12. Which major European city lies on the Amstel River?

13. In which country would you find the Murray-Darling River?

14. The Bering Sea separates which two continents?

15. Hokkaido is the biggest island of which country?

16. The Atlas Mountains are located on which continent?

17. The Azores are found in which ocean?

18. Astana is the capital city of which former Soviet Republic?

19. Which river forms the border between Germany, Liechtenstein and Switzerland?
    a) Rhine
    b) Rhone
    c) Oder

20. Lake Tiberias is also known as the Sea of
    a) Bethlehem
    b) Galilee
    c) Nazareth

Answers to Quiz 74: Pot Luck

1. Spaghetti Junction
2. Very Superior Old Pale
3. Offenbach
4. Roxy Music
5. Tom Stoppard
6. Jersey, York, Hampshire and Mexico
7. Jean-Jacques Rousseau
8. Moat
9. Helicopters
10. Speed
11. 1968
12. Indonesia
13. Emily Davison
14. Ghana
15. John Kerry
16. Hereford
17. Coffee
18. Carousel
19. 1956
20. Kesteven

Quiz 76: Pot Luck

1. What connects a legendary king and the winner of The Derby in 2012?

2. Who died in a plane crash, aged 22, alongside Ritchie Valens and the Big Bopper?

3. Charles Taylor was formerly the president of which country?

4. Angola and Mozambique were formerly colonies of which European country?

5. Which novelist wrote Chitty Chitty Bang Bang?

6. Amman is the capital city of which country?

7. The axilla is the medical name for what part of the body?

8. What is the most common blood group?

9. What railway runs between Moscow and Vladivostock?

10. What is the largest castle in Wales?

11. Warsaw was the original name of which Manchester group?

12. What nationality was the composer Berlioz?

13. 'That's right, that's right – attaboy Clarence' is the last line of which classic Christmas film?

14. What animal lives in a den called a holt?

15. Cambria was the Roman name for which country?

16. In January 1942 comedian Vic Oliver became the first person to appear on what long-running radio programme?

17. Which member of Monty Python made a guest appearance in TV comedy Cheers?

18. Which singer launched her own fragrances called Xpose and Inspire?

19. How many horns does the white rhino have?
    a) 0
    b) 1
    c) 2

20. On the Beaufort Scale, what is represented by the number 12?
    a) strong gale
    b) storm
    c) hurricane

MEDIUM

Answers to Quiz 75: Geography

1. K2
2. Bavaria
3. Denver
4. Grampians
5. Italy
6. Loch Lomond
7. Cape Town
8. Ecuador
9. Spain and France
10. Brazil
11. Saigon
12. Amsterdam
13. Australia
14. Asia and North America
15. Japan
16. Africa
17. Atlantic
18. Kazakhstan
19. Rhine
20. Galilee

Quiz 77: TV Comedies

1. Martin and Ann Bryce, Paul Ryman and Howard and Hilda Hughes were characters in which 80s sitcom?

2. What was the name of the housekeeper in Father Ted?

3. Which character in The Big Bang Theory can't talk to women without alcohol?

4. Rik Mayall played Alan B'stard in which political comedy?

5. In Absolutely Fabulous, what is Patsy's surname?

6. George Costanza, Elaine Benes and Cosmo Kramer were characters in which US sitcom?

7. Which Abba song provided the title to an Alan Partridge chat show?

8. Who played Timothy Lumsden in Sorry?

9. What was the name of the sitcom that starred Steve Coogan as a roadie turned pest controller?

10. Who plays foul mouthed spin doctor Malcolm Tucker in The Thick Of It?

11. Adam Smallbone is the lead character in which ecclesiastical comedy?

12. Who starred alongside Judi Dench in As Time Goes By?

13. What was the name of Victor Meldrew's wife in One Foot In The Grave?

14. What is the name of the family in My Family?

15. Which nurse was the object of Arkwright's affections in Open All Hours?

16. The fictional Manchester Medlock University is the setting for which comedy drama?

17. Brendan O'Carroll plays which foul mouthed, Irish matriarch?

18. In Everybody Loves Raymond what is Ray's job?

19. In 'Allo, 'Allo what was the name of Rene's wife?
    a) Edith
    b) Michelle
    c) Yvette

20. Ruth Jones played the lead role in which sitcom?
    a) Cilla
    b) Della
    c) Stella

MEDIUM

Answers to Quiz 76: Pot Luck

1. Camelot
2. Buddy Holly
3. Liberia
4. Portugal
5. Ian Fleming
6. Jordan
7. Armpit
8. O
9. Trans-Siberian
10. Caerphilly
11. Joy Division
12. French
13. It's A Wonderful Life
14. Otter
15. Wales
16. Desert Island Discs
17. John Cleese
18. Christina Aguilera
19. 2
20. Hurricane

Quiz 78: Pot Luck

1. Which cartoon couple were the first to be shown in bed together on US prime time TV?

2. Who was the original host of Family Fortunes?

3. Rabat is the capital city of which African country?

4. Which group took their name from a 1960 film starring Robert Wagner and Natalie Wood?

5. Bulgarian defector Georgi Markov was poisoned in London from poison dispensed from what?

6. The Levant region borders which sea?

7. The volcanic Mount Teide is found on which of the Canary Islands?

8. Who wrote the Thomas the Tank Engine books?

9. Helvetia was the Roman name for which country?

10. Which Aldous Huxley novel takes its name from a line from Shakespeare's The Tempest?

11. Carisbrooke Castle was used as a prison to hold which English Monarch in 1647 and 1648?

12. Which two US states start with the word North?

13. What is the name of the computerised scoreboard in Family Fortunes?

14. What type of gift is traditionally associated with a 55th wedding anniversary?

15. Who had a van called The Mystery Machine?

16. In what year was the Magna Carta signed?

17. Which actor's autobiography was Boy Wonder: My Life in Tights?

18. Hydroponics involves growing plants without what?

19. Which heavy metal band are named after a medieval torture device?
a) Black Sabbath
b) Iron Maiden
c) Slayer

20. Queen Boudicca was the leader of which tribe?
a) Iceni
b) Mercians
c) Picts

MEDIUM

Answers to Quiz 77: TV Comedies

1. Ever Decreasing Circles
2. Mrs Doyle
3. Raj
4. The New Statesman
5. Stone
6. Seinfeld
7. Knowing Me, Knowing You
8. Ronnie Corbett
9. Saxondale
10. Peter Capaldi
11. Rev.
12. Geoffrey Palmer
13. Margaret
14. Harper
15. Nurse Gladys Emmanuel
16. Fresh Meat
17. Agnes Brown in Mrs Brown's Boys
18. Sportswriter
19. Edith
20. Stella

Quiz 79: Connections part 1

1. Dave Hill was guitarist with which glam rock band?

2. Who hosted TV gameshow Lucky Ladders?

3. What substance is used to seal the gaps between bathroom tiles?

4. Who succeeded Graham Taylor as manager of the England football team?

5. In 2011 Jenson Button and Lewis Hamilton drove for which Formula One team?

6. Which football team play their home games at the Crown Stadium?

7. Isabella Rossellini is the daughter of which Swedish actress?

8. Which playwright wrote Up 'n' Under, Bouncers and Teechers?

9. Which Cornish town is home to a Tate Gallery?

10. What is someone who makes arrows called?

11. Who succeeded David Coleman as the presenter of A Question of Sport?

12. What is the Spanish word for white?

13. What was the name of the Commission charged with investigating the assassination of President Kennedy?

14. Who won I'm a Celebrity, Get Me Out of Here in 2007?

15. Portmeirion served as The Village in which 1960s drama?

16. Which eccentric English lord formed a Formula One motor racing team in the 1970s?

17. What links authors Jeffrey Archer, William Blake, Oscar Wilde and Alexander Solzhenitsyn?

18. The crest of which Scottish clan is a dagger held erect?
    a) McClean
    b) McKay
    c) McLeod

19. Another word for tepid is?
    a) Johnwarm
    b) Lukewarm
    c) Markwarm

20. What connects the answers to the above questions?

MEDIUM

Answers to Quiz 78: Pot Luck

1. Fred and Wilma Flintstone
2. Bob Monkhouse
3. Morocco
4. Fine Young Cannibals
5. An umbrella
6. Mediterranean
7. Tenerife
8. Reverend Wilbert Awdry
9. Switzerland
10. Brave New World
11. Charles I
12. Dakota and Carolina
13. Mr Babbage
14. Emerald
15. Scooby Doo and Friends
16. 1215
17. Burt Ward
18. Soil
19. Iron Maiden
20. Iceni

Quiz 80: Pot Luck

MEDIUM

1. What does Kraftwerk mean in English?

2. A web address ending .de comes from which country?

3. Composer Edward Elgar was born in which English county?

4. Which River flows through Germany, Austria, Slovakia, Hungary, Croatia, Serbia, Bulgaria, Moldova and Ukraine?

5. Leopold and Molly Bloom and Stephen Daedalus are characters in which Irish classic?

6. What sort of railways are designed to go up and down steep hills or mountains?

7. A car from which country would have the registration initials IL?

8. Jesus of Nazareth was crucified on which mountain?

9. The Roman emperor Claudius died after eating which poisonous vegetable?

10. Who is the patron saint of children?

11. Which 80s group took its name from the French for 'fast fashion'?

12. Abuja is the capital city of which country?

13. Detectives Crockett and Tubbs appeared in which TV cop show?

14. Which actor's dying words were 'I should never have switched from scotch to Martini'?

15. How many pairs of chromosomes are there in the human body?

16. What is the largest gland in the human body?

17. Which two US states start with the word South?

18. What was the name of the disciple who replaced Judas Iscariot?

19. What is the name of the professor in Pygmalion?
    a) Henry Higgins
    b) William Wiggins
    c) Dandy Diggins

20. A ten pin bowling pin has to tilt by how many degrees to fall over?
    a) 7.5
    b) 17.5
    c) 27.5

MEDIUM

Answers to Quiz 79: Connections part 1

1. Slade
2. Lennie Bennett
3. Grout
4. Terry Venables
5. McLaren
6. Accrington Stanley
7. Ingrid Bergman
8. John Godber
9. St Ives
10. Fletcher
11. Sue Barker
12. Blanco
13. Warren Commission
14. Christopher Biggins
15. The Prisoner
16. Lord Hesketh
17. They've all been in prison
18. McKay
19. Lukewarm
20. TV comedy Porridge

Quiz 81: Connections part 2

1. What is another name for a traditional beer mug made out of stoneware?

2. Which novel by Charles Dickens is also known as The Parish Boy's Progress?

3. What is the most common surname in the United Kingdom?

4. Which soul singer had 1967 hits with Knock On Wood and Things Get Better?

5. Chris Barrie played which character in TV sitcom Red Dwarf?

6. In EastEnders, what was Kat Moon's maiden name?

7. What is the French word for white?

8. Which singer's real name is Anna Mae Bullock?

9. What film company was founded by siblings Jack, Harry, Albert and Sam in 1918?

10. Who was Chancellor of the Exchequer from 1983 until 1989?

11. What was the name of the character played by David Mitchell in TV sitcom Peep Show?

12. Who captained the England cricket team between 1993 and 1998?

13. Michael Douglas played which character in the 1987 film Wall Street?

14. Venice Airport is named after which traveller and explorer?

15. What is the largest of the Greek Dodecanese Islands?

16. In cooking, what is a mixture of equal parts fat and flour used for thickening sauces and soups?

Answers – page 167

17. What do Americans call a bum bag?

18. In the book of Genesis, who was the second son of Jacob and Zilpah?
a) Asher
b) Dinah
c) Judah

19. Which actor's film debut was in The Man In Grey?
a) Stewart Granger
b) David Niven
c) Errol Flynn

20. What connects the above answers?

MEDIUM

Answers to Quiz 80: Pot Luck

1. Power station
2. Germany
3. Worcestershire
4. The Danube
5. Ulysses
6. Funicular
7. Israel
8. Golgotha
9. Mushrooms
10. St Nicholas
11. Depeche Mode
12. Nigeria
13. Miami Vice
14. Humphrey Bogart
15. 23
16. The liver
17. Dakota and Carolina
18. Matthias
19. Henry Higgins
20. 7.5

Quiz 82: Pot Luck

1. Port of Spain is the capital city of which Caribbean country?

2. Oxygen has what atomic number?

3. Which pair of aviators were the first to fly across the Atlantic Ocean?

4. Mr Lockwood and Nelly Deane are the narrators in which classic novel?

5. The US state of Virginia was named after which English monarch?

6. What does a deltiologist collect?

7. What is the only muscle in the body that is attached at only one end?

8. What is the name of the bone that extends from the shoulder to the elbow?

9. What is the only American state that is one syllable long?

10. What does a founder traditionally make?

11. What is the only London Underground station that doesn't contain any of the letters from the word badger?

12. The Sandwich Islands was the former name of which island group?

13. What is the only letter of the alphabet that has three syllables?

14. Frank Sinatra and George Clooney both played which fictional movie conman?

15. What is the only continent that doesn't have a desert?

16. The Caretaker, The Homecoming and The Birthday Party were written by which Nobel prize winner?

17. Which folk rock band share a name with an 18th century agriculturalist?

18. In which city would you find the opera house La Scala?

19. What is the rapid transit system in Chicago called?
    a) L
    b) M
    c) N

20. Mary Anderson invented which car component?
    a) seat belt
    b) electric windows
    c) windscreen wiper

MEDIUM

Answers to Quiz 81: Connections part 2

1. Stein
2. Oliver Twist
3. Smith
4. Eddie Floyd
5. Arnold Rimmer
6. Slater
7. Blanc
8. Tina Turner
9. Warner Bros.
10. Nigel Lawson
11. Mark Corrigan
12. Michael Atherton
13. Gordon Gekko
14. Marco Polo
15. Rhodes
16. A roux
17. A fanny pack
18. Asher
19. Stewart Granger
20. They all contain the name of a chef

Quiz 83: Brothers and Sisters

1. Which two brothers played for England in the 1966 World Cup final?

2. Which group's first number one hit was All I Have To Do Is Dream?

3. Jake Shears and Ana Matronic are vocalists with which group?

4. In 1986, Michael Caine won a Best Supporting Actor Oscar for which film?

5. Which of the acting Baldwin brothers is the only one never to have been nominated for a Razzie?

6. Which group had a 1980 top ten hit with a song called Stomp?

7. What were the Christian names of flight pioneers the Wright brothers?

8. In the cartoon The Wacky Races, who drove the Bouldermobile?

9. Which Oscar-winning actress is the sister of Warren Beatty?

10. Which brother and sister starred in the 2001 film Donnie Darko?

11. Who in the Bible asked, 'Am I my brother's keeper?'?

12. What are Drizella and Anastasia Tremaine more commonly known as?

13. Which of the Bronte sisters wrote Agnes Grey?

14. Craig Phillips was the first winner of which reality TV series?

15. What nationality were the fairytale writers the Brothers Grimm?

16. Who directed The Big Lebowski, Fargo and Miller's Crossing?

17. Sisters Goneril, Regan and Cordelia are characters in which Shakespeare play?

18. Writer Margaret Drabble is the sister of which Booker prize-winning author?

19. The Smiths had a 1986 hit singing about whose sister?
    a) Byron's
    b) Keats's
    c) Shakespeare's

20. Which group was made up of four sisters called Kim, Debbie, Joni and Kathy?
    a) Pointer Sisters
    b) Sister Sledge
    c) Beverley Sisters

MEDIUM

Answers to Quiz 82: Pot Luck

1. Trinidad and Tobago
2. 8
3. Alcock and Brown
4. Wuthering Heights
5. Elizabeth I (The Virgin Queen)
6. Postcards
7. The tongue
8. Humerus
9. Maine
10. Bells
11. Pimlico
12. Hawaiian Islands
13. W
14. Danny Ocean
15. Europe
16. Harold Pinter
17. Jethro Tull
18. Milan
19. L
20. Windscreen wiper

Quiz 84: Pot Luck

1. Maggie and Brick are the central characters in which play by Tennessee Williams?

2. Who was the first man to fly solo across the Atlantic?

3. Kiev is the capital city of which country?

4. Bradshaw's is a guide to what form of transport?

5. Which golfer is known as The Great White Shark?

6. What is the largest organ of the human body?

7. Whose final words were 'Et tu, Brute?'?

8. Springtime For Hitler is a song from which musical?

9. Which city, that shares a name with a Yorkshire town, was the capital of the Confederacy during the American Civil War?

10. Harrison Ford, Alec Baldwin and Ben Affleck have all played which on-screen action hero?

11. The purchase of which state of America was known as Seward's Folly?

12. Where would an almoner work?

13. A colporteur sells what type of books?

14. What does a conchologist collect?

15. The fabric denim takes its name from which French town?

16. What was the scheduled destination of The Titanic on its ill-fated voyage?

17. A 1965 newspaper advertisement asking for 'four insane boys, aged 17-21' led to the creation of which pop group?

18. The Magna Carta was signed by which king?

19. How long is the M25 motorway?
    a) 97 miles
    b) 107 miles
    c) 117 miles

20. What was the name of the computer in sitcom Red Dwarf?
    a) Dolly
    b) Holly
    c) Molly

MEDIUM

Answers to Quiz 83: Brothers and Sisters

1. Jack and Bobby Charlton
2. Everly Brothers
3. Scissor Sisters
4. Hannah and Her Sisters
5. Daniel
6. Brothers Johnson
7. Wilbur and Orville
8. The Slag Brothers
9. Shirley MacLaine
10. Jake and Maggie Gyllenhaal
11. Cain
12. The Ugly Sisters
13. Anne
14. Big Brother
15. German
16. The Coen Brothers
17. King Lear
18. AS Byatt
19. Shakespeare's Sister
20. Sister Sledge

Quiz 85: Movies

1. Who directed Clerks, Chasing Amy and Red State?

2. Who starred alongside Jackie Chan in the 1998 film Rush Hour?

3. What character did Alan Rickman play in Die Hard?

4. The Departed was a remake of what Hong Kong thriller?

5. Tyrannosaur was the directorial debut of which British actor?

6. Which American actor starred alongside Brendan Gleeson in The Guard?

7. Which English actor, comedian and radio DJ directed Attack The Block?

8. What were Emilio Estevez, Rob Lowe, Ally Sheedy, Demi Moore, Andrew McCarthy, Mare Winningham and Judd Nelson collectively known as?

9. Who provides the voice of Puss in the 2011 animation Puss In Boots?

10. Which musician played Feyd-Rautha in the film version of Dune?

11. What nationality are Jim Carrey, Michael J Fox and William Shatner?

12. Which former Neighbour played King Edward VIII in The King's Speech?

13. What movie creatures should never be fed after midnight?

14. What was the name of the cat in Alien?

15. What are Will McKenzie, Simon Cooper, Jay Cartwright and Neil Sutherland collectively known as?

16. The Hangover II is mostly set in which Asian country?

17. Who directed the 2011 film Thor?

18. Alphonse d'Abruzzo is the real name of which alliterative actor?

19. David Bowie played Nikola Tesla in which magically inspired film?
    a) The Prestige
    b) The Illusionist
    c) The Craft

20. What was the name of the 2011 comedy starring Simon Pegg and Nick Frost?
    a) Paul
    b) George
    c) Ringo

MEDIUM

Answers to Quiz 84: Pot Luck

1. Cat on a Hot Tin Roof
2. Charles Lindbergh
3. Ukraine
4. Railways
5. Greg Norman
6. The skin
7. Julius Caesar
8. The Producers
9. Richmond, Virginia
10. Jack Ryan
11. Alaska
12. Hospital
13. The Bible
14. Shells
15. Nîmes (de Nîmes)
16. New York
17. The Monkees
18. King John
19. 117 miles
20. Holly

Quiz 86: Pot Luck

1. What ocean liner, nicknamed The Great White Whale, served as a hospital ship in the Falklands War?

2. What is the name of the flowergirl in the play Pygmalion?

3. Which 1994 Eurovision Song Contest interval performance went on to become an international sensation?

4. What is the capital city of Canada?

5. What is the largest internal organ in the human body?

6. In which century did the Black Death sweep through Europe?

7. The operas of which composer are performed at the Bayreuth Festival?

8. Who is the youngest artist to enjoy a UK number one hit single?

9. In the name of the sports car manufacturer, what do the initials MG stand for?

10. Which fashion designer was famous for his H line and A line looks?

11. Which band were selected to represent England at the concert to mark the start of the 2012 Olympics?

12. What was the name of the policeman in Top Cat?

13. Which country was the first to give women the vote?

14. In Watership Down, what are Bigwig, Fiver, General Woundwort and Hazel?

15. What was the first song played on Radio 1?

Answers – page 177

16. Which actor and hellraiser's dying words were 'I've had a hell of a lot of fun and enjoyed every minute of it'?

17. Which antipodean band took their name from their cramped rented accommodation?

18. The decibel was named after which inventor and engineer?

19. In what year was the wearing of seat belts made compulsory in Britain?
    a) 1979
    b) 1981
    c) 1983

20. In TV drama The Professionals, Bodie and Doyle worked for what organisation?
    a) CI4
    b) CI5
    c) CI6

MEDIUM

Answers to Quiz 85: MOVIES

1. Kevin Smith
2. Chris Tucker
3. Hans Gruber
4. Infernal Affairs
5. Paddy Considine
6. Don Cheadle
7. Joe Cornish
8. The Brat Pack
9. Antonio Banderas
10. Sting
11. Canadian
12. Guy Pearce
13. Gremlins
14. Jones
15. The Inbetweeners
16. Thailand
17. Kenneth Branagh
18. Alan Alda
19. The Prestige
20. Paul

Quiz 87: James Bond

1. What was the name of author Ian Fleming's Jamaican home?

2. Which comedian wrote the Young Bond series of novels?

3. Norwegian popsters A-Ha recorded the theme to which Bond film?

4. What is Major Boothroyd from the James Bond films more commonly known as?

5. Matt Monro sang the theme tune to which Bond film?

6. Bernard Lee, Robert Brown and Judi Dench have all played which character?

7. What is Bond villain Buonaparte Ignacio Gallia more commonly known as?

8. Who is M's personal secretary?

9. Oddjob was the personal bodyguard of which Bond villain?

10. Which Bond baddie had three nipples?

11. Who wrote Colonel Sun, the first Bond novel after Ian Fleming's death?

12. Grace Jones played May Day in which film?

13. Le Chiffre was the villain in which Bond film?

14. Which Avenger played Bond's ill-fated wife?

15. Bond attended which Scottish public school?

16. What was the first Bond film that wasn't based on a novel by Ian Fleming?

17. Louis Armstrong sang the theme tune to which Bond film?

18. Who wrote the 2008 Bond novel, Devil May Care?

19. Which gameshow host had previously played Bond in a radio play?
    a) Leslie Crowther
    b) Bob Holness
    c) Bruce Forsyth

20. What was the first Bond theme to make the top 10 in the UK singles chart?
    a) Goldfinger
    b) Live and Let Die
    c) Diamonds Are Forever

MEDIUM

Answers to Quiz 86: Pot Luck

1. Canberra
2. Eliza Doolittle
3. Riverdance
4. Ottawa
5. The liver
6. 14th
7. Wagner
8. Little Jimmy Osmond
9. Morris Garages
10. Christian Dior
11. Duran Duran
12. Officer Dibble
13. New Zealand
14. Rabbits
15. Flowers In The Rain by The Move
16. Errol Flynn
17. Crowded House
18. Alexander Graham Bell
19. 1983
20. CI5

Quiz 88: Pot Luck

1. What is biltong?

2. Why do icebergs float?

3. Nassau is the capital city of which country?

4. With what song did Katrina and the Waves win the Eurovision Song Contest?

5. Dr Who comes from which planet?

6. What was the name of Lord Nelson's flagship at the Battle of Trafalgar?

7. Who designed Princess Diana's wedding dress?

8. What was TV detective Inspector Morse's Christian name?

9. What is the highest mountain in the USA?

10. Which French heroine was known as the Maid of Orleans?

11. Which Canadian topped the charts in 2012 with Call Me Maybe?

12. Who founded The Body Shop?

13. What were used for the first time at Newmarket racecourse on 8 July 1965?

14. What song, heard millions of times every day, was written by Mildred Hill and published by Clayton F Summy?

15. The highest ranking Roman Catholic clergyman in England and Wales is the Bishop of where?

16. The Scotsman newspaper is published in which city?

17. Police drama Bergerac was set on which of the Channel Islands?

18. Which two US states don't have a border with any other state?

19. In 1906, which country became the first in Europe to give women the vote?
    a) Denmark
    b) Finland
    c) Norway

20. The original Crystal Palace was erected in which London Park?
    a) Green Park
    b) Hyde Park
    c) Regent's Park

MEDIUM

Answers to Quiz 87: James Bond

1. Goldeneye
2. Charlie Higson
3. The Living Daylights
4. Q
5. From Russia With Love
6. M
7. Mr Big
8. Miss Moneypenny
9. Goldfinger
10. Scaramanga
11. Kingsley Amis
12. A View To A Kill
13. Casino Royale
14. Diana Rigg
15. Fettes
16. The Spy Who Loved Me
17. On Her Majesty's Secret Service
18. Sebastian Faulks
19. Bob Holness
20. Live and Let Die

Quiz 89: Doctors

1. Which Nazi doctor was known as The Angel of Death?

2. Which Serbian doctor was charged with war crimes at the International Criminal Court?

3. Which doctor-turned-author wrote The Master and Margarita?

4. Danish popsters Aqua had a number one hit song about which doctor?

5. Who played Dr Who in the 1965 film Dr Who and the Daleks?

6. Which Welsh rugby legend is an orthopaedic surgeon?

7. Dr Hans Zarkov appears in which science fiction film?

8. What was the name of the doctor who was convicted of the involuntary manslaughter of Michael Jackson?

9. Dr Salvadore Allende was president of which South American country?

10. What are doctors Egon Spengler, Raymond Stantz and Peter Venkman collectively known as?

11. Dr Evil is the arch-nemesis of which movie character?

12. Which film was subtitled How I Learned to Stop Worrying and Love the Bomb?

13. Dr Bunsen Honeydew is the resident scientist on which TV show?

14. Which British surgeon, born in 1827, was a pioneer of antiseptic surgery?

15. What oath is traditionally taken by doctors?

16. Played by Hugh Laurie, what is the first name of Doctor House?

17. Who wrote the children's book The Cat in the Hat?

18. Who wrote the play Dr Faustus?

19. Who played Dr Kilmore in the film Carry On Doctor?
    a) Sid James
    b) Jim Dale
    c) Kenneth Williams

20. Dr Lee Nelson is a top professional in which game?
    a) bridge
    b) chess
    c) poker

MEDIUM

Answers to Quiz 88: Pot Luck

1. Dried meat
2. Because they are made from fresh water which is less dense than sea water
3. The Bahamas
4. Love Shine A Light
5. Galifrey
6. HMS Victory
7. David and Elizabeth Emanuel
8. Endeavour
9. Mt McKinley
10. Joan of Arc
11. Carly Rae Jepsen
12. Anita Roddick
13. Starting stalls
14. Happy Birthday to You
15. Westminster
16. Edinburgh
17. Jersey
18. Alaska and Hawaii
19. Finland
20. Hyde Park

Quiz 90: Pot Luck

1. What was the artist Domenico Theotocopoulos more commonly known as?

2. Is human blood slightly acid or slightly alkaline?

3. Mrs Hudson is the landlady of which fictional sleuth?

4. In 2012, the Qatari Royal Family paid a world record £158.4m for a painting by which artist?

5. How much is the most expensive square in the board game Monopoly?

6. What is the sum of the internal angles in a hexagon?

7. The maxilla and mandible are the two bones that make up what?

8. Which children's TV show was written by Sid Waddell and featured a football team called the Glipton Grasshoppers?

9. In what decade was the MoT test for cars introduced?

10. Which football team play their home matches at Edgeley Park?

11. Axel F was the instrumental theme to which 1984 film?

12. Moorfields Hospital in London specialises in treating injuries to what part of the body?

13. Who wrote the Jimi Hendrix song All Along the Watchtower?

14. The Cuban Missile Crisis occurred in what year?

15. The abandoned Mayan city of Chichen Itza lies in which modern-day country?

16. La Paz is the administrative capital city of which country?

17. Razz, stud and Omaha are versions of which card game?

18. The kuna is the currency of which European country?

19. In cooking, what does the French word brouillé mean?
    a) poach
    b) fry
    c) scramble

20. What size paper measures 297 x 420mm?
    a) A2
    b) A3
    c) A4

MEDIUM

Answers to Quiz 89: Doctors

1. Josef Mengele
2. Radovan Karadzic
3. Mikhail Bulgakov
4. Dr Jones
5. Peter Cushing
6. JPR Williams
7. Flash Gordon
8. Dr Conrad Murray
9. Chile
10. Ghostbusters
11. Austin Powers
12. Dr Strangelove
13. The Muppet Show
14. Joseph Lister
15. Hippocratic
16. Gregory
17. Dr Seuss
18. Christopher Marlowe
19. Jim Dale
20. Poker

Quiz 91: Days of the Week

1. On what day of the week were The Cure in love?

2. What 2004 American football film starred Billy Bob Thornton?

3. What was the name of the character played by John Travolta in Saturday Night Fever?

4. What colour was New Order's Monday?

5. What name is commonly given to the day when Britain was forced to leave the ERM in 1992?

6. In the 1987 the massive stock market crash is known as Black?

7. What right wing pressure group takes its name from a day of the week?

8. According to the nursery rhyme, which child has far to go?

9. On what day of the week does the US Presidential election take place?

10. Who had a 1973 hit with Drive-In Saturday?

11. Which day of the week is associated with Mars?

12. Which band had hits with Step On and Loose Fit?

13. Complete the title of this book by Mitch Albom: Tuesdays with…?

14. Which group had a 1986 hit with Manic Monday?

15. Where did The Drifters like to spend Saturday night?

16. Which Danish popster had a 1994 hit with Saturday Night?

17. What was the B side to the 1967 Rolling Stones hit Let's Spend The Night Together?

18. In 1980, The Undertones had a hit singing about what day of the week?

19. Complete the 2004 Will Young song: Friday's...?
    a) Child
    b) Here
    c) Alive

20. In America, the first day of the Christmas shopping season is known as Black?
    a) Friday
    b) Saturday
    c) Sunday

Answers to Quiz 90: Pot Luck

1. El Greco
2. Slightly alkaline
3. Sherlock Holmes
4. Paul Cezanne
5. £400.00
6. 720 degrees
7. The jaw
8. Jossy's Giants
9. 1960s
10. Stockport County
11. Beverly Hill's Cop
12. The eyes
13. Bob Dylan
14. 1962
15. Mexico
16. Bolivia
17. Poker
18. Croatia
19. Scramble
20. A3

Quiz 92: Pot Luck

1. What African country has the largest population?

2. Winston Smith is the central character in which novel?

3. Tramar Dillard is the real name of which rapper who topped the charts with Good Feeling?

4. What was the name of Dr Who's mechanical dog?

5. What is the capital city of Croatia?

6. Not Tonight, Josephine was the working title of which classic comedy?

7. Which Oscar-winning actress went on to become MP for Hampstead and Kilburn?

8. Which US state is nicknamed the Volunteer State?

9. 'Punctured bicycle on a hillside desolate' is the opening line to which song by The Smiths?

10. Nicolae Ceaucescu was the long-time leader of which country?

11. What form of entertainment takes its name from the Japanese for empty orchestra?

12. What are the five boroughs of New York City?

13. Which Austrian director's films include The White Ribbon, Funny Games and Amour?

14. What salad takes its name from a New York hotel?

15. What ship was found abandoned in the Atlantic Ocean in 1872?

16. What is the closest Commonwealth country to the UK?

17. The play Journey's End is set during which war?

18. What would you do with a jingling johnny?

19. Which patriotic song was written by James Thomson to music by Thomas Arne?
    a) Land of Hope and Glory
    b) Jerusalem
    c) Rule, Britannia!

20. Someone suffering from myopia is
    a) long sighted or
    b) short sighted

MEDIUM

Answers to Quiz 91: Days of the Week

1. Friday
2. Friday Night Lights
3. Tony Manero
4. Blue
5. Black Wednesday
6. Monday
7. The Monday Club
8. Thursday's
9. Tuesday
10. David Bowie
11. Tuesday
12. Happy Mondays
13. Morrie
14. The Bangles
15. At The Movies
16. Whigfield
17. Ruby Tuesday
18. Wednesday
19. Child
20. Friday

Quiz 93: Education

1. What is the oldest university in Britain?

2. In which UK city would you find Queen's University?

3. De Montfort University is located in which British city?

4. Mrs McCluskey was the head teacher at which fictional school?

5. What educational establishment has the initials LSE?

6. Sidney Sussex, Downing and Homerton are colleges at which British university?

7. Keble, Wadham and Nuffield are colleges at which British university?

8. St Aidan's, St Chad's and St Cuthbert's Society are colleges at which British university?

9. In education, what does the acronym UCAS stand for?

10. In which British city would you find Heriot-Watt University?

11. William of Wykeham founded which famous public school?

12. Prince William met his wife, Kate Middleton, while studying at what university?

13. What was the name of ancient Greek school founded by Aristotle?

14. Founded in 1284, what is the oldest college at Cambridge University?

15. In education, what do the letters GCSE represent?

16. In Common People by Pulp, what was studied at St Martin's College?

17. Seymour Skinner is the principal at which fictional school?

18. Plug, Smiffy and Spotty are pupils at which fictional school?

19. Dieu le ward (God Protect Him) is the motto of which
    English public school?
    a) Ampleforth College
    b) Eton
    c) Harrow

20. Poet Philip Larkin was a librarian at which university?
    a) Oxford
    b) Cambridge
    c) Hull

Answers to Quiz 92: Pot Luck

1. Nigeria
2. 1984
3. Flo Rida
4. K9
5. Zagreb
6. Some Like It Hot
7. Glenda Jackson
8. Tennessee
9. This Charming Man
10. Romania
11. Karaoke
12. Bronx, Manhattan, Queens, Brooklyn, Staten Island
13. Michael Haneke
14. Waldorf
15. Marie Celeste
16. Malta
17. First World War
18. Play it – it's a Turkish musical instrument
19. Rule, Britannia!
20. Short sighted

Quiz 94: Pot Luck

1. Which former Miss Ohio won the Oscar for Best Actress in 2002?

2. Which comedians had a hit with the Funky Gibbon?

3. The Cod Wars involved the UK and what other country?

4. What organisation is the largest employer in the UK?

5. Aquamarina was the theme music to which puppet-based TV show?

6. Havana is the capital city of which country?

7. A tricenarian describes somebody between which ages?

8. What was the name of the plane that dropped the first atomic bomb?

9. The Finkler Question was written by which author?

10. What fruit is a cross between grapefruit, tangerine and orange?

11. 'It takes leadership to confront a nation's fear. It takes friendship to conquer your own' was the tagline to which Oscar-winning film?

12. Who comes next in this list? Kenneth Clarke, Gordon Brown, Alistair Darling

13. The musical Jersey Boys is based on the works of which group?

14. In the Wacky Races, the Chuggabug was from which American state?

15. Sancho Panza was the squire of which fictional character?

16. In what month is the earth closest to the sun?

17. What is the largest landlocked country in the world?

18. How many syllables are in a Japanese haiku poem?
    a) 13
    b) 15
    c) 17

19. What is the nickname of the US state of New Hampshire?
    a) Granite State
    b) Rock State
    c) Concrete State

MEDIUM

Answers to Quiz 93: Education

1. Oxford
2. Belfast
3. Leicester
4. Grange Hill
5. London School of Economics
6. Cambridge
7. Oxford
8. Durham
9. Universities and Colleges Admissions Service
10. Edinburgh
11. Winchester
12. St Andrews
13. Lyceum
14. Peterhouse
15. General Certificate of Secondary Education
16. Sculpture
17. Springfield Elementary
18. Bash Street
19. Ampleforth College
20. Hull University

Quiz 95: Reality TV

1. Who is the only X Factor judge to appear in every series since it started?

2. Which singer won the first series of Britain's Got Talent?

3. David Sneddon and Alex Parks were winners of which short-lived TV talent show?

4. Who is the only judge to appear in the first seven series of Dancing On Ice?

5. Which actress won Celebrity Big Brother in 2007?

6. Which member of Take That has also appeared as a judge on The X Factor?

7. Who did Alesha Dixon replace as a judge on Strictly Come Dancing?

8. Who was the winner of the first series of The X Factor?

9. Prokofiev's Montagues and Capulets is the theme music to which reality TV show?

10. Which EastEnder won Strictly Come Dancing in 2010?

11. Which X Factor finalist won I'm A Celebrity...Get Me Out of Here in 2010?

12. Which husband and wife appeared in series five of Strictly Come Dancing?

13. What is the name of the band leader on Strictly Come Dancing?

14. Girls Aloud were created from which reality TV show?

15. What nationality is Strictly dancer Brendan Cole?

16. The daughter of which politician won I'm A Celebrity... Get Me Out of Here! in 2005?

17. Who hosts the American version of The Apprentice?

18. Strictly Come Dancing winner Harry Judd is a member of which band?

19. Which of the following hasn't won Britain's Got Talent?
    a) Spellbound
    b) Susan Boyle
    c) Jai McDowall

20. Which of the following is not a reality TV show?
    a) Desperate Scousewives
    b) Geordie Shore
    c) Yummy Brummies

MEDIUM

Answers to Quiz 94: Pot Luck

1. Halle Berry
2. The Goodies
3. Iceland
4. The NHS
5. Stingray
6. Cuba
7. 30 to 39
8. Enola Gay
9. Howard Jacobson
10. Ugli
11. The King's Speech
12. George Osborne (Chancellors of the Exchequer)
13. Frankie Valli and the Four Seasons
14. Arkansas
15. Don Quixote
16. January
17. Mongolia
18. 17
19. Granite State

Quiz 96: Pot Luck

1. What song, composed by P Degeteyer, was the official anthem of Communist Russia until 1944?

2. In the High Street fashion shop what do the initials H&M stand for?

3. Addis Ababa is the capital city of which country?

4. What is measured using a hygrometer?

5. What tea clipper was seriously damaged in a fire in Greenwich in 2007?

6. In the classic TV sitcom Rising Damp, what was Rigsby's first name?

7. Who won the 2012 PDC World Darts Championship at Alexandra Palace?

8. The food sweetbreads come from which part of the body?

9. The Stars Look Down, Born to Boogie, and Electricity are songs from which musical?

10. Excluding royalty, who was the first woman to appear on a British banknote?

11. Two Pints of Lager and a Packet of Crisps is set in which town?

12. Arte et labore is the motto of which English football club?

13. During the Cold War, what did the acronym MAD stand for?

14. Suicide is Painless was the theme tune to which long-running TV comedy?

15. Motorists in Bangladesh, Barbados, Bermuda and Botswana drive on which side of the road?

16. What do Americans call the herb coriander?

17. Inhabitants of which country are known as Monegasques?

18. The Pilton Pop, Blues and Folk Festival was the original name of which music festival?

19. In what year was Prince Charles born?
    a) 1946
    b) 1948
    c) 1950

20. Which of the following is not a time zone in America?
    a) Mountain
    b) Pacific
    c) Western

MEDIUM

Answers to Quiz 95: Reality TV

1. Louis Walsh
2. Paul Potts
3. Fame Academy
4. Robin Cousins
5. Shilpa Shetty
6. Gary Barlow
7. Arlene Phillips
8. Steve Brookstein
9. The Apprentice
10. Kara Tointon
11. Stacey Solomon
12. Kenny and Gabby Logan
13. Dave Arch
14. Popstars: The Rivals
15. New Zealander
16. Margaret Thatcher (Carol)
17. Donald Trump
18. McFly
19. Susan Boyle
20. Yummy Brummies

Quiz 97: TV Gameshows

MEDIUM

1. What was the first TV programme to appear on Channel 4?

2. What is the smallest prize that can be won on Deal or No Deal?

3. Total Wipeout was filmed at a course in which country?

4. Which author and poker player hosts Only Connect?

5. Mark Labbett, Shaun Wallace, Paul Sinha and Anne Heggerty are regulars on which quiz show?

6. What was the name of the animated character in Catchphrase?

7. Jimmy Tarbuck hosted which golf-inspired game show?

8. Feel The Sportsman was a regular round in which TV quiz show?

9. What programme links Terry Wogan, Les Dawson and Lily Savage?

10. The late Bob Holness hosted which quiz show?

11. How many tasks must a contestant complete in order to win the jackpot on The Cube?

12. What Euro-quiz show was hosted by Henry Kelly?

13. Who succeeded Bob Monkhouse as host of Family Fortunes?

14. Who was the original host of University Challenge?

15. What is the name of the electronic score board on Family Fortunes?

16. Who was the original host of Never Mind The Buzzcocks?

17. In Bullseye, contestants needed to score how much in six darts to win the star prize?

18. Which award winning DJ hosted Confessions?

19. Complete the title of the antiques-based TV show: Dealing with...?
    a) Barbie
    b) Dickinson
    c) Serrell

20. Which of the following wasn't a zone on the Crystal Maze?
    a) Incan
    b) Industrial
    c) Medieval

MEDIUM

Answers to Quiz 96: Pot Luck

1. Internationale
2. Hennes & Mauritz
3. Ethiopia
4. Humidity
5. Cutty Sark
6. Rupert
7. Adrian Lewis
8. Pancreas
9. Billy Elliott
10. Florence Nightingale
11. Runcorn
12. Blackburn Rovers
13. Mutually Assured Destruction
14. M.A.S.H.
15. Left
16. Cilantro
17. Monaco
18. Glastonbury
19. 1948
20. Western

Quiz 98: Pot Luck

1. Olfactory means relating to which human sense?

2. What is the common childhood disease varicella more commonly known as?

3. In 1952, George Jorgensen underwent the first operation to change what?

4. According to naval superstition, any sailor who sees which ghost ship will die within a day?

5. Which song by the Beatles ends with a note sustained for 40 seconds?

6. The focal point of the 2011 political uprising in Cairo, what does Tahrir in Tahrir Square mean?

7. Which Frenchman resigned as head of the International Monetary Fund in 2011?

8. Suva is the capital city of which Asian country?

9. Jarlsberg cheese comes from which country?

10. The 2011 movie Melancholia was directed by which controversial film maker?

11. What Latin named Roman Catholic organisation translates into English as Work of God?

12. Plantain is the cooking variety of which fruit?

13. Which children's TV show featured characters called Timothy Claypole, Hubert Davenport and Miss Nadia Popov?

14. What name is given to a selection of different Indian dishes, usually served in small steel bowls on a round tray?

15. The Golden Temple is in which Indian city?

16. Fanfare for the Common Man was written by which composer?

17. If someone is singing a capella they are doing it without what?

18. Strictly Come Dancing judge Bruno Tonioli appeared in the video to which Elton John hit?

19. What was missing from the 2011 Sports Personality of the Year award shortlist?
    a) Athletes
    b) Golfers
    c) Women

20. What is the nickname of the US state of Minnesota?
    a) East Star State
    b) North Star State
    c) South Star State

MEDIUM

Answers to Quiz 97: TV Gameshows

1. Countdown
2. 1p
3. Argentina
4. Victoria Coren
5. The Chase
6. Mr Chips
7. Full Swing
8. They Think It's All Over
9. Blankety Blank
10. Blockbusters
11. 7
12. Going For Gold
13. Max Bygraves
14. Bamber Gascoigne
15. Mr Babbage
16. Mark Lamarr
17. 101
18. Simon Mayo
19. Dickinson
20. Incan

Quiz 99: History part 1

1. Which Scottish prince was known as 'The Young Pretender'?

2. Who was the British Prime Minister during the Suez Crisis?

3. Which French monarch was known as the 'Sun King'?

4. Who was the first Plantagenet king of England?

5. Founded in 1645, what was the name of the parliamentary army commanded by Thomas Fairfax and then Oliver Cromwell?

6. What was Nazi propagandist William Joyce more commonly known as?

7. Who, when asked what he thought of Western civilisation said, 'I think it would be a very good idea'?

8. What nationality was the explorer Vasco da Gama?

9. On 14 July each year the French celebrate Bastille Day but what was the Bastille?

10. Idi Amin was the president of which African country?

11. Which battle is also known as Custer's Last Stand?

12. The scene of a famous World War One battle, in what country is Gallipoli?

13. Politician Vidkun Quisling, who collaborated with the Nazis in World War Two, was from which Scandinavian country?

14. Who was the first Prime Minister of Israel?

15. Who was the first Tsar of Russia?

16. Who was Britain's first Labour Party Prime Minister?

17. What flat, currant biscuit is named after an Italian soldier and statesman?

18. In what year did the Act of Union between Scotland and England come into effect?

19. What was the cause of Britain's 19th century wars against China?
    a) cocaine
    b) marijuana
    c) opium

20. What was the name of the secret US project to design the atom bomb?
    a) Delaware Project
    b) Manhattan Project
    c) Washington Project

MEDIUM

Answers to Quiz 98: Pot Luck

1. Smell
2. Chicken Pox
3. His sex
4. Flying Dutchman
5. A Day In The Life
6. Liberation Square
7. Dominique Strauss Khan
8. Fiji
9. Norway
10. Lars von Trier
11. Opus Dei
12. Banana
13. Rentaghost
14. Thali
15. Amritsar
16. Aaron Copland
17. Without musical accompaniment
18. I'm Still Standing
19. Women
20. North Star State

Quiz 100: Pot Luck

1. What is the light sensitive part of the eyeball called?

2. How many teeth are in a full adult set?

3. The lingua is the medical name of what part of the body?

4. What disease takes its name from a pneumonia outbreak at convention in Philadelphia in 1976?

5. Someone with acrophobia fears what?

6. Tbilisi is the capital city of which former Soviet Republic?

7. Chopin's Minute Waltz is the theme music to which radio programme?

8. What is the first name of Sherlock Holmes' sidekick Dr Watson?

9. What edible plant is also known as arugula?

10. In 1945, atomic bombs were dropped on which two Japanese cities?

11. In which city would you find the Rijksmuseum?

12. Michael Keaton, Christian Bale and George Clooney have all played which fictional movie character?

13. Which comedian hosted a TV show called Golden Balls?

14. Which painter designed the logo for sweet company Chupa Chups?

15. What is the most expensive spice in the world?

16. What was the name of the nuclear plant damaged in the Japanese earthquake and tsunami of 2011?

17. What name is given to glass that contains 2/3 of a pint?

18. What cocktail is made using 1 part vodka, 2 parts orange juice and 2 teaspoons of Galliano?

19. Who hasn't appeared on Strictly Come Dancing?
    a) Kate Garraway
    b) Lorraine Kelly
    c) Fiona Phillips

20. Potophobia is the fear of what?
    a) alcohol
    b) potatoes
    c) caves

Answers to Quiz 99: History part 1

1. Bonnie Prince Charlie (Charles Edward Stuart)	11. The Battle of Little Bighorn
2. Sir Anthony Eden	12. Turkey
3. Louis XIV	13. Norway
4. Henry II	14. David Ben-Gurion
5. The New Model Army	15. Ivan the Terrible
6. Lord Haw Haw	16. Ramsay MacDonald
7. Mahatma Gandhi	17. Garibaldi
8. Portuguese	18. 1707
9. A prison	19. Opium
10. Uganda	20. Manhattan Project

Quiz 101: Religion

1. What book of the New Testament comes after the four gospels?

2. The Hadith is a sacred text in which religion?

3. What festival marks the Jewish New Year?

4. What religion was founded in the 15th century by Guru Nanak?

5. Who is Siddhartha Gautama more commonly known as?

6. Which two books of the Bible are named after women?

7. The tomb of the prophet Muhammad is in which city?

8. Who did Rowan Williams succeed as Archbishop of Canterbury?

9. What is the name of the Muslim pilgrimage to Mecca?

10. What are members of the Church of Jesus Christ of Latter Day Saints known as?

11. The leader of the Roman Catholic Church in England is the Archbishop of where?

12. Sangha Day and Vesak are holidays observed by followers of what religion?

13. Which clergyman's traditional residence was Fulham Palace?

14. What order of monks are known as the Black Friars?

15. Which of the 12 Apostles was the brother of Peter?

16. What is the last word written in the Bible?

17. The Bible was written in which three languages?

18. What name is given to the seven-branched candelabrum which is a symbol of Judaism?

19. Who is the patron saint of Spain?
    a) St James
    b) St John
    c) St Peter

20. How many books are in the New Testament?
    a) 17
    b) 27
    c) 37

MEDIUM

Answers to Quiz 100: Pot Luck

1. Retina
2. 32
3. The tongue
4. Legionnaires' Disease
5. Heights
6. Georgia
7. Just A Minute
8. John
9. Rocket
10. Hiroshima and Nagasaki
11. Amsterdam
12. Batman
13. Jasper Carrott
14. Salvador Dali
15. Saffron
16. Fukushima
17. Schooner
18. Harvey Wallbanger
19. Lorraine Kelly
20. Alcohol

Quiz 102: Pot Luck

1. Footballer Cristiano Ronaldo was born on which island?

2. What substance is rubbed across the bows of string instruments to enhance friction?

3. Which US state is known as the Hoosier State?

4. Which British ship was torpedoed off the coast of Ireland on 7 May 1915, resulting in the loss of 1,198 lives?

5. Stanley is the capital city of which Atlantic archipelago?

6. What nickname is given to a politician who runs for office in an area where he or she has no ties?

7. What fruit, cream and meringue dessert was named after a Russian ballerina?

8. Which snooker player is known as the Wizard of Wishaw?

9. Captain Benjamin Willard is the central character in which Vietnam war film?

10. Ablutophobia is the fear of what?

11. Which rapper played Huggy Bear in the big-screen version of Starsky and Hutch?

12. Who resigned as manager of the England rugby union team in November 2011?

13. Which group recorded the theme tune to The Big Bang Theory?

14. Before embarking on a solo career Belinda Carlisle was lead singer with which group?

15. Who is the only Spice Girl never to have had a solo number one?

Answers – page 209

16. Who were Scooby Doo's two male companions?

17. Which is bigger – England or the American region of New England?

18. What are the Northern Lights also known as?

19. What is the nickname of the British 7th Armoured Division?
    a) Desert Dogs
    b) Desert Camels
    c) Desert Rats

20. Who played a guitar solo on Michael Jackson's Beat It?
    a) Slash
    b) Jon Bon Jovi
    c) Eddie Van Halen

Answers to Quiz 101: Religion

1. Acts of the Apostles
2. Islam
3. Rosh Hashana
4. Sikhism
5. Buddha
6. Ruth and Esther
7. Medina
8. George Carey
9. Hajj
10. Mormons
11. Westminster
12. Buddhism
13. Bishop of London
14. Dominicans
15. Andrew
16. Amen
17. Greek, Aramaic and Hebrew
18. Menorah
19. St James
20. 27

MEDIUM

Quiz 103: Night and Day

1. 'If music be the food of love, play on' is the opening line of which Shakespeare play?

2. A car called KITT appeared in which TV show?

3. What religious feast is also called Lady Day?

4. Which group had hits with American Idiot and Boulevard of Broken Dreams?

5. Who won the Best Actor Oscar for My Left Foot and There Will Be Blood?

6. What long running programme first aired on 22 August 1964?

7. Which actress and singer's real surname was Kappelhoff?

8. Freddy Krueger was a character in which series of horror films?

9. What is the Jewish festival of Yom Kippur also known as?

10. Who played James Bond in Die Another Day?

11. Which Russian author wrote One Day in the Life of Ivan Denisovich?

12. What night is celebrated in Scotland on 25 January?

13. Which nurse was known as 'The Lady with the Lamp'?

14. What poisonous plant has drooping purple flowers and a black, cherry-like fruit?

15. In TV comedy Friends, Joey played Dr Jake Ramoray in which soap opera?

Answers – page 211

16. Tom Cruise and Nicole Kidman starred in which 1990 motorsport inspired film?

17. Who was the target of the assassination attempt in the film The Day of the Jackal?

18. Which singer was nicknamed Lady Day?

19. Which group recorded albums called A Day at the Races and A Night At The Opera?
a) Pink Floyd
b) Queen
c) Slade

20. In 1994, M People spent One Night In...?
a) Heaven
b) Hell
c) Purgatory

MEDIUM

Answers to Quiz 102: Pot Luck

1. Madeira
2. Rosin
3. Indiana
4. Lusitania
5. Falkland Islands
6. Carpetbagger
7. Pavlova
8. John Higgins
9. Apocalypse Now
10. Bathing
11. Snoop Dogg
12. Martin Johnson
13. The Barenaked Ladies
14. The Go-Go's
15. Victoria Beckham
16. Fred and Shaggy
17. New England
18. Aurora Borealis
19. Desert Rats
20. Eddie Van Halen

Quiz 104: Pot Luck

1. Prime minister David Cameron is a fan of which football club?

2. Who created Cloud Cuckoo Land?

3. The Agnelli family are associated with which make of car?

4. Who composed the opera The Barber of Seville?

5. What is the oldest theatre in Moscow?

6. What was the name of Captain Smollett's ship in Treasure Island?

7. George Clooney's only Oscar win to date came for his performance in which film?

8. Riga is the capital city of which country?

9. Who played Hunter S Thompson in the 1998 film Fear and Loathing in Las Vegas?

10. Phasmophobia is a fear of what?

11. What was Take That's first top ten single?

12. What connects the US state of North Carolina and a British bicycle manufacturer?

13. The 2009 sci-fi thriller District 9 is set in which city?

14. Which mass murderer recorded an album called LIE: The Love & Terror Cult?

15. Which US president delivered the Gettysburg Address?

16. The Tablet and The Universe are periodicals from which religion?

17. Which actor and comedian ran 43 marathons in 51 days in 2009 to raise money for Sport Relief?

18. What was James Brown's only UK top ten single?

19. Where does the spice cinnamon come from?
    a) ground nuts
    b) tree bark

20. Gammon comes from which part of a pig?
    a) belly
    b) thigh
    c) trotter

MEDIUM

Answers to Quiz 103: Night and Day

1. Twelfth Night
2. Knight Rider
3. Feast of the Annunciation
4. Green Day
5. Daniel Day Lewis
6. Match of the Day
7. Doris Day
8. A Nightmare on Elm Street
9. Day of Atonement
10. Pierce Brosnan
11. Alexandr Solzhenitsyn
12. Burns Night
13. Florence Nightingale
14. Deadly Nightshade
15. Days of Our Lives
16. Days of Thunder
17. Charles de Gaulle
18. Billie Holiday
19. Queen
20. Heaven

Quiz 105: London

1. What is sold at Smithfield Market?

2. The tomb of The Unknown Warrior is in which London church?

3. Which district of London has tube stations called Bec and Broadway?

4. What location is used as the point to measure distances to London?

5. What building is officially known as No. 1 Canada Square?

6. What is the only London Underground Station to contain the letter Z?

7. What London body was created in 1965 and abolished in 1985?

8. What is the oldest theatre in London?

9. What London landmark, designed by Sir Christopher Wren, commemorates where the Great Fire of London started?

10. What is the name of the Catholic cathedral in Southwark?

11. What are the six Roman Gates of London Wall?

12. St James's Palace was built by which monarch?

13. Josef Jakobs was the last person executed at which London landmark?

14. What is London's oldest professional football club?

15. Weighing 13.5 tonnes, what is found in St Stephen's Tower in the Houses of Parliament?

16. What is the only tube station that doesn't have of the letters in the word mackerel in it?

17. Who had a 1974 hit with The Streets of London?

18. Which famous cellist in 2001 became the first official busker on the London Underground?

19. What building, designed in the 18th century by Sir William Chambers, is situated on the Strand?
    a) Devonshire House
    b) Gloucestershire House
    c) Somerset House

20. What London thoroughfare was traditionally home to the music publishing industry?
    a) Denmark Street
    b) Norway Street
    c) Sweden Street

MEDIUM

Answers to Quiz 104: Pot Luck

1. Aston Villa
2. Aristophanes
3. Fiat
4. Rossini
5. The Bolshoi Theatre
6. Hispaniola
7. Syriana
8. Latvia
9. Johnny Depp
10. Ghosts
11. It Only Takes A Minute Girl
12. Raleigh
13. Johannesburg
14. Charles Manson
15. Abraham Lincoln
16. Roman Catholicism
17. Eddie Izzard
18. Living In America
19. Tree bark
20. Thigh

Quiz 106: Pot Luck

1. Japanese company YKK is the world's largest manufacturer of what?

2. What was the name of the oil tanker that ran aground off the coast of Alaska in 1989 spilling millions of gallons of oil?

3. Which composer wrote The Flight of the Bumblebee?

4. Stretching some 225 miles, what is the longest motorway in the UK?

5. What is the capital city of Oman?

6. In the Wacky Races, who drove a car called The Compact Pussycat?

7. Which country star sang the theme tune to 1980s drama The Dukes of Hazzard?

8. Musophobia is the fear of what creature?

9. In railways, what does Maglev stand for?

10. In what decade was the FA Cup final broadcast live for the first time?

11. The Ballad of the Unknown Stuntman was the theme song to which TV show?

12. Cassis is flavoured using which fruit?

13. What is the only sign of the zodiac represented by an inanimate object?

14. What is the only word that when capitalised turns from a verb or noun into a nationality?

15. What does the abbreviation e.g. stand for?

16. What is the Spanish word for navy?

17. The Formula One circuit Spa Francorchamps is in which country?

18. What is an eagle's nest called?

19. The Kaiser Chiefs take their name from a football team from which country?
    a) Ivory Coast
    b) Ghana
    c) South Africa

20. Plumbism is poisoning caused by what?
    a) lead
    b) mercury
    c) arsenic

MEDIUM

Answers to Quiz 105: London

1. Meat
2. Westminster Abbey
3. Tooting
4. Charing Cross
5. Canary Wharf Tower
6. Belsize Park
7. The Greater London Council (GLC)
8. Theatre Royal, Drury Lane (1812)
9. Monument
10. St George's

11. Aldgate, Aldersgate, Bishopsgate, Cripplegate, Ludgate and Newgate
12. Henry VIII
13. The Tower of London
14. Fulham
15. Big Ben
16. St John's Wood
17. Ralph McTell
18. Julian Lloyd Webber
19. Somerset House
20. Denmark Street

Quiz 107: Military

1. Which country has the largest army in the world?

2. The Charge of the Light Brigade took place during which war?

3. What is the highest military honour in the UK?

4. What are the five guards regiments in the British Army?

5. In World War Two, Clifford James acted as a double for which British figure?

6. The British Army Officer Training School is in which town?

7. The Red Devils is the nickname of which regiment of the British Army?

8. The US Military Academy at West Point is in which state?

9. What is the highest rank in the Royal Navy?

10. Legio Patria Nostra is the unofficial motto of which fighting force?

11. The Battle of Agincourt was part of which war?

12. In what country was Lord Kitchener born?

13. The Battles of Lexington and Concord were the first military engagements in which war?

14. Which famous general wrote The Art of War?

15. What was Field Marshall Montgomery's first name?

16. Which German soldier was known as The Desert Fox?

17. Gettysburg was a battle in which conflict?

18. Edgehill, the site of a famous battle in the English Civil War, is in which county?

19. A Kepi is worn by soldiers in the army of which country?
    a) Britain
    b) France
    c) Germany

20. What is the higher rank in the British Army?
    a) corporal
    b) sergeant

MEDIUM

Answers to Quiz 106: Pot Luck

1. Zips
2. Exxon Valdez
3. Nikolai Rimsky-Korsakov
4. M6
5. Muscat
6. Penelope Pitstop
7. Waylon Jennings
8. Mice
9. Magnetic Levitation
10. 1930s
11. The Fall Guy
12. Blackcurrant
13. Libra (scales)
14. Polish
15. Exempli gratia (for example)
16. Armada
17. Belgium
18. An eyrie
19. South Africa
20. Lead

Quiz 108: Pot Luck

1. In which European country can you catch a train called the Glacier Express?

2. In heraldry, what colour is sable?

3. Sinophobia is a fear of things associated with which country?

4. What animal is the offspring of a male horse and a female donkey?

5. Who played Batman and Robin in the original 1960s TV series?

6. What is the capital city of Lithuania?

7. What was the first American city to host the Olympic Games?

8. Cricketers from which country were jailed for spot fixing in the 2010 Lord's Test against England?

9. Who scored the first goal for England under the reign of Roy Hodgson?

10. Des Moines is the capital of which US state?

11. What Latin phrase means let the buyer beware?

12. Which Benedictine monk invented sparkling wine?

13. In which Italian city would you ride a vaporetto?

14. An email address ending in .hr is for people from which country?

15. The 2004 film The Aviator was based on the life of which pioneer of flight?

16. Cliff Richard came second in the 1968 Eurovision Song Contest with which song?

17. Don Alfonso, Dorabella and Fiordiligi are characters in which Mozart opera?

18. Dear Old Shiz, I'm Not That Girl, and As Long As You're Mine, are songs from which West End Musical?

19. How many feet are in a mile?
    a) 2,850
    b) 5,280
    c) 8,250

20. On which side of a ship is port?
    a) front
    b) left
    c) right

Answers to Quiz 107: Military

1. China
2. The Crimean War
3. The Victoria Cross
4. Grenadier, Coldstream, Scots, Irish and Welsh
5. Field Marshall Montgomery
6. Sandhurst
7. The Parachute Regiment
8. New York
9. Admiral of the Fleet
10. The French Foreign Legion
11. The Hundred Years' War
12. Ireland
13. The American War of Independence
14. Sun Tzu
15. Bernard
16. Erwin Rommel
17. The American Civil War
18. Warwickshire
19. France
20. Sergeant

Quiz 109: History part 2

1. The Battle of the Bulge was fought in which war?

2. Adolf Hitler was born in what country?

3. What was the name of the census compiled by William the Conqueror?

4. Who was the last Tudor monarch?

5. Who was Henry VIII's fourth wife?

6. Born in 1769, what is the soldier and statesman Arthur Wellesley more commonly known as?

7. Which Egyptian queen died after being bitten by an asp?

8. Which Scottish outlaw was immortalised in a novel by Sir Walter Scott?

9. Who founded the Holy Roman Empire?

10. What was the name of Napoleon Bonaparte's wife?

11. Which English king was victorious in the Battle of Agincourt?

12. Haile Selassie was the emperor of which African country?

13. What treaty established the European Economic Community which later became the European Union?

14. Who killed presidential assassin Lee Harvey Oswald?

15. Which Basque town, heavily bombed by the Luftwaffe in the Spanish Civil War, was portrayed in a painting by Picasso?

16. Which Conservative Prime Minister founded the Metropolitan Police?

17. What were the Dorset labourers who formed a union in 1833 and were later deported to Australia known as?

18. California, Victoria, Witwatersrand and Klondike were all scenes of what?

19. What was the name of the US aid programme which helped the economies of Western Europe after World War Two?
a) Eisenhower Plan
b) Marshall Plan
c) Roosevelt Plan

20. What name was given to supporters of the deposed Stuart royal line?
a) Jacobites
b) Henryites
c) Williamites

MEDIUM

Answers to Quiz 108: Pot Luck

1. Switzerland
2. Black
3. China
4. Hinny
5. Adam West and Burt Ward
6. Vilnius
7. St Louis
8. Pakistan
9. Ashley Young
10. Iowa
11. Caveat emptor
12. Dom Perignon
13. Venice
14. Croatia
15. Howard Hughes
16. Congratulations
17. Cosi fan tutte
18. Wicked
19. 5,280
20. Left

Quiz 110: Pot Luck

1. Suntory whisky is distilled in which country?

2. What is the hottest planet in the solar system?

3. In mathematics what does LCM stand for?

4. Apple pips contain which poisonous compound?

5. Brian O'Nolan was the real name of which Irish author?

6. The Daily Herald is the former name of which newspaper?

7. Many of the cast from TV comedy Hi De Hi appeared in which railway-set sitcom?

8. What Latin phrase is used to describe the justification for a war?

9. Artist Spartacus Chetwynd was nominated for the 2012 Turner Prize for her recreation of a scene featuring which science fiction film character?

10. Leonardo da Vinci Airport is in which city?

11. In music, if something is andante, at what pace should it be played?

12. Which cowboy rode a horse called Silver?

13. Tallahassee is the capital of which US state?

14. We Started Nothing was a 2008 number one album for which synth pop duo?

15. In computing what does the acronym MPEG stand for?

16. In what decade were dog licences abolished in the UK?

17. What character did Sean Bean play in The Lord of the Rings film?

18. The Latin motto Superbia in proelia appears on the crest of which English football club?

19. What was the name of the BBC's teletext service?
    a) Oracle
    b) Ceefax
    c) 4Tel

20. What is the name of the railway operating company in America?
    a) Amrail
    b) Amride
    c) Amtrak

Answers to Quiz 109: History part 2

1. World War II
2. Austria
3. The Domesday Book
4. Elizabeth I
5. Anne of Cleves
6. Duke of Wellington
7. Cleopatra
8. Rob Roy
9. Charlemagne
10. Josephine
11. Henry V
12. Ethiopia
13. Treaty of Rome
14. Jack Ruby
15. Guernica
16. Robert Peel
17. The Tolpuddle martyrs
18. Gold rushes
19. Marshall Plan
20. Jacobites

Quiz 111: Pop Music 2000 and Beyond

1. Who reached number 1 in 2001 with a cover of Uptown Girl?

2. Which Spice Girl had a 2001 hit with It's Raining Men?

3. What George Harrison song topped the charts in 2002, 31 years after it first reached number one?

4. Which group Crashed The Wedding in November 2003?

5. Adam Levine is the lead singer of which group?

6. What sort of boy did Estelle sing about on her 2008 hit?

7. What was Take That's first hit after they reformed in 2006?

8. Changes was a 2003 number one hit for which father and daughter?

9. The Suburbs was a number 2010 number one album by which group?

10. Which Greek goddess gave its name to a 2010 album by Kylie Minogue?

11. Billie Joe Armstrong is the lead singer with which group?

12. The Defamation of Strickland Banks was a best selling album by which artist?

13. The band Sigur Ros are from which country?

14. Which indie rockers had the Golden Touch in 2004?

15. Which female singer reached number one in the charts with an album called Lights?

16. Which group recorded West Ryder Pauper Lunatic Asylum?

17. What sort of Age did The Strokes sing about in 2001?

18. Which music veteran sang at the half-time show of Super Bowl XLV?

19. What is the award winning singer Adele's surname?
    a) Adkins
    b) Armstrong
    c) Ashton

20. Who topped the charts in 2012 with Twilight?
    a) Forward Defence
    b) Cover Drive
    c) Late Cut

MEDIUM

Answers to Quiz 110: Pot Luck

1. Japan
2. Venus
3. Lowest Common Multiplier
4. Cyanide
5. Flann O'Brien
6. The Sun
7. Oh, Dr Beeching
8. Casus belli
9. Jabba the Hutt
10. Rome
11. Walking pace
12. The Lone Ranger
13. Florida
14. The Ting Tings
15. Moving Picture Experts Group
16. 1980s
17. Boromir
18. Manchester City
19. Ceefax
20. Amtrak

Quiz 112: Pot Luck

1. Eurostar trains from London terminate at which Paris station?

2. Clint Eastwood won Best Director Oscars for which two films?

3. Which team won the Scottish League Cup in 2012?

4. Which British actor played US Marine Nicholas Brody in the American TV drama Homeland?

5. What was the Baader-Meinhof Group also known as?

6. Roquefort cheese is made from the milk of which animal?

7. The cartoon Doonesbury appears in which daily newspaper?

8. Anything You Can Do is a song from which musical?

9. Which two cricketers have won Strictly Come Dancing?

10. Politician Boris Johnson was born in which city?

11. Who was President Obama talking about when he said, 'We got him' in May 2011?

12. Which two English counties share a border with Scotland?

13. Port Moresby is the capital city of which country?

14. Star of Hitchcock's The Birds, Tippi Hedren is the mother of which Hollywood actress?

15. Which fictional character rode a donkey called Dapple?

16. How many Oscars did Steve McQueen, Marilyn Monroe and Robert Mitchum win combined?

17. Which football club changed the name of its ground to

the Sports Direct Arena?

18. Slaghoopal was the maiden name of which famous cartoon wife?

19. The first public steam railway was operated between Stockton and which town?
    a) Darlington
    b) Hartlepool
    c) Middlesbrough

20. What was the name of the Duke of Wellington's horse?
    a) Copenhagen
    b) Stockholm
    c) Oslo

MEDIUM

Answers to Quiz 111: Pop Music 2000 and Beyond

1. Westlife
2. Geri Halliwell
3. My Sweet Lord
4. Busted
5. Maroon 5
6. American
7. Patience
8. Ozzy and Kelly Osbourne
9. Arcade Fire
10. Aphrodite
11. Green Day
12. Plan B
13. Iceland
14. Razorlight
15. Elie Goulding
16. Kasabian
17. Modern
18. Madonna
19. Adkins
20. Cover Drive

Quiz 113: Oscars

1. Who was the first woman to win a Best Director Oscar?

2. Robert Redford won the Best Director Oscar in 1980 for which film?

3. Which actor won the Best Actor award in both 1993 and 1994?

4. Forest Whitaker won an Oscar in 2006 for his portrayal of which African ruler?

5. What was the first X-rated film to be nominated for the Best Picture award?

6. Philip Seymour Hoffman won the Best Actor award in 2005 for his portrayal of which writer?

7. Which actor received posthumous nominations in 1956 and 1957 for the Best Actor award?

8. How many Best Director Oscars did Alfred Hitchcock win?

9. Who received two Best Director nominations in 2000 for Traffic and Erin Brokovich?

10. How long do Oscar winners have to make a speech?

11. Marlon Brando is one of two Oscar winners to refuse the award. Who was the other?

12. Who, in 2012, became the oldest winner of an acting Oscar for his performance in Beginners?

13. Who won the Best Actor Oscar in 2004 for his portrayal of soul singer Ray Charles?

14. What was the first colour film to win the Best Picture Oscar?

15. The Academy Awards ceremony was delayed in 1968 after the assassination of which person?

16. The Color Purple was nominated for 11 Oscars in 1985. How many did it win?

17. Who won the Best Actor Oscar in 2008 for his portrayal of gay rights activist Harvey Milk?

18. Who won an Oscar in 2007 for her portrayal of Edith Piaf?

19. Which of the following wasn't nominated for Best Picture in 2012?
    a) Moneyball
    b) Drive
    c) The Help

20. Which film won 8 Oscars in 1972 but missed out on Best Picture?
    a) Cabaret
    b) The Godfather
    c) Butterflies Are Free

Answers to Quiz 112: Pot Luck

1. Gare du Nord
2. Unforgiven and Million Dollar Baby
3. Kilmarnock
4. Damien Lewis
5. The Red Army Faction
6. Ewe
7. The Guardian
8. Annie Get Your Gun
9. Darren Gough and Mark Ramprakash
10. New York
11. Osama Bin Laden
12. Cumbria and Northumberland
13. Papua New Guinea
14. Melanie Griffiths
15. Sancho Panza
16. None
17. Newcastle United
18. Wilma Flintstone
19. Darlington
20. Copenhagen

MEDIUM

Quiz 114: Pot Luck

1. Who is the first character to speak in the original Star Wars film?

2. What is the capital city of Pakistan?

3. Who invented the bagless vacuum cleaner?

4. In which English city would you find Lime Street station?

5. In which country would you find the highest waterfall in the world?

6. Complete the title of the 2012 film: Jeff, Who Lives ... ?

7. The longest bridge in the world lies in which Asian country?

8. Which cyclist is known as The Manx Missile?

9. In a set of numbers, what word describes the number that occurs the most often?

10. What Indian curried soup literally means 'pepper water'?

11. Which Disney character's original name was Dippy Dawg?

12. The capital of the US state of Delaware has the same name as which Kent town?

13. Which Beatle's middle name is Winston?

14. What is the pigment that makes plants green?

15. Who succeeded John Major as leader of the Conservative Party in 1997?

Answers – page 233

16. Which US President was a former Director of the CIA?

17. What 1927 film was the first to feature sound?

18. Who topped the album charts for a record-breaking 12th time with the 2012 release MDNA?

19. What sort of building was the Pharos of Alexandria?
    a) library
    b) lighthouse
    c) temple

20. British railways were privatised under which prime minister?
    a) Thatcher
    b) Major
    c) Blair

Answers to Quiz 113: Oscars

1. Kathryn Bigelow
2. Ordinary People
3. Tom Hanks
4. Idi Amin
5. Midnight Cowboy
6. Truman Capote
7. James Dean
8. None
9. Steven Soderbergh
10. 45 seconds
11. George C Scott
12. Christopher Plummer
13. Jamie Foxx
14. Gone With The Wind
15. Martin Luther King
16. None
17. Sean Penn
18. Marion Cotillard
19. Drive
20. Cabaret

Quiz 115: Myth and Legend

1. In Roman mythology, who was the messenger of the gods?

2. To whom did Apollo bestow the gift of prophecy?

3. Which Titan carried the world on his shoulders?

4. What ship carried Jason on his quest for the golden fleece?

5. What was the name of the Roman slave who befriended a lion which later saved his life?

6. In Greek mythology, where do the souls of the righteous go after death?

7. Who was the Greek and Roman god of the moon, music and poetry?

8. Who was the Greek god of wine?

9. In Egyptian mythology, Ra was the god of what?

10. Which Norse warrior killed The Grendel in a wrestling match?

11. The mythical creature the centaur is half man, half what?

12. Who turned Atlas into stone when he showed him the head of Medusa?

13. What was the name of the vast maze built by Daedalus at Knossos?

14. Which Ancient Greek king was murdered by his wife, Clytemnestra?

15. In Greek mythology, what was the food of the gods?

16. What were Tisiphone, Alecto and Megaera collectively known as?

17. Who was the Roman god of the sea?

18. Who were the Dioscuri?

19. In Greek mythology, which giant had 100 eyes?
    a) Argus
    b) Goliath
    c) Apollo

20. Marduk was the king of the gods in which ancient civilisation?
    a) Babylonian
    b) Incan
    c) Aztec

MEDIUM

Answers to Quiz 114: Pot Luck

1. C3PO
2. Islamabad
3. James Dyson
4. Liverpool
5. Venezuela
6. At Home
7. Japan
8. Mark Cavendish
9. Mode
10. Mulligatawny
11. Goofy
12. Dover
13. John Lennon
14. Chlorophyll
15. William Hague
16. George H W Bush
17. The Jazz Singer
18. Madonna
19. Lighthouse
20. Major

Quiz 116: Pot Luck

1. Which author wrote the 2012 novel Capital?

2. Which fictional milkman rode a horse called Trigger?

3. Since 1974, the Green Line has divided the north and south of which island?

4. What name describes a train that runs on a single rail rather than a track?

5. What is measured using a pedometer?

6. Which country has the longest coastline in the world?

7. The Royal and Ancient Golf Club is in which town?

8. How many British Prime Ministers have served under Queen Elizabeth II?

9. What is the highest civilian honour in the UK?

10. Mozart's Eine kleine Nachtmusik is the theme tune to what radio quiz?

11. Which sitcom couple lived in Popular Avenue, Purley?

12. In Greek mythology, the minotaur had a human body and the head of which animal?

13. What is the capital of the US state of California?

14. Which two boxers were involved in a brawl in Munich after a World Heavyweight fight featuring Vitali Klitschko?

15. Who comes next in this list? Bernard Wetherill, Betty Boothroyd, Michael Martin?

16. Brisbane is the capital city of which Australian state?

17. In what decade was the BBC formed?

18. Whose full name is Barbara Millicent Roberts?

19. Who did Icelandic singer Björk describe as her 'rock star' when growing up?
    a) David Attenborough
    b) David Bowie
    c) David Hockney

20. Bucharest is the capital of which country?
    a) Bulgaria
    b) Hungary
    c) Romania

MEDIUM

Answers to Quiz 115: Myth and Legend

1. Mercury
2. Cassandra
3. Atlas
4. Argo
5. Androcles
6. Elysian Fields
7. Apollo
8. Dionysus
9. The sun
10. Beowulf
11. Horse
12. Perseus
13. Labyrinth
14. Agamemnon
15. Ambrosia
16. The Furies
17. Neptune
18. Castor and Pollux
19. Argus
20. Babylonian

Quiz 117: Animals

1. Starting from the front, what is the first animal you will find in a dictionary?

2. How many humps does a Bactrian camel have?

3. What type of animal is a caribou?

4. What is the largest member of the primate family?

5. What bird is the Pica Pica more commonly known as?

6. What name describes an animal with a vertebra that spends some of its life in water?

7. A squab is a young of which bird?

8. What is the largest marine mammal in the world?

9. What are the only insects that make food that is eaten by humans?

10. Who rode a horse called Aethenoth?

11. An entomologist studies what type of animals?

12. What is the offspring of a hare called?

13. Trumpeter, whooper and mute are types of what bird?

14. What animal is a cross between a female horse and a male donkey?

15. Which poet owned a dog called Boatswain?

16. A dingo is what type of animal?

17. London was the name of the dog in which Canadian children's TV programme?

18. The piranha fish is native to which continent?

19. What type of animal is a chinchilla?
    a) rodent
    b) marsupial
    c) reptile

20. What name is used to describe a female donkey?
    a) Jacky
    b) Jenny
    c) Joni

Answers to Quiz 116: Pot Luck

1. John Lanchester
2. Ernie
3. Cyprus
4. Monorail
5. Walking distance
6. Canada
7. St Andrews
8. 12
9. The George Cross
10. Brain of Britain
11. Terry and June
12. Bull
13. Sacramento
14. Dereck Chisora and David Haye
15. John Bercow (Speakers of the House of Commons)
16. Queensland
17. 1920s
18. Barbie
19. David Attenborough
20. Romania

Quiz 118: Pot Luck

1. Which film director said, 'There is no terror in the bang, only in the anticipation of it'?

2. Which brothers invented the first hot air balloon?

3. What word describes items thrown overboard by a ship in distress?

4. According to Mark Twain, what is a good walk spoiled?

5. What was Karol Jozef Wojtyla better known as?

6. Genghis Khan was the ruler of which empire?

7. Khartoum is the capital city of which African country?

8. Who was the last Tsar of Russia?

9. US politician Sarah Palin is from which state?

10. Whose sculpture entitled Golden Calf sold for a then record price of £10.3m in 2008?

11. Hobart is the capital of which Australian state?

12. Who were the runners-up in the 2011 Rugby World Cup?

13. What are members of the Society of Jesus known as?

14. What was the name of the horse in Steptoe and Son?

15. True or false. There's a town in Norway called Hell?

16. Which dinosaur had the longest tail?

17. Rusty, Poppa, Greaseball and Electra are characters in which hit musical?

18. What Japanese word means 'divine wind' in English?

19. Who were the Germanic tribes of the 4th and 5th century who invaded the Roman Empire?
    a) Emos
    b) Goths
    c) Punks

20. What Swiss city gives its name to a series of conventions on the conduct of wars?
    a) Berne
    b) Geneva
    c) Zurich

Answers to Quiz 117: Animals

1. Aardvark
2. Two
3. Deer
4. Gorilla
5. Magpie
6. Amphibian
7. Pigeon
8. Blue whale
9. Honeybees
10. Lady Godiva
11. Insects
12. Leveret
13. Swan
14. Mule
15. Lord Byron
16. Dog
17. The Littlest Hobo
18. South America
19. Rodent
20. Jenny

MEDIUM

Quiz 119: Sport

1. True or false – Tug of War was formerly an Olympic sport?

2. What was the first city in Asia to host the Olympic Games?

3. How many times have Wales qualified for the European Football Championships?

4. Which cyclist was named BBC Sports Personality of the Year in 2011?

5. Which Welshman won the first World Darts Championship?

6. Which Essex cricketer was the first Englishman to be found guilty of spot fixing?

7. What colour jersey is worn by the leader of the Giro d'Italia cycle race?

8. Which rugby league team play their home matches at Odsal Stadium?

9. Tannadice Park is the home ground of which Scottish football club?

10. What links Shakespeare's A Midsummer Night's Dream and ice hockey?

11. Which dart player is nicknamed the Bronzed Adonis?

12. How many matches did the England football team lose in 2011?

13. 2011 film The Goon was about which sport?

14. At what ground do the Northern Ireland football team play their home internationals?

15. In rugby union, which countries compete for the Bledisloe Cup?

16. In what sport do teams compete for the Stanley Cup?

17. How many players are on a hurling team?

18. Which Asian city hosted the 2011 World Athletics Championships?

19. Which of the following is not an event in the decathlon?
    a) shot put
    b) hammer
    c) discus

20. David Haye put his heavyweight championship defeat to Wladimir Klitschko down to a broken what?
    a) little finger
    b) little toe
    c) gumshield

MEDIUM

Answers to Quiz 118: Pot Luck

1. Alfred Hitchcock
2. Montgolfier brothers
3. Jetsam
4. Golf
5. Pope John Paul II
6. Mongol Empire
7. Sudan
8. Nicholas II
9. Alaska
10. Damien Hirst
11. Tasmania
12. France
13. Jesuits
14. Hercules
15. True
16. Diplodocus
17. Starlight Express
18. Kamikaze
19. Goths
20. Geneva

Quiz 120: Pot Luck

1. That's Living Alright was the theme tune to what popular drama?

2. What is the capital of the US state of Arizona?

3. What religion was founded in America in 1830 by Joseph Smith?

4. In 2009, Jennifer Figge became the first woman to swim which body of water?

5. Which is the largest of the five North American Great Lakes?

6. According to the proverb, whose wife must be above suspicion?

7. Griffin Park is the home ground of which football club?

8. Which South American country was formerly known as Dutch Guiana?

9. Who is the patron saint of carpenters?

10. Black Agnes was the horse of which Scottish monarch?

11. What are the Donmar Warehouse, Menier Chocolate Factory and Young Vic?

12. Kampala is the capital city of which country?

13. In the Magic Roundabout, what type of animal was Brian?

14. In Greek and Roman mythology, who was the god of dreams?

15. Where would you find the Hang Seng Stock Exchange?

16. The OSS was the forerunner of what American organisation?

Answers – page 245

17. Papa Doc and Baby Doc Duvalier were rulers of which country?

18. Where is the Tynwald the parliament?

19. Hebrew script is written in which direction?
    a) left to right
    b) right to left
    c) vertically

20. What number President was Obama?
    a) 42nd
    b) 43rd
    c) 44th

Answers to Quiz 119: Sport

1. True
2. Tokyo
3. None
4. Mark Cavendish
5. Leighton Rees
6. Mervyn Westfield
7. Pink
8. Bradford Bulls
9. Dundee United
10. Puck
11. Steve Beaton
12. None
13. Ice Hockey
14. Windsor Park
15. Australia and New Zealand
16. Ice Hockey
17. 15
18. Daegu
19. Hammer
20. Little toe

Quiz 121: Opera and Classical Music

1. Which Verdi opera is about a Shakespearian knight?

2. Who composed the opera Porgy and Bess?

3. What did the composers Beethoven, Faure and Smetana have in common?

4. The Chorus of the Hebrew Slaves is from which Verdi opera?

5. Since 2004, Peter Maxwell Davies has held which post?

6. Vladimir Ashkenazy is associated with which musical instrument?

7. Figaro, Fiorello and Bartolo are characters in which Rossini opera?

8. What nationality was the composer Jean Sibelius?

9. Which composer's ballets include The Rite of Spring and The Firebird?

10. Bizet's opera The Pearl Fishers is set in which Asian country?

11. Captain Vere, Claggart and Arthur Jones are characters in which opera?

12. Lilliburlero is the signature tune for which radio station?

13. Fidelio, or The Triumph of Married Love was the only opera by which composer?

14. The opera Eugene Onegin is based on a novel by which author?

15. The CBSO is an orchestra from which city?

16. Which Gilbert and Sullivan operetta is also known as The Lass That Loved a Sailor?

17. Which British composer was the first to be made a life peer in the House of Lords?

18. Which composer wrote the operas Nixon in China and The Death of Klinghoffer?

19. In Wagner's Tristan und Isolde, Marke is the king of where?
    a) Cornwall
    b) Devon
    c) Mercia

20. Which of the following is an opera by Wagner?
    a) The Flying Belgian
    b) The Flying Dutchman
    c) The Flying German

MEDIUM

Answers to Quiz 120: Pot Luck

1. Auf Wiedersehen, Pet
2. Phoenix
3. The Mormon Church (Church of Jesus Christ of Latter-Day Saints)
4. Atlantic Ocean
5. Lake Superior
6. Caesar's
7. Brentford
8. Suriname
9. St Joseph
10. Mary Queen of Scots
11. London theatres
12. Uganda
13. Snail
14. Morpheus
15. Hong Kong
16. The CIA
17. Haiti
18. Isle of Man
19. Right to left
20. 44th

Quiz 122: Pot Luck

1. Which three gospels are referred to as the synoptic gospels?

2. Who led the mutiny on the Bounty?

3. What is the capital city of Turkey?

4. Who designed the Mini car?

5. Who was the Roman goddess of the moon?

6. Which teams compete for golf's Solheim Cup?

7. The faces of four US presidents are carved into which American mountain?

8. Don Draper is the central character in which TV drama?

9. Gold and frankincense were two of the three gifts brought by the three wise men, what was the third?

10. Which Scot won the 2011 World Snooker Championship?

11. What is the penultimate letter in the Greek alphabet?

12. Approaching Menace is the name of the theme tune to what television show?

13. The phrase 'pass the buck' derives from which card game?

14. Montgomery is the capital of which US state?

15. What headwear takes its name from a Black Sea port on the Crimea?

16. What does an odometer measure?

17. Who are the five permanent members of the UN Security Council?

18. Who was the last president of Czechoslovakia and also the first president of the Czech Republic?

19. The aromatic substance musk comes from what animal?
    a) cow
    b) deer
    c) cat

20. What is the main ingredient in tabbouleh?
    a) pasta
    b) rice
    c) bulgur wheat

MEDIUM

Answers to Quiz 121: Opera and Classical Music

1. Falstaff
2. George Gershwin
3. They were all deaf
4. Nabucco
5. Master of the Queen's Music
6. Piano
7. The Barber of Seville
8. Finnish
9. Igor Stravinsky
10. Sri Lanka (Ceylon)
11. Billy Budd
12. BBC World Service
13. Beethoven
14. Alexander Pushkin
15. Birmingham
16. HMS Pinafore
17. Benjamin Britten
18. John Adams
19. Cornwall
20. The Flying Dutchman

Quiz 123: Connections part 3

1. Who plays Brian Lane in detective drama New Tricks?

2. Which country singer's only number one hit was Distant Drums?

3. In the TV cartoon, who lives next door to The Simpsons?

4. Which Englishman refereed the 2010 World Cup Final?

5. Which Jamaican-born TV chef stood as a candidate for UKIP in the 2005 General Election?

6. Who succeeded Max Bygraves as host of Family Fortunes?

7. Which Lancastrian football club are nicknamed The Shrimps?

8. What is the symbol of clothes manufacturer Fred Perry?

9. Which bespectacled singer had a backing band called The Attractions?

10. Which actor played David Wicks in Eastenders?

11. Who was the host of TV shows Think Of A Number and Think Again?

12. Who reached number one in the charts in 1972 with Long Haired Lover From Liverpool?

13. What is the most common surname in Wales?

14. Which female prison reformer, who died in 1845, has appeared on the £5 note since 2001?

15. Which English theologian was beatified by Pope Benedict in 2010?

16. Stuart Goddard is the real name of which 1980s pop star?

17. What is the small piece of gummed paper that is used to attach stamps in an album?

18. Which England cricketer plays in a band called Dr Comfort and the Lurid Revelations?
    a) Graeme Swann
    b) Ian Bell
    c) James Anderson

19. Which American golfer won the US Open in 1974, 1979 and 1990?
    a) Jack Nicklaus
    b) Tom Watson
    c) Hale Irwin

20. What is the connection between the above answers?

Answers to Quiz 122: Pot Luck

1. Matthew, Mark and Luke
2. Fletcher Christian
3. Ankara
4. Sir Alec Issigonis
5. Luna
6. Europe and the USA
7. Mount Rushmore
8. Mad Men
9. Myrrh
10. John Higgins
11. Psi
12. Mastermind
13. Poker
14. Alabama
15. Balaclava
16. Distance (in vehicles)
17. USA, UK, China, Russia and France
18. Vaclav Havel
19. Deer
20. Bulgur wheat

Quiz 124: Pot Luck

1. The TV comedy MASH was set during which conflict?

2. Which of the 12 disciples was known as The Twin and is the patron saint of architects?

3. The car manufacturer Daewoo is based in which country?

4. Caracas is the capital city of which country?

5. Which Brazilian footballer, who died in 2011, shared his name with a Greek philosopher?

6. The inventor of the Rubik's Cube came from which country?

7. Who is the patron saint of France?

8. Solanum tuberosum is the botanical name for which food?

9. On what date is St David's Day celebrated?

10. Constantinople was the former name of which city?

11. Which country hosted the 2011 Rugby World Cup?

12. Pascal, Fortran and Basic are examples of what?

13. Which US President's middle name was Milhous?

14. Belmarsh, Winson Green and Styal what type of establishments?

15. Venus was the Roman goddess of love. Who is her Greek equivalent?

16. Shall We Dance comes from which Rodgers and Hammerstein musical?

Answers – page 253

17. Mike Joyce and Andy Rourke were the lesser known members of which seminal 80s band?

18. What nationality is tennis star Novak Djokovic?

19. The High Numbers was the former name of which group?
    a) The Who
    b) The Move
    c) The Jam

20. What is Bodensee more commonly known as in Britain?
    a) Lake Geneva
    b) Lake Constance
    c) Lake Zurich

Answers to Quiz 123: Connections part 3

1. Alun Armstrong
2. Jim Reeves
3. Ned Flanders
4. Howard Webb
5. Rustie Lee
6. Les Dennis
7. Morecambe
8. Laurel wreath
9. Elvis Costello
10. Michael French
11. Johnny Ball
12. Little Jimmy Osmond
13. Jones
14. Elizabeth Fry
15. Cardinal John Henry Newman
16. Adam Ant
17. Hinge
18. Graeme Swann
19. Hale Irwin
20. They contain the name of half of a comedy double act

Quiz 125: Read All About It

1. The Guardian newspaper was founded in which city?

2. What type of columns are written by Justin Toper, Jonathan Cainer and Peter Watson?

3. What was the UK's first colour newspaper?

4. Which newspaper was founded by a trio of journalists from The Daily Telegraph in 1986?

5. Max Aitken was the real name of which newspaper baron?

6. Funny Old World, Ad nauseam and Signal Failures are regular columns in which publication?

7. In which country would you find newspapers called El Pais, ABC and Marca?

8. The crusader is the logo of which newspaper?

9. In newspapers what are Tramp, Enigmatist and Gemini?

10. What free newspaper was launched in 1999?

11. Leonard Barden, Raymond Keene and Jon Speelman write newspaper columns on what?

12. Jan Hoch was the real name of which newspaper proprietor?

13. Which newspaper is nicknamed The Thunderer?

14. In which English city would you find a newspaper called the Express and Star?

15. What newspaper was founded by Irishman WS Bourne in 1791?

16. La Stampa and La Repubblica are newspapers from which country?

17. What name comes next? Stuart Higgins, David Yelland, Rebekah Brooks.

18. Which newspaper was the first to publish a colour supplement?

19. Asahi Shimbun is a newspaper in which country?
    a) China
    b) Japan
    c) Korea

20. The first what was published in the Daily Express on 2 November 1924?
    a) cartoon
    b) crossword
    c) horoscope

Answers to Quiz 124: Pot Luck

1. Korean War
2. St Thomas
3. Korea
4. Venezuela
5. Socrates
6. Hungary
7. St Denis
8. Potato
9. 1st March
10. Istanbul
11. New Zealand
12. Computer programming languages
13. Richard Nixon
14. Prisons
15. Aphrodite
16. The King and I
17. The Smiths
18. Serbian
19. The Who
20. Lake Constance

Quiz 126: Pot Luck

1. En passant is a manoeuvre in which game?

2. What is the capital city of Vietnam?

3. What is the wife of a Sultan known as?

4. What the name of the prisoner who was released by Pontius Pilate in place of Jesus?

5. What was the name of Captain Nemo's submarine?

6. Which musician's Rolls Royce sold for $2,229,000 when auctioned off in 1985?

7. Juneau is the capital of which American state?

8. Which fashion designer was dismissed from Christian Dior after saying 'I love Hitler'?

9. Which jockey won his first Grand National in 2010 riding Don't Push It?

10. Barwick Green is the theme tune to which long-running radio programme?

11. The biggest-selling English language newspaper in the world is published in which country?

12. Which famous chef made the cake that appeared on the front of the Rolling Stones' album Let It Bleed?

13. Which London tube station contains six consecutive consonants?

14. How many members sit in the US Senate?

15. What is the lower house of the Russian parliament called?

16. Which jazz legend is the oldest man to have a UK number one single?

17. What was the first name of TV's Sergeant Bilko?

18. Fontina cheese comes from which country?

19. Who designed the Volkswagen Beetle?
    a) Gottfried Daimler
    b) Karl Benz
    c) Ferdinand Porsche

20. What major river flows through Baghdad?
    a) Tigris
    b) Euphrates
    c) Ganges

MEDIUM

Answers to Quiz 125: Read All About It

1. Manchester
2. Horoscopes
3. Today
4. The Independent
5. Lord Beaverbrook
6. Private Eye
7. Spain
8. Daily Express
9. Crossword setters
10. Metro
11. Chess
12. Robert Maxwell
13. The Times
14. Wolverhampton
15. The Observer
16. Italy
17. Dominic Mohan (Sun editors)
18. The Sunday Times
19. Japan
20. Crossword

Quiz 127: Organisations

1. What children's organisation was founded by William Smith in 1883?

2. The BND is the secret intelligence service of which country?

3. The Camorra organised crime family originates from which city?

4. Based in Geneva, CERN is the European Centre of what?

5. The CIA is based in which American state?

6. The Diet is the legislature in which Asian country?

7. How many countries were in the original European Economic Community?

8. Between 1937 and 1977, the Falange was a right wing nationalist political party in which European country?

9. The Chetniks were a guerrilla movement from which country?

10. Which Irish political party's name is the Gaelic for 'ourselves alone'?

11. The World Health Organisation is based in which city?

12. The Yakuza are a criminal organisation from which country?

13. The International Court of Justice is based in which city?

14. What popular British institution was founded by Octavia Hill in 1895?

15. The Securitate was the secret police in which Communist state?

16. The Mau Mau was a nationalist organisation in which

African country?

17. The name of which extreme right conservative American organisation derives from a US intelligence worker killed in China in 1945?

18. What decade saw the creation of the National Health Service?

19. What is the name of the body made up of back-bench MPs of the Conservative Party?
a) 1912 Committee
b) 1922 Committee
c) 1932 Committee

20. What was the name of the British anarchist group of the late 1960s and early 1970s?
a) Angry Brigade
b) Mad Brigade
c) Tirade Brigade

MEDIUM

Answers to Quiz 126: Pot Luck

1. Chess
2. Hanoi
3. Sultana
4. Barabbas
5. Nautilus
6. John Lennon
7. Alaska
8. John Galliano
9. Tony McCoy
10. The Archers
11. India
12. Delia Smith
13. Knightsbridge
14. 100
15. Duma
16. Louis Armstrong with What a Wonderful World
17. Ernie
18. Italy
19. Ferdinand Porsche
20. Tigris

Quiz 128: Pot Luck

1. What does as seismograph measure?

2. Jagged Little Pill was a number one album for which Canadian singer?

3. What name is given to words that are pronounced the same but are spelled differently and have different meanings?

4. Who wrote the ancient Greek poems The Iliad and The Odyssey?

5. Where is the San Andreas Fault?

6. What is the highest mountain in Japan?

7. How many sides does a dodecahedron have?

8. What is the longest river in Ireland?

9. The Everglades are in which American state?

10. Detective drama Wallander is set in which country?

11. What does pH stand for?

12. 'In space, no one can hear you scream' is the tagline to which classic sci-fi film?

13. What was the name of the ship that took the Pilgrim Fathers from Plymouth to America in 1620?

14. Who succeeded William Hague as leader of the Conservative Party?

15. What classic Christmas film was based on a short story called The Greatest Gift?

16. What is the name of the US Presidential car?

17. What does the Latin phrase veni, vidi, vici mean?

18. Web addresses ending .se are from which country?

19. What is Queen Elizabeth II's second name?
    a) Margaret
    b) Victoria
    c) Alexandra

20. In Waking The Dead, Trevor Eve plays which character?
    a) Boyd
    b) Floyd
    c) Lloyd

Answers to Quiz 127: Organisations

1.	The Boys' Brigade	11.	Geneva
2.	Germany	12.	Japan
3.	Naples	13.	The Hague
4.	Nuclear Research	14.	The National Trust
5.	Virginia	15.	Romania
6.	Japan	16.	Kenya
7.	Six	17.	John Birch Society
8.	Spain	18.	1940s
9.	Serbia	19.	1922 Committee
10.	Sinn Fein	20.	Angry Brigade

Quiz 129: British Politics

1. David Cameron is the MP for which constituency?

2. Who, in 2010, became the Green Party's first Westminster MP?

3. Who is the current MP for the Doncaster North Constituency?

4. On what day of the week does Prime Minister's Questions take place?

5. In what decade was Parliament first televised?

6. Who played Margaret Thatcher in The Iron Lady?

7. What title is given to the MP with the longest unbroken service in the House of Commons?

8. Shirley Williams, David Owen and Roy Jenkins were three members of the so called Gang of Four. Who was the fourth?

9. Who was the British prime minister during the first Gulf War?

10. Which house has more members? The House of Commons or the House of Lords?

11. Pierce Brosnan played the fictional former Prime Minister Adam Lang in which 2010 film?

12. Tony Blair was born in which country?

13. Prior to 2010, in what year was the last hung parliament elected?

14. Which long time Labour MP wrote a diary called A View From the Foothills?

15. Which former Fleet Street editor presents The Daily Politics?

16. George Galloway was elected as MP in Bradford West in

2012 representing which party?

17. The person holding which post is the head of the British Civil Service?

18. The Scottish Parliament is located in which part of Edinburgh?

19. What is the minimum age at which a person can stand for the UK Parliament?

20. What colour are the benches in the House of Lords?
    a) blue
    b) green
    c) red

21. How many members sit in the Scottish Parliament?
    a) 99
    b) 129
    c) 149

MEDIUM

Answers to Quiz 128: Pot Luck

1. Earthquakes
2. Alanis Morissette
3. Homophone
4. Homer
5. California
6. Mount Fuji
7. 12
8. Shannon
9. Florida
10. Sweden
11. potential Hydrogen
12. Alien
13. The Mayflower
14. Ian Duncan Smith
15. It's A Wonderful Life
16. Cadillac One
17. I came, I saw, I conquered
18. Sweden
19. Alexandra
20. Boyd

Quiz 130: Pot Luck

1. Ascorbic acid is another name for what vitamin?

2. The Brenner Pass links which two European countries?

3. What was Lord Byron's first name?

4. American Idiot is a musical based on the music of which band?

5. Who played Marilyn Monroe in the 2011 film My Week With Marilyn?

6. What does an altimeter measure?

7. What is the process of splitting atoms called?

8. The film True Grit was based on a novel by which author?

9. What is the only active volcano in mainland Europe?

10. Which Norwegian was the first man to reach the South Pole?

11. Who played Captain Jonathan Archer in Star Trek Enterprise?

12. What is the name of the desert that separates Egypt and Israel?

13. What battle, according to the Duke of Wellington, was 'a close run thing'?

14. The Bank of England is located on which London thoroughfare?

15. Who was the youngest member of The Beatles?

16. Who was named Time magazine's Man of the Year in 1938?

17. Which ancient Greek mathematician is known as the 'Father of Geometry'?

18. In the nursery rhyme who killed Cock Robin?

19. What word represents Y in the International Radio Alphabet?
    a) Yankee
    b) Yeti
    c) Yodel

20. What is the name of the film festival founded by Robert Redford?
    a) Moondance
    b) Raindance
    c) Sundance

MEDIUM

Answers to Quiz 129: British Politics

1.	Witney	12.	Scotland
2.	Caroline Lucas	13.	1974
3.	Ed Miliband	14.	Chris Mullin
4.	Wednesday	15.	Andrew Neil
5.	1980s	16.	Respect
6.	Meryl Streep	17.	Cabinet Secretary
7.	The Father of the House	18.	Holyrood
8.	Bill Rogers	19.	18
9.	John Major	20.	Red
10.	The House of Lords	21.	129
11.	The Ghost		

Quiz 131: Black and White

1. What cocktail is made using equal measures of champagne and stout?

2. Tony Iommi, Geezer Butler and Bill Ward are members of which rock group?

3. Who rode a horse called Black Bess?

4. Which group had a hit album called It's Great When You're Straight ... Yeah?

5. What is the name of the official who acts as a messenger between the House of Commons and the House of Lords?

6. The Kepi Blanc is the monthly magazine of which military organisation?

7. Who beat Jimmy White to win his only World Snooker Championship title?

8. What was soul singer Barry White's only UK number one hit?

9. What was Joe Gargery's occupation in Charles Dickens' Great Expectations?

10. Which actor played the lead role in the film The Man In The White Suit?

11. Which English football team are nicknamed The Lillywhites?

12. Alan White was the drummer with which Manchester band?

13. Is This Love and Here I Go Again were which heavy rock group's only top ten hits?

14. Italian football team Juventus modelled their black and white striped shirts on which English football club?

15. Which group topped the UK charts in 2006 with the single Welcome To The Black Parade?

16. The White Sox are a baseball team from which American city?

17. Which reggae group takes its name from the Arabic word for black?

18. Which major African city's name derives from the Spanish for white house?

19. The Black Swan appears on the badge of which Australian state?
    a) New South Wales
    b) South Australia
    c) Western Australia

20. The White Peacock was the first published novel by which author?
    a) Graham Greene
    b) DH Lawrence
    c) Henry James

MEDIUM

Answers to Quiz 130: Pot Luck

1. Vitamin C
2. Italy and Austria
3. George
4. Green Day
5. Michelle Williams
6. Altitude
7. Fission
8. Charles Portis
9. Vesuvius
10. Roald Amundsen
11. Scott Bakula
12. The Negev
13. Waterloo
14. Threadneedle Street
15. George Harrison
16. Adolf Hitler
17. Euclid
18. The sparrow
19. Yankee
20. Sundance

Quiz 132: Pot Luck

1. Which group topped the charts for 15 weeks in 1995 with Love Is All Around?

2. Which comedian provided the voice of the speaking clock to raise money for 2012's Sport Relief campaign?

3. On what date is St Andrew's Day celebrated?

4. Which Ancient Greek philosopher founded the Academy?

5. Hindi is one of India's two official languages. What is the other?

6. In Japan they drive on what side of the road?

7. What was the nickname of American cowboy William F Cody?

8. Which Grammy award winning singer starred in The No. 1 Ladies' Detective Agency?

9. What was the name of the protest camp set up outside St Paul's Cathedral in 2011 and 2012?

10. True or false? Cricket was formerly an Olympic sport?

11. In Christianity, what day is celebrated 40 days after Easter Sunday?

12. Pittodrie is the home ground of which British football club?

13. Where in the world is Margaret Thatcher Day celebrated?

14. Which town in Derbyshire is famous for its church with a crooked spire?

15. Berlin replaced which town as German capital in 1990?

16. Who, in 1955, replaced Winston Churchill as British prime minister?

17. The phrase 'back to square one' originates from commentary of what sport?

18. The Caribbean island of Guadeloupe is an overseas territory of which European country?

19. What is the small circle of paper that is removed by a hole punch called?
    a) brad
    b) chad
    c) vlad

20. In Devon, a grockle is another word for what?
    a) winkle
    b) tourist
    c) cream cake

MEDIUM

Answers to Quiz 131: Black and White

1. Black Velvet
2. Black Sabbath
3. Dick Turpin
4. Black Grape
5. Black Rod
6. The French Foreign Legion
7. John Parrott
8. You're The First, The Last, My Everything
9. Blacksmith
10. Alec Guinness
11. Tottenham Hotspur
12. Oasis
13. Whitesnake
14. Notts County
15. My Chemical Romance
16. Chicago
17. Aswad
18. Casablanca
19. Western Australia
20. DH Lawrence

Quiz 133: Ireland

1. Which three counties from the province of Ulster are in the Irish Republic?

2. What are the four Irish counties that start with the letter W?

3. Galway, Mayo, Leitrim, Sligo and Roscommon make up which Irish province?

4. What is the official emblem of the Irish Republic?

5. The traditional Irish dish champ is made using potato and what vegetable?

6. What river runs through the city of Belfast?

7. Rock band The Undertones were from which Irish city?

8. In what part of Belfast is the Northern Ireland Assembly located?

9. Which Irish province shares its name with a town in Germany?

10. Which manager steered Ireland to qualification to the 2012 European Championships?

11. Eamon de Valera, the first President of Ireland, was born in which country?

12. What is the name of the lake that borders five of Northern Ireland's six counties?

13. Who did Enda Kenny succeed as Taoiseach in March 2011?

14. What is the name of the group of islands situated off the coast of Galway Bay?

15. How many counties are there on the island of Ireland?

16. In what year did the Easter Rising take place?

17. Which Irish poet was awarded the Nobel Prize in 1923?

18. In which city was author Bram Stoker born?

19. Who is the only Irishman to win the Tour de France?
    a) Sean Kelly
    b) Paul Kimmage
    c) Stephen Roche

20. In what decade of the 19th century did the Irish Potato Famine occur?
    a) 1830s
    b) 1840s
    c) 1850s

MEDIUM

Answers to Quiz 132: Pot Luck

1.	Wet Wet Wet	11.	Ascension Day
2.	David Walliams	12.	Aberdeen
3.	30th November	13.	Falkland Islands
4.	Plato	14.	Chesterfield
5.	English	15.	Bonn
6.	Left	16.	Anthony Eden
7.	Buffalo Bill	17.	Football
8.	Jill Scott	18.	France
9.	Occupy	19.	Chad
10.	True	20.	Tourist

Quiz 134: Pot Luck

1. What is St Stephen's Day more commonly known as?

2. Who played The Singing Detective in Dennis Potter's classic TV series?

3. What word describes food cooked in accordance with Muslim law?

4. What does PVC stand for?

5. In American currency, how much is a nickel worth?

6. Which author created the fictional world of Narnia?

7. What is the biggest-selling single in history in the UK?

8. Which former Dr Who actor played aristocratic TV detective Campion?

9. In 1892, Keir Hardie became the the first elected MP from which political party?

10. What was The Beatles' first number one hit single?

11. In the Bible, who was the second son of Adam and Eve?

12. What Latin phrase describes doing something for the public good without charging?

13. What sort of victory involves such terrible losses for the winner that it's almost as bad as a defeat?

14. Which Egyptian leader was overthrown during the Arab Spring?

15. Before becoming President of the USA, Ronald Reagan was governor of which state?

16. How old is somebody who is a quadragenarian?

17. What are the four main blood groups?

18. Vincent Furnier is the real name of which rock legend?

19. Which of the following isn't one of the Mr Men?
    a) Mr Bounce
    b) Mr Bump
    c) Mr Bubbly

20. A hostage who comes to empathise with his captors is said to have what syndrome?
    a) Oslo
    b) Copenhagen
    c) Stockholm

Answers to Quiz 133: Ireland

1. Cavan, Donegal and Monaghan
2. Waterford, Westmeath, Wexford and Wicklow
3. Connacht (Connaught)
4. The harp
5. Spring onion
6. River Lagan
7. Derry
8. Stormont
9. Munster
10. Giovanni Trapattoni
11. USA
12. Lough Neagh
13. Brian Cowen
14. Aran Islands
15. 32
16. 1916
17. WB Yeats
18. Dublin
19. Stephen Roche
20. 1840s

DiFFiCULT QUIZZES

Quiz 135: Food and Drink

1. What berry forms the basis of Cumberland sauce?

2. What baked dish takes its name from the German word for whirlpool?

3. Which two types of fish would you find in a salad Niçoise?

4. What is the fruit granadilla more commonly known as?

5. A loganberry is a hybrid of which two types of berry?

6. What flavouring gives Earl Grey tea its distinctive taste?

7. Solanum lycopersicum is the Latin name for which food?

8. What does the flavour intensifier MSG stand for?

9. Stilton cheese can only be made in which three English counties?

10. Chianti wine comes from which Italian region?

11. What type of Japanese fish cane be deadly if not cooked properly?

12. What fruit is a cross between grapefruit, tangerine and orange?

13. Which orange flavoured red wine takes its name from the Spanish for 'a bleeding'?

14. What fruit is used in the brandy Kirsch?

15. Which famous author said that 'Wine is the most civilised thing in the world'?

16. Iskra sparkling wine comes from which country?

17. Yarg cheese comes from which English county?

Answers – page 277

18. If an American chef broils something what would a British cook do with it?
    a) boil
    b) scramble
    c) grill

19. How many gallons are in a firkin of beer?
    a) 5
    b) 7
    c) 9

Answers to Quiz 200: Pot Luck

1. James Brown
2. Mexico City
3. Cecil Day-Lewis
4. Beard of the Year
5. TS Eliot
6. Gilbert and George
7. Andalusia
8. John Peel
9. Engelbert Humperdinck
10. QPR
11. Nice
12. George Robertson
13. The Matterhorn
14. Poker
15. Oxford United and Swindon Town
16. Thursday
17. JMW Turner
18. Arabic
19. Manchester
20. Elephant

DIFFICULT

Quiz 136: Pot Luck

1. After how many years would a couple celebrate their crystal anniversary?

2. Dodoma is the capital city of which African country?

3. The Massachusetts Institute of Technology is located in which American city?

4. In the board game Monopoly, what is the only property that is located south of the River Thames?

5. What is the smallest city in Wales with a cathedral?

6. Which playwright got his first writing credit on Coronation Street in 1961?

7. What was the first National Park to be created in Britain?

8. The Dada movement was founded in which European city?

9. In military aviation what does the acronym AWACS stand for?

10. What is the second oldest university in Britain?

11. What is the first term in the legal year?

12. Which London Underground line serves the most stations?

13. The curie is an SI unit used to measure what?

14. John Francis Wade wrote the words and music to which famous Christmas carol?

15. Who was the first Secretary General of the UN?

16. In which country would you find the Cliffs of Moher?

17. Which Frenchman won the Best Director award at the 2012 Oscars?

18. Queen Alexandra's Birdwing is the largest type of which insect?

19. In which European city would you find Guell Park
    a) Madrid
    b) Barcelona
    c) Valencia

20. What castle is known as the Key of England?
    a) Dover
    b) Windsor Castle
    c) Warwick

Answers to Quiz 135: Food and Drink

1. Redcurrant
2. Strudel
3. Tuna and anchovy
4. Passion fruit
5. Raspberry and Blackberry
6. Bergamot
7. Tomato
8. Monosodium glutamate
9. Leicestershire, Nottinghamshire, Derbyshire
10. Tuscany
11. Puffer fish (fugu)
12. Ugli
13. Sangria
14. Cherries
15. Ernest Hemingway
16. Bulgaria
17. Cornwall
18. Grill
19. 9

DIFFICULT

Quiz 137: Geography part 1

1. Batavia is the former name of which Asian capital?

2. What is the smallest country in mainland Africa?

3. Milwaukee Deep is the deepest point of which ocean?

4. Which Caribbean country, takes its name from the Spanish for ancient and bearded?

5. Kinder Scout is the highest point in which British National Park?

6. The longest road and rail bridge in Europe connects which two countries?

7. Dahomey is the former name of which African country?

8. The tallest dam in the world is in which former Soviet republic?

9. What river, meaning 'plenty of eels' flows through Sydney, Australia?

10. The Canary Islands take their name from which animal?

11. Which Shipping Forecast Area was formerly known as Heligoland?

12. Cotopaxi, the highest active volcano in the world is in which South American country?

13. What is the Fremantle Doctor?

14. Lunescastrum was the Roman name for which English city?

15. Which country has the shortest coastline in the world?

16. Which is longer, the Panama Canal or the Suez Canal?

Answers – page 281

17. Conakry is the capital city of which African country?

18. The name of which African capital city means 'new flower'?

19. Coombe Hill is the highest point in which range of English hills?
    a) Malverns
    b) Chilterns
    c) Cheviots

20. What is the largest sea in the world?
    a) Caribbean Sea
    b) Mediterranean Sea
    c) South China Sea

Answers to Quiz 136: Pot Luck

1. 15
2. Tanzania
3. Cambridge
4. Old Kent Road
5. St David's
6. Jack Rosenthal
7. The Peak District National Park
8. Vienna
9. Airborne Warning And Control System
10. Cambridge
11. Michaelmas
12. Piccadilly (53)
13. Radiation
14. O Come All Ye Faithful
15. Trygve Lie
16. Ireland
17. Michel Hazanavicius
18. Butterfly
19. Barcelona
20. Dover

DIFFICULT

Quiz 138: Pot Luck

1. Lome is the capital city of which African country?

2. American painter Mark Rothko was born in which European country?

3. Who starred in BBC comedy White Van Man?

4. Mercalli is a unit used to measure what?

5. The Oscar-winning film A Separation was set in which country?

6. In taxonomy, what comes between family and species?

7. The original version of the board game Monopoly was based on which city?

8. Black-bellied, whiskered and roseate are types of which seabird?

9. What is the busiest station on the London Underground?

10. Which Scottish band took their name from a French TV show featuring a small boy and an enormous white dog?

11. Author William Makepeace Thackeray was born in which country?

12. Which Italian architect designed London's tallest building, the Shard?

13. While at Oxford University at the same time as Bill Clinton, which British-based broadcaster was voted The American Most Likely to Succeed?

14. What is the only painting that Vincent Van Gogh sold in his lifetime?

15. In 1964, which actor and comedian became the first man to appear on the cover of Playboy magazine?

16. Bruce Lee, Joan Collins, Liberace and Zsa Zsa Gabor all had guest roles in which superhero inspired TV show?

17. Which singer launched a range of chocolates called Chakalates?

18. Which two famous film directors have children called Satchel?

19. Who were the first British band to top the US singles chart?
    a) The Animals
    b) The Beatles
    c) The Tornados

20. What is the most powerful type of solar flare called?
    a) X flare
    b) Y flare
    c) Z flare

Answers to Quiz 137: Geography part 1

1. Jakarta
2. Gambia
3. Atlantic
4. Antigua and Barbuda
5. Peak District
6. Denmark and Sweden
7. Benin
8. Tajikistan
9. Parramatta
10. Dog
11. German Bight
12. Ecuador
13. A wind
14. Lancaster
15. Monaco
16. Suez Canal
17. Guinea
18. Addis Ababa
19. Chilterns
20. South China Sea

DIFFICULT

Quiz 139: Fashion

1. On what part of the body would a babouche be worn?

2. Billycock and biggin are examples of what type of clothing?

3. Which designer created Queen Elizabeth II's wedding dress?

4. On a clothes care label, what does a circle mean?

5. Barbara Hulanicki was the founder of which fashion label?

6. Which brightly coloured cotton fabric takes its name from the Hindi word for spatter or stain?

7. Who would wear a chasuble and a calotte?

8. Which French fashion designer hosted the TV show Eurotrash?

9. Which English city gives its name to styles of shoes, shirts and trousers?

10. Where would you wear an aigrette?

11. A castor was a hat made from the fur of which animal?

12. Which fashion designer was shot dead outside his Miami mansion in July 1997?

13. A chogori is a jacket traditionally worn in which Asian country?

14. Which Welsh designer succeeded Alexander McQueen at the fashion house Givenchy?

15. Which style of checked cloth takes its name from the Malay word meaning 'striped'?

16. In what two months of the year does London Fashion Week take place?

17. Fashion designer Paul Smith is from which city?

18. The cravat takes its name from the people of which country?

19. Which of the following was a famous London tailor?
    a) Tommy Nutter
    b) Tommy Wildman
    c) Tommy Maniac

20. David Shilling is famous for designing what type of clothing?
    a) dresses
    b) shoes
    c) hats

Answers to Quiz 138: Pot Luck

1. Togo
2. Latvia
3. Will Mellor
4. Earthquake intensity
5. Iran
6. Genus
7. Atlantic City
8. Tern
9. Waterloo
10. Belle and Sebastian
11. India
12. Renzo Piano
13. Paul Gambaccini
14. The Red Vineyard
15. Peter Sellers
16. Batman
17. Chaka Khan
18. Woody Allen and Spike Lee
19. The Tornados
20. X flare

DIFFICULT

Quiz 140: Pot Luck

1. Which US president's real name was Leslie King?

2. Which five London Underground stations contain the letter X?

3. A Dudelsack is a German variety of what type of musical instrument?

4. What is measured using the mohs scale?

5. Who was the only artist to have a top 40 hit in the US and the UK every year from 1971 to 1999?

6. In what decade was the Boy Scout movement founded?

7. Which playwright wrote the farce Noises Off?

8. The father of which tennis great represented Iran at boxing in the 1948 and 1952 Olympic Games?

9. Chisinau is the capital city of which country?

10. What was the first song played on Top of the Pops?

11. Former US Vice President Al Gore was a roommate of which Oscar-nominated actor?

12. Which French painter briefly worked on the construction of the Panama Canal?

13. Which Alfred Hitchcock film was the first to show a flushing toilet on screen?

14. In 1971 Caroline Davidson invented which famous logo?

15. The first ice cream cones were eaten in which decade of the twentieth century?

16. The first escalator in Britain was installed in which department store?

17. John McEnroe, Gyles Brandreth and Lucien Freud were all born in which country?

18. In the board game Monopoly, how much do you win for coming second in a beauty contest?

19. What is the length of the London Underground network?
    a) 129 miles
    b) 229 miles
    c) 329 miles

20. Before finding fame as a singer Matt Monro used to drive what for a living?
    a) bus
    b) taxi
    c) train

Answers to Quiz 139: Fashion

1. On the feet
2. Hat
3. Sir Norman Hartnell
4. Suitable for dry cleaning
5. Biba
6. Chintz
7. A Catholic priest
8. Jean-Paul Gaultier
9. Oxford
10. On the head
11. Beaver
12. Gianni Versace
13. Korea
14. Julien Macdonald
15. Gingham
16. February and September
17. Nottingham
18. Croatia
19. Tommy Nutter
20. Hats

DIFFICULT

Quiz 141: TV Gameshows

1. Who presents TV quiz The Bank Job?

2. The theme to which long-running quiz show is College Boy by Derek New?

3. How many questions must a pair correctly answer to win money on the Million Pound Drop?

4. Which future King of the Jungle previously hosted a children's game show called On Safari?

5. What is the name of the spoof game show on BBC comedy That Mitchell and Webb Look?

6. In what Ant and Dec-hosted game show was one lucky contestant given the opportunity to win £1 million on a 50/50 gamble?

7. Who succeeded Richard Whiteley as host of Countdown?

8. Which world athlete became the the first person to complete TV gameshow The Cube?

9. Which comedian hosted Lucky Ladders and Punchlines?

10. Who hosts sports quiz show A League of Their Own?

11. Pointless co-host Richard Osman's brother Mat was bass player with which indie rockers?

12. How many boxes are in play at the start of a game on Deal or No Deal?

13. Which two sportsmen have been captains on Hole in the Wall?

14. Richard O'Brien was the first host of The Crystal Maze but who was the second?

15. Who succeeded David Dickinson as the host of TV's Bargain Hunt?

16. 'The heat is on, the time is right' was the opening line to the theme tune to which classic quiz show?

17. Which Watchdog presenter hosts The Exit List?

18. In what game show did members of the losing team receive a photograph of them and their opponents?

19. Which radio DJ appeared on the very first episode of 3-2-1?
    a) Annie Nightingale
    b) Liz Kershaw
    c) Janice Long

20. What is the name of the TV game show hosted by Jeremy Kyle?
    a) Who's The Daddy
    b) High Stakes
    c) Lie Detector

Answers to Quiz 140: Pot Luck

1. Gerald Ford
2. Brixton, Croxley, Oxford Circus, Uxbridge and Vauxhall
3. Bagpipes
4. Hardness
5. Elton John
6. 1900s
7. Michael Frayn
8. Andre Agassi
9. Moldova
10. I Only Want To Be With You by Dusty Springfield
11. Tommy Lee Jones
12. Paul Gauguin
13. Psycho
14. Nike swoosh
15. 1910s
16. Harrods
17. Germany
18. £10.00
19. 229 miles
20. Bus

DIFFICULT

Quiz 142: Pot Luck

1. Which common pub name derives from the heraldic symbol of King Richard II?

2. In what year did Britain hand Hong Kong back to China?

3. Lilongwe is the capital city of which African country?

4. Which sixth-century saint founded a monastery on Iona?

5. Which country's national anthem has the same tune as God Save the Queen?

6. In Monopoly, how much is the fine for being Drunk In Charge?

7. In which city are there theatres called the Hippodrome, Crescent and Alexandra?

8. What is the largest National Park in the UK?

9. What was the last novel written by Thomas Hardy?

10. What was the first credit card?

11. Which two London Underground stations contain the letter J?

12. What is measured using the Scoville scale?

13. Which comic character is the alter ego of Dan Renton Skinner?

14. In 1994, 3.5 million people in Rio de Janeiro attended a free concert by which British singer?

15. Tokay and Bull's Blood wine come from which country?

16. What is the only letter that doesn't feature on the periodic table?

17. In what decade was Parliament first broadcast live on the radio?

18. Who was nominated for an Oscar for her portrayal of Lisbeth Salander in The Girl With the Dragon Tattoo?

19. Osmology relates to which one of the senses?
    a) sight
    b) hearing
    c) smell

20. How many white keys are on a standard piano?
    a) 42
    b) 52
    c) 62

Answers to Quiz 141: TV Gameshows

1. George Lamb
2. University Challenge
3. 8
4. Christopher Biggins
5. Numberwang
6. Red or Black
7. Des Lynam
8. Mo Farah
9. Lennie Bennett
10. James Corden
11. Suede
12. 22
13. Darren Gough and Austin Healy
14. Ed Tudor-Pole
15. Tim Wonnacott
16. Going For Gold
17. Matt Allwright
18. Family Fortunes
19. Janice Long
20. High Stakes

DIFFICULT

Quiz 143: History

1. The ancient city of Babylon is in which modern-day country?

2. Revolutionary leader Simon Bolivar was from which South American country?

3. The so called Wonga Coup was a plot to overthrow the government of which African country?

4. Who was the oldest monarch to ascend to the British throne?

5. Brian Boru was the king of which country?

6. Which part of the British Isles was the first to give women the vote?

7. Sam Nujoma was the first president of which African country?

8. The Tupamaros were a guerrilla movement from which country?

9. Which wartime leader was described by Winston Churchill as the 'bullfrog of the Pontine marshes'?

10. Which English explorer was executed for treason in 1618?

11. Which king created the Hanging Gardens of Babylon?

12. Who was the only US President to be elected unanimously by the electoral college?

13. Which country's former Prime Ministers include David Lange, Geoffrey Palmer and Mike Moore?

14. Which monarch founded the Order of the Garter?

15. The first woman elected to the British parliament represented which party?

16. The collaborationist government of France in World War Two was based in which town?

17. Which two countries joined the European Economic Community on the same day as the UK?

18. What was the name of the plot to assassinate members of Lord Liverpool's cabinet and then declare a republic?

19. When was the last time that there were two British general elections in the same year?
    a) 1970
    b) 1974
    c) 1979

20. Slavery in the British Empire was outlawed in what year?
    a) 1823
    b) 1833
    c) 1843

Answers to Quiz 142: Pot Luck

1. The White Hart
2. 1997
3. Malawi
4. St Columba
5. Liechtenstein
6. £20.00
7. Birmingham
8. The Cairngorms
9. Jude The Obscure
10. Diners Club
11. St John's Wood and St James's Park
12. The heat of chillies
13. Angelos Epithemiou
14. Rod Stewart
15. Hungary
16. J
17. 1970s
18. Rooney Mara
19. Smell
20. 52

DIFFICULT

Quiz 144: Pot Luck

1. Which animated baddie was the alter ego of Sylvester Sneekley?

2. The first televised Royal Christmas Speech took place in which year?

3. Which Roman emperor's name comes from the Latin for 'little boots'?

4. What was the first country to declare Christianity as state religion?

5. N'Djamena is the capital city of which African country?

6. In what year did the space shuttle make its maiden space flight?

7. Who is the only US President to have been divorced?

8. Anjou Rose wine comes from which region of France?

9. Who sang the line 'I want my MTV' on the Dire Straits hit Money For Nothing?

10. The only existing foot tunnel under the River Thames links the Greenwich and where?

11. A person with polydactylism has extra what?

12. In America, the Mason-Dixon line marks the boundary between which two states?

13. The Peacock Throne was used to describe the monarchy of which Asian country?

14. The House of Commons last sat on a Saturday in 1982. What was the reason?

15. The dong is the currency of which Asian country?

DIFFICULT

Answers – page 295

16. What name is given to the white, crescent-shaped areas at the base of the fingernail?

17. In 1997, Jenny Shipley became the first female prime minister in which Commonwealth country?

18. What is the only American state that borders only one other state?

19. Laverock is another name for which bird?

20. How many stations are served by the London Underground?
    a) 170
    b) 270
    c) 370

21. Which Shipping Forecast Area lies directly south of Irish Sea?
    a) Plymouth
    b) Lundy
    c) Portland

Answers to Quiz 143: History

1. Iraq
2. Venezuela
3. Equatorial Guinea
4. William IV
5. Ireland
6. Isle of Man
7. Namibia
8. Uruguay
9. Mussolini
10. Sir Walter Raleigh
11. Nebuchadnezzar II
12. George Washington
13. New Zealand
14. Edward III
15. Sinn Fein
16. Vichy
17. Ireland and Denmark
18. Cato Street Conspiracy
19. 1974
20. 1833

DIFFICULT

Quiz 145: Real Names

1. Henry McCarty was the real name of which Wild West bandit?

2. What was Louis Armstrong's real first name?

3. Tynian O'Mahoney was the real name of which Irish comedian?

4. Which legendary rock 'n' roller's real name was Ernest Evans?

5. Which actor and dancer's real name was Frederick Austerlitz?

6. Which blonde bombshell's real name was Camille Javal?

7. Christopher Wallace was the real name of which rapper?

8. Alfred Schweider was the real name of which legendary American comedian?

9. Robert LeRoy Parker and Henry Longabaugh were the real name of which American outlaws?

10. Phyllis Primrose-Pechey was the real name of which TV chef?

11. Eric Bishop is the real name of which Oscar-winning actor?

12. Which American union leader had the unfortunate middle name of Riddle?

13. Yvette Marie Stevens is the real name of which American soul singer?

14. Which US singer took his stage name from a blonde bombshell and a serial killer?

15. Issur Danielovitch is the real name of which Hollywood icon?

16. What is the name of the comedian who created the character Keith Lemon?

17. Georgios Krylacos Panayiotou is the real name of which singer?

18. Which Hollywood actress's real name is Demetra Guynes?

19. What does the E in Richard E Grant stand for?
    a) Edward
    b) Ernest
    c) Esterhuysen

20. Tracy Marrow is the real name of which rapper?
    a) Ice T
    b) Ice Cube
    c) Vanilla Ice

Answers to Quiz 144: Pot Luck

1. The Hooded Claw
2. 1957
3. Caligula
4. Armenia
5. Chad
6. 1981
7. Ronald Reagan
8. Loire valley
9. Sting
10. The Isle of Dogs
11. Fingers
12. Maryland and Pennsylvania
13. Iran
14. Falkland Islands Invasion
15. Vietnam
16. Lunula
17. New Zealand
18. Maine
19. Lark
20. 270
21. Lundy

DIFFICULT

Quiz 146: Pot Luck

1. Who were Bill Clinton's two opponents in the 1992 US Presidential election?

2. Which playwright wrote A Doll's House, The Master Builder and Peer Gynt?

3. Excluding London stations, what is the busiest railway station in Britain?

4. Yosemite Falls are in which American state?

5. Prohibition in America occurred between which years?

6. Nyasaland is the former name of which African country?

7. Which four London Underground stations contain the colour of the line that they are on?

8. In English law, what is the third term of the legal year known as?

9. In 1992, which band became the first winners of the Mercury Music Prize?

10. The Shipping Forecast Area Fastnet lies off the coast of which country?

11. Which comedian endured 'a week from hell' to raise money for Sport Relief?

12. Gabarone is the capital city of which African country?

13. Taking 72 days, in 1998 Benoit Lecomte was the first person to swim what body of water?

14. Year Zero was the slogan adopted by the murderous leaders of which Asian country?

15. Which alliterative author won the 2012 Orange Prize for her novel The Song of Achilles?

16. A koto is a musical instrument originating from which country?

17. Tanganyika is the former name of which African country?

18. The Irish Derby is held at which track?

19. Which cartoon character appeared on the cover of Playboy magazine in 2009?

20. What would you do with a baldric?
    a) eat it
    b) wear it
    c) smoke it

21. Pasteurisation occurs at what temperature?
    a) 63°C
    b) 73°C
    c) 83°C

Answers to Quiz 145: Real Names

1. Billy The Kid
2. Daniel
3. Dave Allen
4. Chubby Checker
5. Fred Astaire
6. Brigitte Bardot
7. Notorious B.I.G.
8. Lenny Bruce
9. Butch Cassidy and the Sundance Kid
10. Fanny Craddock
11. Jamie Foxx
12. Jimmy Hoffa
13. Chaka Khan
14. Marilyn Manson
15. Kirk Douglas
16. Leigh Francis
17. George Michael
18. Demi Moore
19. Esterhuysen
20. Ice T

DIFFICULT

Quiz 147: Movies

1. The Average Joes and The Purple Cobras were sports teams in which 2004 comedy?

2. Which Turner Prize-winning artist directed Hunger and Shame?

3. 'The longer you wait, the harder it gets' is the tagline to what 2005 comedy?

4. Which Spielberg film had the working title A Boy's Life?

5. What was the first Carry On Film?

6. A woman in a toga holding a torch is the logo of which film studio?

7. Who played Dennis Thatcher in the 2011 film The Iron Lady?

8. A dream sequence by Salvador Dali appeared in which Hitchcock film?

9. Which action star's real name is Mark Vincent?

10. Star Beast was the working title of which sci-fi classic?

11. Complete the sequence. European, Christmas, Vegas...?

12. Which villainous creature had a pet called Salacious Crumb?

13. Antoine Doinel is a recurring character in the films of which director?

14. Which actor wrote the novels Ash Wednesday and The Hottest State?

15. The Dead Rabbits, The Night Walkers of Ragpickers Row and The Frog Hollows are gangs from which film?

16. 'Check in. Relax. Take a shower' is the tagline to which film?

17. Which action star represented Britain at the Diving World Championships in 1992?

18. Who are the only two actors to have played James Bond just once?

19. Which Hollywood actor played bass in a band called Dogstar?
    a) Keanu Reeves
    b) Kiefer Sutherland
    c) Val Kilmer

20. What was the first film that Elvis Presley starred in?
    a) Love Me Tender
    b) King Creole
    c) Jailhouse Rock

Answers to Quiz 146: Pot Luck

1. George H W Bush and Ross Perot
2. Henrik Ibsen
3. Birmingham New Street
4. California
5. Madeline Miller
6. Malawi
7. Parsons Green, Redbridge, Stepney Green and Turnham Green
8. Easter
9. Primal Scream
10. Ireland
11. John Bishop
12. Botswana
13. Atlantic Ocean
14. Cambodia
15. Madeline Miller
16. Japan
17. Tanzania
18. The Curragh
19. Marge Simpson
20. Wear it
21. 63°C

DIFFICULT

Quiz 148: Pot Luck

1. Who replaced George Dawes as the scorer on TV gameshow Shooting Stars?

2. Amos Hart, Kitty Baxter, and Mary Sunshine are characters in which musical?

3. Thimphu is the capital city of which Asian country?

4. What group has had the most UK chart hits without reaching number 1?

5. The actor playing which role in a Shakespeare play has the most lines to learn?

6. Which Canadian city was formerly known as Ville Marie?

7. What was exceptional about Ernest Vincent Wright's novel Gadsby?

8. What is the only station name shared by both the London Underground and Paris Metro?

9. In English law, what is the second term of the legal year?

10. In what year was MTV launched?

11. Six Men Under Dry Things is an anagram of which popular group from the 1980s?

12. In Ireland, a gombeen man would lend you what?

13. A gricer likes to take pictures of what?

14. An ikebanist is a Japanese practitioner of what?

15. In 2006, which chef became the first man since King George VI to appear on the cover of Good Housekeeping magazine?

Answers – page 303

16. Apart from the UK, what are the two Commonwealth countries in Europe?

17. The popliteal fossa is found at the back of which joint of the human body?

18. Which toy takes its name from the Danish for 'play well'?

19. Under EU law what is the minimum alcohol content a wine must have?
    a) 7%
    b) 13%
    c) 17%

20. Who would most commonly wear an alb?
    a) barrister
    b) priest
    c) king

Answers to Quiz 147: Movies

1. Dodgeball
2. Steve McQueen
3. The 40 Year Old Virgin
4. ET
5. Carry on Sergeant
6. Columbia
7. Jim Broadbent
8. Spellbound
9. Vin Diesel
10. Alien
11. American (National Lampoon travel sequels)
12. Jabba The Hutt
13. Francois Truffaut
14. Ethan Hawke
15. The Gangs of New York
16. Psycho
17. Jason Statham
18. David Niven and George Lazenby
19. Keanu Reeves
20. Love Me Tender

DIFFICULT

Quiz 149: Pop Music

1. What is the only palindromic song by a palindromic band to reach the top 10 in the UK singles chart?

2. Apart from the Beatles, what is the only other group to top the UK singles charts on seven consecutive occasions?

3. Which songwriter and bass player was captain of the Wales under-16 football team?

4. What song reached number 18 when released in 1971 but went on to top the charts in 2005?

5. Which 1960s group were the first to reach number one with their first three releases?

6. What is the only song to top the UK charts by four different artists?

7. Film director Baz Luhrmann topped the charts in 1999 with Everyone's Free (To Wear...) what?

8. The soundtrack to which film was the biggest-selling album in America in the 1960s?

9. Who is the only female solo artist to have had 13 UK number one hits?

10. Which group's only number one hit was The Model?

11. Which Welsh group have reached the UK top 40 19 times but never had a top ten single?

12. Which Colonel was Trapped in 1985?

13. Who was the first artist to have a posthumous UK number one single?

14. At 9m 38s, what Oasis song is the longest-running track to reach number one?

15. Andy Williams reached the charts in 2002 with an unlikely duet with which TV presenter?

16. Who are the only father and son combo to have both topped the UK singles chart with solo releases?

17. Which 80's singer's stage name is an anagram of his real-life surname of Hamill?

18. The blues album Let Them Talk was recorded by which actor?

19. Guns N' Roses guitarist Slash grew up in which English city?
a) Hull b) Bradford c) Stoke

20. In 2000 George Michael paid £1.45m for whose upright piano?
a) Elvis Presley b) John Lennon c) Ludwig van Beethoven

Answers to Quiz 148: Pot Luck

1. Angelos Epethemiou
2. Chicago
3. Bhutan
4. Depeche Mode
5. Hamlet
6. Montreal
7. None of its 50,000 words contained the letter E
8. Temple
9. Trinity term
10. 1981
11. Dexy's Midnight Runners
12. Money
13. Trains
14. Flower arranging
15. Jamie Oliver
16. Malta and Cyprus
17. The knee
18. LEGO
19. 7%
20. Priest

DIFFICULT

Quiz 150: Pot Luck

1. With a capacity of almost 2,500, what is the largest theatre in London's West End?

2. What musical instrument takes its name from the Greek for wooden sound?

3. Nicholas Bardon established what in London in 1684?

4. In ballet, what term describes leaping from one foot to another?

5. Which African country was, until 1984, known as Upper Volta?

6. Belmopan is the capital city of which country?

7. Which Wimbledon tennis champion also danced on Strictly Come Dancing?

8. Where in America would you find the Getty Museum?

9. Tim Brabants is an Olympic champion at which sport?

10. Which actress said, 'I'm prouder of my weight loss than my Oscar'?

11. The highest temperature on earth, 58°C, was recorded in which African country?

12. Who is the oldest female to top the UK singles chart?

13. The longest vehicular tunnel in the world is in which country?

14. What geological era came after the Palaeozoic era?

15. Which businessman had cameo roles in both Friends and Only Fools and Horses?

16. What does a numismatist collect?

17. What name is given to someone who makes artificial eyes?

18. What is the least commonly used letter in the English language?

19. McKinley Morganfield is the real name of which legendary Blues singer?
a) Muddy Waters
b) Leadbelly
c) Howlin' Wolf?

20. A vexillologist studies and collects what type of objects?
a) musical instruments
b) flags
c) magazines

Answers to Quiz 149: Pop Music

1. SOS by Abba
2. Westlife
3. Nicky Wire
4. (Is This The Way To) Amarillo?
5. Gerry and the Pacemakers
6. Unchained Melody
7. Sunscreen
8. West Side Story
9. Madonna
10. Kraftwerk
11. Super Furry Animals
12. Colonel Abrams
13. Buddy Holly
14. All Around The World
15. Denise Van Outen
16. Julio and Enrique Iglesias
17. Limahl
18. Hugh Laurie
19. Stoke
20. John Lennon

DIFFICULT

305

Quiz 151: Oscars

1. Who, in 2010, became the first actress to win the Best Actress Oscar and Golden Raspberry for Worst Actress in the same year?

2. Who is the only person named Oscar to win an Oscar?

3. Which Irish playwright is the only person to win an Oscar and a Nobel prize?

4. Who is the only actor to win an Oscar for a performance in a Shakespeare play?

5. Which sisters were nominated for the Best Actress award in 1967?

6. Who is the only Beatle to be individually nominated for an Oscar?

7. The Beatles won the Best Score Oscar for which film?

8. Who holds the record for the most acting nominations without actually winning an award?

9. Which three films each won 11 Academy Awards?

10. In 2005, who became the first Asian to win the award for Best Director?

11. Who was the first Australian to win a Best Actor or Best Actress Oscar?

12. Who are the only actors to win an Oscar for playing the same role?

13. With four wins, who has won the most Best Director Oscars?

14. Which living person has received the most Oscar nominations?

15. How did Robert Opal interrupt the 1974 Academy Awards ceremony?

16. In 2002, who became the youngest winner of the Best Actor Oscar?

17. What is the official name of the Oscar statue?

18. Who is the only person to be nominated for producing, writing, acting and directing Oscars in the same year?

19. How many Oscars did Citizen Kane win?
    a) 0
    b) 1
    c) 5

20. Edith Head won eight Oscars in which category?
    a) Cinematography
    b) Costume Design
    c) Visual Effects

Answers to Quiz 150: Pot Luck

1. The Coliseum
2. Xylophone
3. Fire Brigade
4. Jete
5. Burkina Faso
6. Belize
7. Martina Hingis
8. Los Angeles
9. Canoeing
10. Jennifer Hudson
11. Libya
12. Cher (with Believe at the age of 52)
13. Japan
14. Mesozoic
15. Richard Branson
16. Coins and medals
17. Ocularist
18. Q
19. Muddy Waters
20. flags

DIFFICULT

Quiz 152: Pot Luck

1. The Apollo, Lyric and Queen's Theatre are located on what London thoroughfare?

2. Which X Factor finalist had previously appeared on Deal or No Deal, winning just £10?

3. In 1912, Albert Berry was the first person to do what?

4. Which female film icon was only ever played by males?

5. What was the first state to secede from the union prior to the American Civil War?

6. In what month is the earth furthest away from the sun?

7. Didactics is the art and science of what?

8. An ecdysiast has what saucy occupation?

9. What is strathspey?

10. What type of clouds are often anvil shaped and accompany thunder storms?

11. Which actor played Arthur Miller in the 2011 film, My Week With Marilyn?

12. In which decade were traffic wardens and parking tickets introduced in the UK?

13. What term is used to describe classical music from from 1600 to around 1760?

14. How many black keys are on a standard piano?

15. Which London Underground station was formerly called Gillespie Road?

16. Which of the Channel Islands did the Romans call Caesaria?

17. What are the prongs at the end of a fork called?

18. What does a philumenist collect?

19. Where would you find a spelunker?
    a) in the air
    b) on the sea
    c) in a cave

20. What would you do with Aquavit?
    a) drink it
    b) eat it
    c) smoke it

Answers to Quiz 151: Oscars

1. Sandra Bullock
2. Oscar Hammerstein
3. George Bernard Shaw
4. Laurence Olivier
5. Lynn and Vanessa Redgrave
6. Paul McCartney (for Best Song for Live and Let Die and Vanilla Sky)
7. Let It Be
8. Peter O'Toole (he did receive an honorary Oscar though)
9. Ben Hur, Titanic and The Lord of the Rings: The Return of the King
10. Ang Lee
11. Nicole Kidman
12. Marlon Brando and Robert de Niro for Vito Corleone
13. John Ford
14. Composer John Williams
15. He streaked on stage
16. Adrien Brody
17. The Academy Award of Merit
18. Warren Beatty
19. One
20. Costume design

DIFFICULT

Quiz 153: Sport

1. In 1981, Dick Beardsley and Inge Simonsen became the winners of which annual sporting event?

2. Which English footballer spent £30,000 on a Harley St hair transplant in 2011?

3. A statue of Michael Jackson can be found outside which English football ground?

4. Which racing driver was made a CBE in 2012 for his work with education charity UK Youth?

5. Who won the Super Bowl in January 2012?

6. Prince Charles is a fan of which football club?

7. Canadian James Naismith is credited with inventing which sport?

8. Broadhall Way is the home of which football club?

9. Langtree Park is the home ground of which rugby league team?

10. Which American city was awarded the 1976 Winter Olympics but refused to host the games?

11. What colour jersey is worn by the leader of Vuelta a Espana?

12. Sara Stevenson is a World Champion at which Olympic sport?

13. Notts County's Neil Mackenzie was the first professional footballer to appear on which TV programme?

14. Which two teams compete for cricket's Frank Worrell Trophy?

15. Which Masters-winning golfer, noted for his bushy moustache, was nicknamed the Walrus?

16. In what sport do teams compete for the Sam Maguire trophy?

17. Consilio et animis is the Latin motto of which football club?

18. What is the name of the Women's World amateur team championship in tennis?

19. Which of the following isn't the name of a team in the MLS?
    a) Real Salt Lake
    b) Inter Indiana
    c) DC United

20. The Thomas Cup is awarded in which sport?
    a) badminton
    b) squash
    c) tennis

Answers to Quiz 152: Pot Luck

1. Shaftesbury Avenue
2. Olly Murs
3. A parachute jump from a plane
4. Lassie the dog
5. South Carolina
6. July
7. Teaching
8. A striptease artist
9. A Scottish dance
10. Cumulonimbus
11. Dougray Scott
12. 1960s
13. Baroque
14. 36
15. Arsenal
16. Jersey
17. Tines
18. Matchbox labels
19. In a cave
20. Drink it (it's a Scandinavian spirit)

DIFFICULT

Quiz 154: Pot Luck

1. In which European capital would you find the Kunsthistorisches Museum?

2. John Dryden was the first person to hold which post?

3. What shape are vegetable chopped julienne style?

4. What Asian city was originally known as Edo?

5. The Aldeburgh Festival was founded by which English composer?

6. Which two London Underground Lines run entirely in zone 1?

7. To the nearest 100km, what is the diameter of the moon?

8. Luanda is the capital city of which African country?

9. In 2002, 88-year-old Raymond David Jr became the oldest recipient of what award?

10. What do the initials TARDIS stand for?

11. Which planet of the solar system was discovered in 1781 by Sir William Herschel?

12. Which country has more lakes than the rest of the world combined?

13. Which two authors have won the Booker Prize twice?

14. What is the longest word in English containing just one vowel?

15. Which US state has borders with all of the Great Lakes apart from Lake Ontario?

16. What type of fabric takes its name from the French for cloth of the king?

17. In what decade were the FM Radio, Nylon and the Richter Scale invented?

18. In English law, what is the second term of the legal year known as?

19. A spodomancer makes predictions by looking at what?
    a) tea leaves
    b) tarot cards
    c) ashes

20. Who hit Rupert Murdoch with a foam pie at a parliamentary select committee meeting?
    a) Jonnie Marbles
    b) Jonnie Dominoes
    c) Jonnie Checkers

Answers to Quiz 153: Sport

1. London Marathon
2. Wayne Rooney
3. Craven Cottage (Fulham)
4. Nigel Mansell
5. New York Giants
6. Burnley
7. Basketball
8. Stevenage
9. St Helens
10. Denver
11. Red
12. Taekwondo
13. Countdown
14. Australia and West Indies
15. Craig Stadler
16. Gaelic football
17. Sheffield Wednesday
18. Federation Cup
19. Inter Indiana
20. Badminton

DIFFICULT

Quiz 155: Anatomy and Medicine

1. The Salk vaccine is used to prevent which disease?

2. Geneticist Gregor Mendel made his discoveries using what vegetable?

3. Keshan disease is caused by a deficiency of which element?

4. What is a synchronous, diaphragmatic flutter more commonly known as?

5. The first stethoscope was made of what material?

6. In what part of the body would you find bones called malleus and incus?

7. Insulin is produced in which gland of the human body?

8. What is the biggest cavity in the human body?

9. Calcaneus is another name for what bone of the human body?

10. The bane of many a teenager, what is a comedo more commonly known as?

11. Hemicrania is another name for what?

12. What is the lower jaw bone called?

13. The Snellen Chart is used to test what?

14. Epistaxis is another name for what?

15. In what part of the body would you find alveoli?

16. Where in the body are the adrenal glands located?

17. What is the hallux more commonly known as?

18. Meniere's Syndrome is a disease afflicting which part of the body?

19. Someone with hypermetropia is
    a) long sighted or
    b) short sighted

20. People of what group can receive blood from any other blood group?
    a) A
    b) AB
    c) O

Answers to Quiz 154: Pot Luck

1. Vienna
2. Poet Laureate
3. Matchstick
4. Tokyo
5. Benjamin Britten
6. Waterloo and City and Circle
7. 3476km
8. Angola
9. A Nobel Prize
10. Time And Relative Dimension In Space
11. Uranus
12. Canada
13. JM Coetzee and Peter Carey
14. Strengths
15. Michigan
16. Corduroy
17. 1930s
18. Hilary term
19. Ashes
20. Jonnie Marbles

DIFFICULT

Quiz 156: Pot Luck

1. Which two tube station contain all five vowels?

2. Anthony Perkins and Vince Vaughn have both played which movie character?

3. Which UK rapper topped the charts in 2011 with Stay Awake?

4. In 2005, Hilary Spurling won the Whitbread Prize for her biography of which artist?

5. Joseph K was the central character in which novel?

6. Topeka is the capital of which US state?

7. Who was the first actor to play Dr Who who was born after the show first aired in 1963?

8. What colour dresses do Chinese brides traditionally wear on their wedding day?

9. Ralph Fiennes directorial debut was a film version of which play?

10. St John's is the capital city of which Caribbean country?

11. In the croquet game in Alice in Wonderland what animal was used for the mallets?

12. And what animals were used for the balls?

13. What organisation, whose name means Circle of Brothers, was formed in Pulaski, Tennessee in 1865?

14. What was Abba's only number 1 hit in America?

15. Which city did the poet Milton describe as 'mother of arts and eloquence'?

16. What car did Dick Dastardly and Muttley drive in The Wacky Races?

17. Who was the last monarch to live at the Tower of London?

18. Prokofiev's opera The Gambler was based on a story by which author?

19. The national anthem of which country contains 158 verses?

20. The Griffin Prize is awarded in which field?
    a) architecture
    b) poetry
    c) gardening

21. A durzi is an Indian what?
    a) chef
    b) waiter
    c) tailor

Answers to Quiz 155: Anatomy and Medicine

1. Polio
2. Pea
3. Selenium
4. A hiccup
5. Wood
6. Ear
7. Pancreas
8. Abdomen
9. Heel bone
10. A blackhead
11. A migraine
12. Mandible
13. Eyesight
14. A nose bleed
15. Lung
16. On top of the kidneys
17. Big toe
18. The ear
19. Long sighted
20. AB

DIFFICULT

Quiz 157: Eurovision

1. Hard Rock Hallelujah was a 2006 Eurovision-winning song for which group?

2. Which five countries don't have to qualify for Eurovision?

3. In 1978, which country became the first to receive nul points in the Eurovision Song Contest?

4. Who was the first UK artist to win the Eurovision Song Contest?

5. Abba won Eurovision in which English city?

6. Which singer won Eurovision singing Boom Bang-A-Bang?

7. Which singer and DJ was runner-up in 1992 with One Step Out of Time?

8. What was the name of the Israeli transsexual who won the 1998 Eurovision Song Contest?

9. Which North African country has appeared in Eurovision?

10. Who is the only singer to win Eurovision twice?

11. Which actress represented the UK in the 1974 Eurovision?

12. Why did France withdraw from the 1974 Eurovision Song Contest?

13. Which X Factor runner-up represented the UK in the 2008 Eurovision Song Contest?

14. Diggi loo-Diggi ley was a winning entry from which country?

15. Celine Dion represented which country in the 1988 Eurovision Song Contest?

16. The 1975 winning entry Ding A Dong was from which country?

17. What dubious honour did Jemini, with their song Cry Baby, achieve for the first time in 2003?

18. Which former Soviet Republic hosted the 2012 contest?

19. Which children's favourites were the interval act in the 1974 Eurovision Song Contest?
    a) The Muppets
    b) The Wombles
    c) Pinky and Perky

20. How many times have the UK finished as runner-up in the Eurovision Song Contest?
    a) 10
    b) 12
    c) 15

Answers to Quiz 156: Pot Luck

1. Mansion House and South Ealing
2. Norman Bates
3. Example
4. Henri Matisse
5. The Trial
6. Kansas
7. Christopher Eccleston
8. Red
9. Coriolanus
10. Antigua and Barbuda
11. Flamingoes
12. Hedgehogs
13. Ku Klux Klan
14. Dancing Queen
15. Athens
16. The Mean Machine
17. James I
18. Dostoevsky
19. Greece
20. Poetry
21. Tailor

DIFFICULT

Quiz 158: Pot Luck

1. Lawrence Bragg is the youngest person to receive what prize?

2. In George Orwell's Animal Farm, what animal was Boxer?

3. Which actress provided the voice of ET?

4. Which author, after winning the 1972 Booker Prize gave half the prize money to the Black Panthers?

5. Everyone's a Little Bit Racist and If You Were Gay are songs from which musical?

6. Joe Keller is the central character in which Arthur Miller play?

7. What family has won the most Nobel prizes?

8. Composer Frederic Chopin grew up in which city?

9. Which of the 12 apostles is the only one believed to have died a natural death?

10. What is the only line on the London Underground that intersects all the other lines?

11. What are the eight universities that make up the Ivy League?

12. Which actor released an album called Highly Illogical?

13. Oranjestad is the capital city of which tiny island in the Caribbean?

14. Which American played Two Face in the 2008 film Batman – The Dark Knight?

15. What is the heaviest internal organ in the human body?

16. On what part of the body would a finnesko be worn?

Answers – page 323

17. The world's first cash dispenser was opened in which decade?

18. What is the dot on top of the letters 'i' and 'j' called?

19. Batrachophobia is the fear of what type of animals?
    a) birds
    b) reptiles
    c) spiders

20. Who was the caretaker in children's TV show Take Hart?
    a) Mr Bennett
    b) Mr Barnett
    c) Mr Bowen

Answers to Quiz 157: Eurovision

1. Lordi
2. UK, Germany, France, Spain and Italy
3. Norway
4. Sandie Shaw
5. Brighton
6. Lulu
7. Michael Ball
8. Dana International
9. Morocco (once in 1980)
10. Johnny Logan
11. Olivia Newton-John
12. The funeral of President Pompidou took place on the same day
13. Andy Abraham
14. Sweden
15. Switzerland
16. Netherlands
17. They were the first UK act to finish last in the Eurovision Song Contest
18. Azerbaijan
19. The Wombles
20. 15

DIFFICULT

Quiz 159: Read All About It

1. The oldest surviving UK newspaper is published in which city?

2. What newspaper merged with the Daily Mail in 1971?

3. The Sunday Sport newspaper was founded by which football club owner?

4. Who played newspaper editor Linda Day in the children's TV drama Press Gang?

5. What newspaper was founded by Robert Maxwell in 1990 but closed in 1999?

6. Alfred Harmsworth was the real name of which newspaper baron?

7. What is the world's oldest Sunday newspaper?

8. Which newspaper tycoon owned a castle called San Simeon?

9. Which American city has a newspaper called the Plain Dealer?

10. What tabloid newspaper was launched on 2 November 1978?

11. Vicky Coren and Nick Szeremeta write newspaper columns on what?

12. The Daily Universal Register is the former name of which British newspaper?

13. The father of which journalist and former MP compiled the first Times Crossword?

14. The Herald newspaper is published in which Scottish city?

15. Which weekly magazine is nicknamed the Staggers?

16. Who edited Milan-based socialist newspaper Avanti from 1912-1914?

17. Who founded the Christian Science Monitor newspaper?

18. Which Italian newspaper translates as Evening Courier even though it's published in the morning?

19. The Sunday Pictorial is the former name of which national newspaper?
    a) Mail On Sunday
    b) The People
    c) Sunday Mirror

20. Newspaper La Vanguardia is based in which European city?
    a) Barcelona
    b) Lisbon
    c) Rome

Answers to Quiz 158: Pot Luck

1. A Nobel Prize
2. Horse
3. Debra Winger
4. John Berger
5. Avenue Q
6. All My Sons
7. The Curies
8. Warsaw
9. St John
10. Jubilee Line
11. Harvard, Yale, Pennsylvania, Princeton, Columbia, Brown, Dartmouth and Cornell
12. Leonard Nimoy
13. Aruba
14. Aaron Eckhart
15. The liver
16. On the foot
17. 1960s
18. Tittle
19. Reptiles
20. Mr Bennett

DIFFICULT

Quiz 160: Pot Luck

1. Which Portuguese football team won the 2011 Europa League?

2. Lansing is the capital of which US state?

3. Which actor starred in the Inspector Alleyn Mysteries as well as playing Sergeant Chisholm in Minder?

4. Which Old Master painted Massacre of the Innocents which sold for £49.5 million in 2002?

5. What is the national flower of Spain, Monaco and Slovenia?

6. Genuphobia is the fear of which body part?

7. Which two American states have borders with eight other states?

8. Porto Novo is the capital city of which African country?

9. Which Hollywood star had an audition to join pop group Boyzone?

10. In a deck of cards, which king is the only one without a moustache?

11. Which university in Britain has the most students?

12. Jodie Foster and Julianne Moore have both played which movie character?

13. What does the T in Star Trek captain James T Kirk stand for?

14. Who wrote the Booker prize winning novel The Line of Beauty?

15. 'The quick brown fox jumps over the lazy dog' is an example of a pangram. But what is a pangram?

16. In January 2012 which pop star gave birth to a baby called Blue Ivy?

17. In which country is government policy based on Gross National Happiness?

18. Which French author declined the Nobel prize for literature in 1964?

19. A pickelhaube would be worn by whom?
    a) priests
    b) lawyers
    c) soldiers

20. What was Detective Kojak's first name?
    a) Leo
    b) Neo
    c) Theo

Answers to Quiz 159: Read All About It

1. Belfast (News Letter)
2. Daily Sketch
3. David Sullivan
4. Julia Sawalha
5. The European
6. Lord Northcliffe
7. The Observer
8. Randolph Hearst
9. Cleveland
10. Daily Star
11. Poker
12. The Times
13. Martin Bell
14. Glasgow
15. New Statesman
16. Benito Mussolini
17. Mary Baker Eddy
18. Corriere della Sera
19. Sunday Mirror
20. Barcelona

DIFFICULT

Quiz 161: Organisations

1. The ICAO is concerned with the safety of what form of transport?

2. What organisation was founded in 1961 by Peter Benenson and Sean Macbride Kropotkin?

3. The Sandanistas were a left wing revolutionary group in which country?

4. The headquarters of African Union are in which country?

5. Which 18th century painter was the first President of the Royal Academy?

6. What Conservative Eurosceptic group takes its name from a town in Belgium?

7. The New Jewel Movement was a left wing political movement on which Caribbean island?

8. What is the only all African state that is not a member of the African Union?

9. The headquarters of the European Court of Justice are in which country?

10. What agreement, signed at a Scottish golf club in 1977, banned sporting links with South Africa?

11. The Tonton Macoutes were a secret police force in which Caribbean country?

12. The EOKA were a nationalist movement in which European country?

13. The Dergue was a military junta that ruled which African country between 1974 and 1987?

14. The DGSE is the external security agency of which European country?

15. The 'Ndragheta crime organisation originated in which region of Italy?

16. The Sejm is the lower house of parliament in which country?

17. United In Diversity is the motto of which organisation?

18. Lok Sabha is the lower house of the parliament of which country?

19. An American Senator faces re-election after how many years?
a) 4 b) 5 c) 6

20. What is the Cambridge Conversazione Society also known as?
a) Cambridge Apostles b) Cambridge Disciples
c) Cambridge Followers

Answers to Quiz 160: Pot Luck

1. Porto
2. Michigan
3. Patrick Malahide
4. Rubens
5. Carnation
6. The knee
7. Missouri and Tennessee
8. Benin
9. Colin Farrell
10. King of hearts
11. The Open University
12. Clarice Starling
13. Tiberius
14. Alan Hollinghurst
15. A sentence that uses all 26 letters of the alphabet
16. Beyonce
17. Bhutan
18. Jean-Paul Sartre
19. Soldiers
20. Theo

DIFFICULT

Quiz 162: Pot Luck

1. What is the only London Underground line without a station in Zone 1?

2. In what European country is The Pulpit Rock?

3. Piccadilly Weepers, Mutton Chops and Franz Josefs are examples of what?

4. A couple celebrating their platinum anniversary would have spent how many years together?

5. In George Orwell's Animal Farm, what animal was Napoleon?

6. What was the name of the diner in TV comedy Happy Days?

7. Kinshasa is the capital city of which African country?

8. What was the only number one hit single for Madness?

9. Steve McQueen and Pierce Brosnan have both played which movie character?

10. Lt Pinkerton and Cio-Cio San are characters in which opera?

11. Alektorophobia is the fear of which bird?

12. Which poet's epitaph reads 'Here lies one whose name was writ in water'?

13. What city was the capital of the USA from 1783 until 1789?

14. In 2011, the Royal Opera House hosted an opera about which glamour model?

15. Which group of 17th century English poets included John Donne, Andrew Marvell and George Herbert?

16. Helena is the capital of which US state?

17. Which rock star was banned from the state of Texas after being caught urinating on the Alamo memorial?

18. In 1967, London Bridge was moved to which American state?

19. Someone with thixophobia doesn't like being what?
    a) looked at
    b) touched c) spoken to

20. In what decade was The Sunday Telegraph launched?
    a) 1940s
    b) 1950s
    c) 1960s

Answers to Quiz 161: Organisations

1. Aviation
2. Amnesty International
3. Nicaragua
4. Ethiopia
5. Joshua Reynolds
6. The Bruges Group
7. Grenada
8. Morocco
9. Luxembourg
10. Gleneagles Agreement
11. Haiti
12. Cyprus
13. Ethiopia
14. France
15. Calabria
16. Poland
17. European Union
18. India
19. 6
20. Cambridge Apostles

DIFFICULT

Quiz 163: US Presidents

1. Which US President won the Nobel Peace Prize in 2002?

2. Which US President's last words were 'Independence for ever'?

3. What is US presidential hopeful Mitt Romney's real first name?

4. US Presidents John Quincy Adams, Rutherford B Hayes, Benjamin Harrison and George W Bush share what dubious distinction?

5. Who are the two US Presidents who have been impeached?

6. George H W Bush and George W Bush were the second father and son US Presidents. Who were the first?

7. Who was the first US President born in the twentieth century?

8. Which US president was previously a male model?

9. Who becomes president of the US if the sitting president and vice-president both die?

10. Who is the only US President buried in Washington DC?

11. Which American politician lives at Number One Observatory Circle?

12. In 1906, which politician became the first American to win the Nobel Peace Prize?

13. Who was the only US president to have previously led a labour union?

14. Which US president appears on a $100 bill?

15. Franklin D Roosevelt, John F Kennedy, George W Bush and Barack Obama all attended which US college?

16. What is the minimum age at which a person can stand as President of the United States?

17. Who is the only US President never to been elected as President or Vice President?

18. George W Bush was born in which state?

19. Who was the first US President to live in the White House?
    a) George Washington
    b) John Adams
    c) Abraham Lincoln

20. Who is the only US President who remained unmarried throughout his life?
    a) James Buchanan
    b) James Munroe
    c) Andrew Johnson

Answers to Quiz 162: Pot Luck

1. East London Line
2. Norway
3. Sidewhiskers
4. 70
5. Pig
6. Arnold's
7. Democratic Republic of Congo
8. House of Fun
9. Thomas Crown
10. Madame Butterfly
11. Chicken
12. Keats
13. Philadelphia
14. Anna Nicole Smith
15. The Metaphysical Poets
16. Montana
17. Ozzy Osbourne
18. Arizona
19. Touched
20. 1960s

DIFFICULT

Quiz 164: Pot Luck

1. What does the acronym ASLEF stand for in relation to a UK trade union?

2. Cayenne is the capital city of which South American country?

3. Which Sunday newspaper was launched on 2 May 1982?

4. In This Light And On This Evening was a number one album for which group?

5. What African country came into existence on 9 July 2011?

6. What was the name of the iPad newspaper launched in 2011 by Rupert Murdoch?

7. What is the largest island in the Mediterranean Sea?

8. The literary Bronte sisters all died of which disease?

9. What famous award was designed by Cedric Gibbons and sculpted by George Stanley?

10. Poet Andrew Marvell and anti slavery campaigner William Wilberforce were MPs in which English city?

11. The Madness song The Prince was a tribute to which Jamaican musician?

12. What is the official language of Liechtenstein?

13. How many letters are in the Greek alphabet?

14. What is the Beau Sancy?

15. Electronic pioneers Kraftwerk are from which German city?

16. Which group's first seven singles went to number one?

17. Which British director's films include Kick Ass, Stardust, and X-Men: First Class?

18. British actor Andrew Lincoln stars in which American zombie series?

19. Which social network was founded in 2005 by Michael and Xochi Birch?
    a) Bebo
    b) Facebook
    c) MySpace

20. A gift of sugar is usually given to celebrate which wedding anniversary?
    a) 4
    b) 6
    c) 8

Answers to Quiz 163: US Presidents

1. Jimmy Carter
2. John Adams
3. Willard
4. They all lost the popular vote
5. Andrew Johnson and Bill Clinton
6. John Adams and John Quincy Adams
7. John F Kennedy
8. Gerald Ford
9. The Speaker of the House
10. Woodrow Wilson
11. The Vice-President
12. Theodore Roosevelt
13. Ronald Reagan (the Screen Actors Guild)
14. Benjamin Franklin
15. Harvard
16. 35
17. Gerald Ford
18. Connecticut
19. John Adams
20. James Buchanan

DIFFICULT

Quiz 165: Religion

1. Pope John Paul II was bishop of which Polish city?

2. In the Christian Church, what are seraphim, cherubim and orphanim?

3. What order of monks are known as Black Monks?

4. What religion is largely based on the teachings of Siddhartha Gautama?

5. Which Christian group was founded by John Thomas in the mid 19th century?

6. Who succeeded David Hope as Archbishop of York in 2005?

7. Which saint was the first Archbishop of Canterbury?

8. St Boniface is the patron saint of which European country?

9. Which country has the largest Muslim population in the world?

10. What church was founded by Korean Sun Myung Moon in 1956?

11. What name comes after John Heenan, Basil Hume and Cormac Murphy-O'Connor?

12. Dismas was one of the two thieves crucified alongside Jesus. Who was the other?

13. Which Archbishop of Canterbury compiled the Book of Common Prayer?

14. What animal is mentioned most frequently in the Bible?

15. Who was the father of the apostles James the great and John?

16. What is the third book of the Old Testament?

17. The Adi Granth is the holy book of which religion?

18. How many books are in the New Testament?

19. Who is the patron saint of accountants?
    a) Matthew
    b) Mark
    c) Luke

20. In the Bible, how old was Noah?
    a) 59
    b) 590
    c) 950

Answers to Quiz 164: Pot Luck

1. Associated Society of Locomotive Engineers and Firemen
2. French Guiana
3. Mail on Sunday
4. Editors
5. South Sudan
6. The Daily
7. Sicily
8. Tuberculosis
9. The Oscar
10. Hull
11. Prince Buster
12. German
13. 24
14. A diamond
15. Dusseldorf
16. Westlife
17. Matthew Vaughn
18. The Walking Dead
19. Bebo
20. 6

DIFFICULT

Quiz 166: Pot Luck

1. In what city does the ceremony to award the Nobel Peace Prize take place?

2. How many members are in the US House of Representatives?

3. Which European country went without a government for a record breaking 541 days in 2010 and 2011?

4. In computing what do the initials GIF stand for?

5. Asmara is the capital city of which east African country?

6. Which Shakespearean character was based on the real life Sir John Oldcastle?

7. What colour are the stars on the New Zealand flag?

8. 01603 is the dialling code for which English city?

9. The wife of which US President wrote an 'autobiography' about the couple's dog, Millie?

10. The largest dam in the world, the Itaipu Dam, lies between which two South American countries?

11. A sculpture by which artist sold for a British record price of £19.1m in February 2012?

12. The Golden Bear award is given to the best film at which film festival?

13. Creator of the wind storm scale Francis Beaufort was born in which country?

14. Jefferson City is the capital of which US state?

15. Anthophobia is a fear of what?

16. Which member of the Rolling Stones studied at the London School of Economics?

17. How many squares are on a Scrabble board?

18. In which Spanish town does the Tomatina festival take place?

19. Which actor released an album called The Futurist in 2004?
    a) Robert Downey Jr
    b) Ben Affleck
    c) George Clooney

20. Which daily paper started life as a newspaper for women?
    a) Daily Mail
    b) Daily Mirror
    c) The Sun

Answers to Quiz 165: Religion

1. Krakow
2. Angels
3. Benedictines
4. Buddhism
5. The Christadelphians
6. John Sentamu
7. St Augustine
8. Germany
9. Indonesia
10. The Unification Church
11. Vincent Nichols
12. Gestas
13. Thomas Cranmer
14. Sheep
15. Zebedee
16. Leviticus
17. Sikhism
18. 27
19. St Matthew
20. 950

DIFFICULT

Quiz 167: Transport

1. Foregate Street and Shrub Hill are railways stations in which English city?

2. What was abolished on British railways in 1956?

3. Robin Hood Airport is in which English town?

4. Piraeus is a port in which European capital?

5. In which American city would you travel on a transport system called the BART?

6. Opened in 1959, what is the oldest motorway service station in the UK?

7. Which newsreader was the first presenter of TV show Top Gear?

8. In terms of passengers, what is the busiest railway station in Britain?

9. The longest railway bridge in the world is in which country?

10. Which Scandinavian popsters had a 1985 hit with Train Of Thought?

11. Who captained a ship called The Black Pig?

12. Which four British cities have underground railways?

13. The Ghan is a passenger train operating from the north to the south of which country?

14. Which trio had a 1970 hit with Leavin' On a Jet Plane?

15. In 1947, Thor Heyerdahl crossed the Pacific Ocean on a boat made of what?

16. Which motorway links Coventry to Leicester?

17. What platform does the Hogwarts Express leave from in the Harry Potter films?

18. Which organisation is the General Lighthouse Authority for England and Wales?

19. Pooley's is a guide to which form of transport?
    a) aviation
    b) rail
    c) shipping

20. What was the name of the 2007 film starring Christian Bale and Russell Crowe?
    a) 2.10 To Yuma
    b) 3.10 To Yuma
    c) 4.10 To Yuma

Answers to Quiz 166: Pot Luck

1. Oslo
2. 435
3. Belgium
4. Graphics Interchange Format
5. Eritrea
6. Sir John Falstaff
7. Red with white trim
8. Norwich
9. George W Bush
10. Peru and Brazil
11. Henry Moore
12. Berlin
13. Ireland
14. Missouri
15. Flowers
16. Mick Jagger
17. 225
18. Bunol
19. Robert Downey Jr
20. Daily Mirror

DIFFICULT

Quiz 168: Pot Luck

1. Malabo is the capital city of which African country?

2. In computing, how many bits make up a byte?

3. Beatrice and Sidney Webb were the founders of which weekly magazine?

4. In 2005, the Tulip Revolution occurred in which former Soviet Republic?

5. Who sits on a throne called the sedia gestatoria?

6. Which newsreader had a cameo in the 2012 film Coriolanus?

7. Nephology is a branch of meteorology dealing with what?

8. Which singer, whose real name is Sarah Joyce, recorded the top 5 album Seasons of My Soul?

9. Who holds the record for winning the most acting Oscars?

10. Which comedy, starring Chris Addison and Jo Enright, was set in a university science department?

11. Carla Borrego is the assistant to which magical TV detective?

12. Which Star Trek captain had a pet fish called Livingston?

13. Sesame Street's Bert and Ernie were named after characters in which classic film?

14. Which sweets were invented by Forrest Mars Sr and Bruce Murrie?

15. What is the lowest number that, when spelled out, contains the letter A?

16. Which fictional hero takes his name from the Spanish for fox?

17. An enneahedron is a solid with how many faces?

18. The Brannock device is used to measure what?

19. Singer Stephen Duffy took his nickname from which comic-strip character?
    a) Asterix
    b) Tin Tin
    c) Homer

20. The Nobel prizes were first awarded in which decade?
    a) 1890s
    b) 1900s
    c) 1910s

Answers to Quiz 167: Transport

1. Worcester
2. Third class carriages
3. Doncaster
4. Athens
5. San Francisco (Bay Area Rapid Transport)
6. Watford Gap
7. Angela Rippon
8. London Waterloo
9. China
10. A-Ha
11. Captain Pugwash
12. London, Glasgow, Liverpool and Newcastle
13. Australia
14. Peter, Paul and Mary
15. Balsa wood
16. M69
17. 9 3/4
18. Trinity House
19. Aviation
20. 3.10 To Yuma

DIFFICULT

Quiz 169: Capital Cities

1. Pago Pago is the capital city of which Pacific Island country?

2. Vientian is the capital city of which Asian country?

3. Abidjan is the capital city of which African country?

4. Paramaribo is the capital city of which South American country?

5. Windhoek is the capital city of which African country?

6. St George's is the capital city of which Commonwealth country?

7. Basse-Terre is the capital city of which French speaking Caribbean island?

8. Doha is the capital city of which country?

9. Georgetown is the capital city of which South American country?

10. Bujumbura is the capital city of which country?

11. Ashkhabad is the capital city of which former Soviet Republic?

12. Thorshavn is the capital city of which European island nation?

13. Santo Domingo is the capital city of which Caribbean country?

14. Apia is the capital city of which Pacific country?

15. Niamey is the capital city of which African country?

16. Podgorica is the capital city of which European country?

17. Antananarivo is the capital city of which African country?

18. Vaduz is the capital city of which European country?

19. Skopje is the capital city of which former Yugoslav republic?

20. Libreville is the capital city of which African country?
    a) Gabon
    b) Guinea
    c) Ghana

21. Tegucigalpa is the capital city of which central American country?
    a) El Salvador
    b) Honduras
    c) Dominican Republic

DIFFICULT

Quiz 170: Pot Luck

1. Approximately how many characters of information are in a terabyte?

2. What order of monks are also known as the Greyfriars?

3. Crab, the only dog to feature in a Shakespeare play, appeared in which play?

4. What is the capital of the Canadian province of New Brunswick?

5. What is the only film to win Best Picture without featuring a single female speaking role?

6. Which British prime minister introduced income tax?

7. Which country declared war on America in 1898?

8. Who was the Roman goddess of sorcery and witchcraft who haunted crossroads and graveyards?

9. What was dropped from a plane called Bock's Car?

10. Who, in 1952 was offered the presidency of Israel?

11. Whose white suit was sold for a record-setting $145,500 at an auction at Christie's?

12. Alif, baa and taa are letters in which alphabet?

13. In computing what does the acronym HTML stand for?

14. What is the German word for satellite (it's also a make of car)?

15. What is the ball on the top of a flagpole called?

16. Which film director's first film was called THX1138?

17. Who comes next in this list? Mark Leckey, Richard Wright, Susan Philips?

18. Who drives a car with the registration plate JGY 280?

19. Who was the first British female singer to perform behind the Iron Curtain?
    a) Sandie Shaw
    b) Lulu
    c) Petula Clark

20. Limacology is the study of what type of creature?
    a) snakes
    b) slugs
    c) seahorses

Answers to Quiz 169: Capital Cities

1. American Samoa
2. Laos
3. Ivory Coast
4. Suriname
5. Namibia
6. Grenada
7. Guadaloupe
8. Qatar
9. Guyana
10. Burundi
11. Turkmenistan
12. Faeroe Islands
13. Dominican Republic
14. Samoa
15. Niger
16. Montenegro
17. Madagascar
18. Liechtenstein
19. Macedonia
20. Gabon
21. Honduras

DIFFICULT

Quiz 171: Nature

1. What flower's name derives from the Turkish word for turban?

2. What climbing shrub is also known as old man's beard?

3. Adam's needle, Joshua Tree and Palm Lily are varieties of which plant?

4. What bird is also known as the puffinet?

5. Self, fancy and picotee are types of which flower?

6. Bract, stipule and pinnate are types of what?

7. What is a young grouse called?

8. Nettle stings are caused by which acid?

9. Which bird has the largest wingspan in the world?

10. How many hearts does an octopus have?

11. Cetti's, Dartford, barbed an icterine are types of what bird?

12. What is the largest bird of prey found in the UK?

13. What is the climex lectularius more commonly known as?

14. John Audobon was a noted painter of which type of animal?

15. Glanville, High Brown and Silver-Washed are examples of what type of creature?

16. What bird is also known as a yaffle?

17. Wild chinchillas are native to which continent?

18. Merle is another name for which bird?

19. The goatfish is also known as
    a) Grey Mullet
    b) Red Mullet
    c) White Mullet

20. How many eyes does a bee have?
    a) 3
    b) 5
    c) 7

Answers to Quiz 170: Pot Luck

1. One thousand billion
2. Franciscans
3. The Two Gentlemen of Verona
4. Fredericton
5. Lawrence of Arabia
6. William Pitt The Younger
7. Spain
8. Trivia
9. An atomic bomb on the city of Nagasaki
10. Albert Einstein
11. John Travolta's from Saturday Night Fever
12. Arabic
13. HyperText Mark-up Language
14. Trabant
15. Truck
16. George Lucas
17. Martin Boyce (Turner Prize winners)
18. HRH The Queen
19. Lulu
20. Slugs

DIFFICULT

Quiz 172: Pot Luck

1. The Stirling Prize is awarded in which discipline?

2. Mars has two moons. Name them.

3. How many bytes are in a kilobyte?

4. Anarchist Leon Czolgosz shot and killed which US president?

5. How many books are in the Hebrew Bible?

6. In heraldry, what colour is gules?

7. Rhinology is the study of what?

8. What TV comedy was set in East Hampton Hospital Trust?

9. The anchor is the hallmark of the Assay Office of which city?

10. In heraldry, what is an escutcheon?

11. Quentin Crisp was the first to do it in 1993. Ali G, Sharon Osborne and President Mahmoud Ahmadinejad have also done it. What have they done?

12. What is the name of the symbol &?

13. What does a tegestologist collect?

14. A googol is 1 followed by how many zeroes?

15. High Above the Young Rhine is the English translation of which country's national anthem?

16. Which website was founded by Steve Chen, Chad Hurley and Jawed Karim in 2005?

17. Did Mary ever visit Brighton Beach? Is a mnemonic to remember what?

18. 104-year-old Taufeek Khanjar in February 2012 became the oldest man to receive what?

19. Which city is closest to London?
    a) Dubai
    b) New York
    c) New Delhi

20. The groundhog is a member of which animal family?
    a) canine
    b) feline
    c) rodent

Answers to Quiz 171: Nature

1. Tulip
2. Wild clematis
3. Yucca
4. Black guillemot
5. Carnation
6. Leaves
7. Poult
8. Formic
9. Andean condor
10. 3
11. Warbler
12. Golden eagle
13. Bedbug
14. Birds
15. Butterfly
16. Green Woodpecker
17. South America
18. Blackbird
19. Red Mullet
20. 5

DIFFICULT

Quiz 173: Money

1. In finance what does the acronym NASDAQ stand for?

2. In what year did the £1 coin replace the £1 note?

3. The lari is the currency of which former Soviet republic?

4. Who was the central character in Martin Amis's 1984 novel Money?

5. In 1879, James J Ritty patented which device?

6. The SGX is the stock exchange in which country?

7. What connects Panama and Sylvester Stallone?

8. What is the name of the cartoon character who appears on the box of the board game Monopoly?

9. Which investor is known as The Sage of Omaha?

10. Which comedian said, 'Money can't buy you friends but you can get a better class of enemy'?

11. Which Nobel prize winning economist wrote There's No Such Thing As A Free Lunch?

12. Which American singer had a hit with I Need a Dollar?

13. The film Moneyball was about which sport?

14. The metical is the currency of which African country?

15. The subtitle to which hit by the Pet Shop Boys was Let's Make Lots of Money?

16. Who did Mervyn King succeed as Governor of the Bank of England?

17. The headquarters of the Royal Mint are in which Welsh town?

18. Which Italian succeeded Jean-Claude Trichet as President of the European Central Bank in 2011?

19. In 2009, what denomination of coin was sold on eBay for £7,100?
    a) 1p
    b) 20p
    c) 50p

20. The Bulgarian Lev is divided into 100 what?
    a) groszy
    b) bani
    c) stotinki

Answers to Quiz 172: Pot Luck

1. Architecture
2. Phobos and Deimos
3. 1024
4. William McKinley
5. 24
6. Red
7. Noses
8. Green Wing
9. Birmingham
10. A shield
11. Delivered Channel 4's
    Alternative Christmas Message
12. Ampersand
13. Beer mats
14. 100
15. Liechtenstein
16. YouTube
17. Order of Nobility
18. British citizenship
19. Dubai
20. Rodent

DIFFICULT

Quiz 174: Pot Luck

1. Which planet in the solar system has the most moons?

2. Which Mexican revolutionary was assassinated on his ranch in Parral in June 1923?

3. Anwar Sadat was the president of which African country?

4. Which US politician was Lyndon Johnson describing when he said, 'He couldn't walk and chew gum at the same time'?

5. David St Hubbins was the lead singer with which fictional band?

6. Nicholas Breakspear was the only British holder of which office?

7. In physics, what is measured using the weber unit?

8. Which technology company was founded by Janus Friis and Niklas Zennström, who sold it to Microsoft for $8.5 billion in 2011?

9. Montpelier is the capital of which US state?

10. What was the name of the Russian nuclear submarine that sank in the Barents Sea in August 2000?

11. Which sitcom was set in Whitbury-Newtown Leisure Centre?

12. Who did Mikhail Gorbachev succeed as leader of the Communist Party of the Soviet Union?

13. Which African country joined the Commonwealth in 2009 despite having no former constitutional ties to Britain?

14. Winnipeg is the capital city of which Canadian province?

15. If a human, a horse and a giraffe fell pregnant on the same day, which would give birth first?

16. Dave Wakeling was the lead singer with which Two Tone band?

17. What is Trisomy 21 more commonly known as?

18. Which Hollywood actor said that British rule of the Falklands was 'colonialist, ludicrous and archaic'?

19. An eremologist is interested in which geographic features?
    a) deserts
    b) oceans
    c) volcanoes

20. Chinese businessman Hu Zhen Yu spent £209,000 on what in January 2012?
    a) a Barbie doll
    b) a pigeon
    c) a pedigree chihuahua

Answers to Quiz 173: Money

1. National Association of Securities Dealers Automatic Quotation
2. 1983
3. Georgia
4. John Self
5. Cash register
6. Singapore
7. Balboa (it's the currency of Panama and the surname of fictional boxer Rocky)
8. Rich Uncle Pennybags
9. Warren Buffett
10. Spike Milligan
11. Milton Friedman
12. Aloe Blacc
13. Baseball
14. Mozambique
15. Opportunities
16. Sir Eddie George
17. Llantrisant
18. Mario Draghi
19. 20p (it was dateless)
20. Stotinki

DIFFICULT

Quiz 175: Words and Language

1. What is the only city in the UK whose name is spelt using only letters from the first half of the alphabet?

2. Gelotology is the study of what?

3. Anguine describes something that is similar to what animal?

4. What is the most commonly used letter in the English language?

5. What does Vorsprung durch Technik mean in English?

6. What is the only US state capital that shares no letters with the name of its state?

7. What common English word contains five consecutive vowels?

8. The words pillion and slogan originate from which language?

9. What five letter word, when written in capitals, looks the same when viewed upside down?

10. Which three US states have names beginning with two consonants?

11. Which Chinese martial art literally translates as boundless fist?

12. Which five countries have only one syllable in their name?

13. What name is given to a word that is spelled and pronounced the same but has different meanings?

14. No plan like yours to study history wisely is a mnemonic to remember what?

15. What does a pogonophile love?

16. A manometer is used to measure what?

17. What is the only European country, when written in upper case, that has no letters that can be coloured in?

18. What three six-letter words are made up of letters in alphabetical order, without repeating any of those letters?

19. The name of which car manufacturer is the Latin for 'I drive'?

20. Who are the rulers in a stratocracy?
    a) clergy
    b) military
    c) royalty

21. Pharology is the study of what?
    a) Pharaohs
    b) lighthouses
    c) racehorses

Answers to Quiz 174: Pot Luck

1. Jupiter
2. Pancho Villa
3. Egypt
4. Gerald Ford
5. Spinal Tap
6. Pope
7. Magnetic flux
8. Skype
9. Vermont
10. Kursk
11. The Brittas Empire
12. Konstantin Chernenko
13. Rwanda
14. Manitoba
15. Human
16. The Beat
17. Down's Syndrome
18. Sean Penn
19. Deserts
20. Pigeon

DIFFICULT

Quiz 176: Pot Luck

1. In December 1972 Harrison Schmitt became the twelfth and last person to do what?

2. The phrase 'often a bridesmaid, never a bride' was originally written as an advert for what type of product?

3. Analects is the most famous work of which philosopher?

4. Which Anglo-Saxon king rode a horse called Lamri?

5. In what decade was the driving test introduced?

6. What type of animal does a hippophile have an interest in?

7. What educational establishment did the students attend in The Young Ones?

8. Complete the title of the American sitcom: How I Met Your...?

9. Which comedian plays Chummy Brown in BBC drama Call The Midwife?

10. What fruit was known by the Ancient Greeks and the 'golden egg of the sun'?

11. Traf-O-Data was the first company of which businessman?

12. In what year was the National Lottery launched?

13. What is the only book of the Bible that doesn't mention god?

14. What was the last year that could be written upside down and appear the same as the right way up?

15. When will this happen again?

16. Which martial art derives from the Japanese for empty hand?

17. In a deck of cards, which king is known as the Suicide King?

18. Who, in 2012, became the first person to win a Razzie for worst actor and worst actress?

19. On a ship, what is a Charley Noble?
    a) galley smokestack
    b) a bell
    c) a sail

20. Lord Plumb is the only Briton to hold what political post?
    a) President of the European Parliament
    b) UN Secretary General
    c) Head of the Commonwealth

Answers to Quiz 175: Words and Language

1. Lichfield
2. Laughter
3. Snake
4. E
5. Progress through technology
6. Pierre (South Dakota)
7. Queueing
8. Gaelic
9. SWIMS
10. Florida, Rhode Island and Wyoming
11. Tai Chi
12. Chad, France, Greece, Laos and Spain (also Wales which is officially part of the UK)
13. Homonym
14. Ruling houses of Britain
15. Beards
16. Pressure
17. LIECHTENSTEIN
18. Abhors, almost and biopsy
19. Volvo
20. Military
21. Lighthouses

DIFFICULT

Quiz 177: Quotes

1. Which politician said, 'I have always made it so that every woman feels, how should I say, special'?

2. Who described an appearance at a parliamentary committee as 'the most humble day of my life'?

3. 'Oh Wow! Oh Wow! Oh Wow!' were the last words of which technological giant?

4. Who said of public sector strikers, 'I'd have them all shot. I would take them outside and execute them in front of their families'?

5. Which actress said of her musician husband, 'He's a musical genius. It's like living with Picasso'?

6. Which British royal said, 'I am not part of the PlayStation generation'?

7. Which tennis player said, 'I can cry like Roger (Federer). It's just a shame I can't play like him'?

8. Which much travelled football manager said, 'I'm a gypsy and I've been a gypsy for many years. It doesn't matter where I live as long as it's a good football project'?

9. Which hard living actor said, 'I'm tired of pretending like I'm not bitchin', a total frickin' rock star from Mars'?

10. Who was Neil Warnock describing when he said, 'I was going to call him a sewer rat, but that might insult the sewer rats'?

11. Who was MP Tom Watson addressing when he said, 'You are the first Mafia boss in history to not know he was running a criminal enterprise'?

12. Which sporting mogul said, 'The only good thing about the Olympics is the opening and closing ceremony. They do a lovely showbiz job. Otherwise, it's complete nonsense'?

13. Which German politician said, 'In view of the fact that God limited the intelligence of man, it seems unfair that he did not also limit his stupidity'?

14. What was FIFA chief Sepp Blatter describing when he said, 'It is energy, it is dance, it is rhythm, it is music and it is Africa!'?

15. 'Blessed is he who expects nothing, for he shall never be disappointed' wrote which English poet?

16. According to George Bernard Shaw's Man and Superman, 'Every man of 40 is a…'?

17. Which football manager said, 'I'm not a wheeler-dealer'?

18. Which reclusive author wrote, 'All we do our whole lives is go from one little piece of Holy Ground to the next'?

19. What was Kenneth Clarke describing when he said, 'Quite a large proportion of them are nuts and extremists – with the honourable exception of the culture secretary'?
a) bloggers b) Tweeters c) Facebook users

20. Who was French President Nicolas Sarkozy talking about when saying, 'I can't stand him, he's a liar'?
a) David Cameron b) Silvio Berlusconi c) Binyamin Netanyahu

Answers to Quiz 176: Pot Luck

1. Walk on the moon
2. Mouthwash
3. Confucius
4. King Arthur
5. 1930s
6. Horses
7. Scumbag College
8. Mother
9. Miranda Hart
10. Apricot
11. Bill Gates
12. 1994
13. Esther
14. 1961
15. 6009
16. Karate
17. King of Hearts
18. Adam Sandler
19. Galley smokestack
20. President of the European Parliament

DIFFICULT

Quiz 178: Pot Luck

1. Launched in 2011, what planet is the destination of NASA's Juno spacecraft?

2. Which Ancient Greek philosopher was known as the laughing philosopher?

3. Cheyenne is the capital of which US state?

4. Which antipodean duet had a hit with Where The Wild Roses Grow?

5. Alan Partridge made his TV debut in which short-lived show?

6. What is the only Irish county that ends in the letter O?

7. Who was the Greek goddess of retribution?

8. What was the name of the Norwegian man who in 2011 killed 77 people in a bombing and mass shooting?

9. The 2012 album Wonky was the first in eight years by which electronic dance group?

10. What are leaplings?

11. Broadcaster Mariella Frostrup was born in which country?

12. What was the breed of the dog that starred in the Oscar-winning film The Artist?

13. TV drama Luck centres around which sport?

14. Mark Wallinger's Ecce Homo, Anthony Gormley's One & Other and Rachel Whitbread's Monument have all been exhibited where?

15. Who played superspy Charlie Bind in Carry On Spying?

16. Which philosopher in 2012 proposed building an atheist temple in London?

17. In 1995, which African country was the first to join the Commonwealth without having any traditional ties to Britain?

18. Who succeeded Leonid Brezhnev as leader of the Communist Party of the Soviet Union?

19. The kakapo is the only type of what bird that cannot fly?
    a) parrot
    b) dove
    c) owl

20. On a ship, what is the head?
    a) sleeping quarters
    b) kitchen
    c) toilet

Answers to Quiz 177: Quotes

1. Silvio Berlusconi
2. Rupert Murdoch
3. Steve Jobs
4. Jeremy Clarkson
5. Gwyneth Paltrow on Chris Martin
6. Prince Charles
7. Andy Murray
8. Sven Goran Eriksson
9. Charlie Sheen
10. El Hadji-Diouf
11. James Murdoch
12. Bernie Ecclestone
13. Konrad Adenauer
14. The vuvuzela
15. Alexander Pope
16. Scoundrel
17. Harry Redknapp
18. JD Salinger
19. Bloggers
20. Binyamin Netanyahu

DIFFICULT

Quiz 179: TV Detectives

1. Sergeant Barbara Havers is the assistant of which Oxford educated Detective Inspector?

2. Who plays Laura Thyme in the detective drama Rosemary and Thyme?

3. Keith Allen played Inspector Hale in which Waking The Dead spin-off?

4. Which actor replaced John Nettles in the lead role in Midsomer Murders?

5. In Monk, Adrian had two assistants. Natalie was the second but who was the first?

6. World War II detective drama Foyle's War is set in which coastal town?

7. Chief Superintendent Jean Innocent appears in which police drama?

8. Cabot Cove was the home of which TV sleuth?

9. Chief Inspector Barney Crozier was the boss of which TV cop?

10. Which Oscar-nominated actress plays the lead role in Vera?

11. Which actor links The Professionals, The Chief and Inspector George Gently?

12. In The Sweeney, what was the name of Regan's boss?

13. The American remake of The Killing was set in which city?

14. Actress Blythe Duff's TV career has spanned over 20 years. In that time she's played one role continuously. In what programme?

15. Which family is the centre of US cop drama Blue Bloods?

16. In New Tricks, Brian supports what football team?

17. Who played the title role in private detective drama Vincent?

18. Which former Coronation Street actress plays DCI Gill Murray in Scott & Bailey?

19. Rycott and Chisholm were detectives in which drama?
    a) The Sweeney
    b) The Professionals
    c) Minder

20. 55 Degrees North was set in which city?
    a) Birmingham
    b) Liverpool
    c) Newcastle

Answers to Quiz 178: Pot Luck

1. Jupiter
2. Democritus
3. Wyoming
4. Kylie Minogue and Nick Cave
5. The Day Today
6. Mayo
7. Nemesis
8. Anders Breivik
9. Orbital
10. People born on 29th February
11. Norway
12. Jack Russell
13. Horse racing
14. On the fourth plinth in Trafalgar Square
15. Charles Hawtrey
16. Alain de Botton
17. Mozambique
18. Yuriy Andropov
19. Parrot
20. Toilet

DIFFICULT

Quiz 180: Pot Luck

1. Which two planets do not rotate in an anticlockwise direction?

2. 'Man is born free; and everywhere he is in chains' is the opening line of which classic work of political philosophy?

3. The busiest airport in the world is in which city?

4. On a ship, at what time does the first dog watch occur?

5. In geometry, an isosahedron has how many faces?

6. What is the smallest county in the Republic of Ireland?

7. The leu is the currency of which country?

8. Dead Belgians Don't Count was the working title for which 1990s TV comedy?

9. What is the first name of the fictional Dr Jekyll?

10. What is the first name of the fictional Mr Hyde?

11. What nationality is the filmaker Jafar Pahani?

12. How many squares are there on a snakes and ladders board?

13. Which UK city has the dialling code 0191?

14. What is LulzSec?

15. Who was the first US President to visit Moscow?

16. The largest obelisk in Europe, the Wellington Monument, is in which city?

17. What is the official motto of the USA?

18. Chet, zayin and vav are letters in which alphabet?

19. The average adult male's body contains approximately how much blood?
    a) 5l
    b) 10l
    c) 15l

20. Tocology is the science of what?
    a) childbirth
    b) old age
    c) knee injuries

Answers to Quiz 179: TV Detectives

1. Inspector Thomas Lynley
2. Pam Ferris
3. The Body Farm
4. Neil Dudgeon
5. Sharona
6. Hastings
7. Lewis
8. Jessica Fletcher (Murder She Wrote)
9. Jim Bergerac
10. Brenda Blethyn
11. Martin Shaw
12. Frank Haskins
13. Seattle
14. Taggart
15. Reagan
16. AFC Wimbledon
17. Ray Winstone
18. Amelia Bullmore
19. Minder
20. Newcastle

DIFFICULT

Quiz 181: US States

Identify the US states by their nickname:

1. Which US state is known as the Empire State?

2. Which US state is nicknamed the Bluegrass State?

3. Which US state is nicknamed the Centennial State?

4. Which US state is known as the Prairie State?

5. Which US state is nicknamed the Magnolia State?

6. Which US state is nicknamed the Peach State?

7. Which US state is nicknamed the Wolverine State?

8. Which US state is known as the Cornhusker State?

9. Which US state is known as the Pine Tree State?

10. Which US state is known as the Buckeye State?

11. Which US state is known as the Sooner State?

12. The nickname of the US state of Connecticut comes from which tree?

13. Which US state is nicknamed the Beaver State?

14. Which US state is known as the Beehive State?

15. Which US state is known as the Sunflower State?

16. Which US state is nicknamed the Cowboy State?

17. Which US state is known as the Buckeye State?

18. Which US state is known as the Old Line State?

19. What is the nickname of the US state of Pennsylvania?
    a) Keystone State
    b) Limestone State
    c) Sandstone State

20. What is the nickname of the US state of South Dakota?
    a) Coyote State
    b) Wolf State
    c) Prairie Dog State

Answers to Quiz 180: Pot Luck

1. Venus and Uranus
2. The Social Contract
3. Atlanta, USA
4. 4pm to 6pm
5. 20
6. Louth
7. Romania
8. Drop The Dead Donkey
9. Henry
10. Edward
11. Iranian
12. 100
13. Newcastle-upon-Tyne
14. A computer hacking activist group
15. Richard Nixon
16. Dublin
17. In God We Trust
18. Hebrew
19. 5l
20. Childbirth

DIFFICULT

Quiz 182: Pot Luck

1. Excluding the sun, what is the nearest star to earth?

2. What nationality was the philosopher Kierkegaard?

3. Which Aussie rock band was formerly known as the Farriss Brothers?

4. Ganymede was the Greek God of what?

5. Barbary Roan was the horse of which English king?

6. The candela is a unit used to measure what?

7. What distance is defined as the distance light travels in a vacuum in $\frac{1}{299792458}$ of a second?

8. King Harald V is the monarch of which European country?

9. Which director's films include Contagion, Solaris and The Good German?

10. Which legendary rocker released an album in 2012 called Wrecking Ball?

11. The Sage arts and music venue is in which English town?

12. Irish Prime Ministers Enda Kenny and Charles Haughey and reality TV judge Louis Walsh are from which Irish county?

13. How much time do MPs have to vote after the division bell is rung?

14. Which Scottish football club play their home games at Glebe Park?

15. In betting what odds are represented by the slang term double carpet?

16. To the nearest 50 miles, what is the driving distance from Land's End to John O'Groats?

17. England's Alistair Brownlee is a world champion in which sport?

18. What are the five cinque ports?

19. Oscar statues were made of what during World War II?
    a) Plaster
    b) Bakelite
    c) Copper

20. What is the shortest-titled song ever to reach number one in the UK?
    a) If
    b) As
    c) Is

Answers to Quiz 181: US States

1. New York	11. Oklahoma
2. Kentucky	12. Nutmeg
3. Colorado	13. Oregon
4. Illinois	14. Utah
5. Mississippi	15. Kansas
6. Georgia	16. Wyoming
7. Michigan	17. Ohio
8. Nebraska	18. Maryland
9. Maine	19. Keystone State
10. Ohio	20. Coyote State

DIFFICULT

Quiz 183: Opening Lines

Identify the books from the following opening lines:

1. Robert Langdon awoke slowly.

2. These two very old people are the father and mother of Mr Bucket.

3. Stately plum Buck Mulligan came from the stairhead, bearing a bowl of lather on which a mirror and a razor lay crossed.

4. The truth is, if old Major Dover hadn't dropped dead at Taunton races Jim would never have come to Thursgood's at all.

5. Ours is essentially a tragic age, so we refuse to take it tragically.

6. Mr and Mrs Dursley, of number 4 Privet Drive, were proud to say that they were perfectly normal, thank you very much.

7. We were somewhere around Barstow on the edge of the desert when the drugs began to take hold.

8. It was 7 minutes after midnight. The dog was lying on the grass in the middle of the lawn in front of Mrs Shears' house.

9. It was a queer, sultry summer, the summer they electrocuted the Rosenbergs, and I didn't know what I was doing in New York.

10. I wish Giovanni would kiss me.

11. Today, I'm five.

12. 'To be born again,' sang Gibreel Farishta tumbling from the heavens, 'first you have to die.'

13. Last night I dreamt I went to Manderley again.

14. This is my favorite book in all the world, though I have never read it.

15. You will rejoice to hear that no disaster has accompanied the commencement of an enterprise which you have regarded with such evil forebodings.

16. Robert Cohn was once middleweight boxing champion of Princeton.

17. As Gregor Samsa awoke one morning from uneasy dreams he found himself transformed in his bed into a gigantic insect.

18. In my younger and more vulnerable years my father gave me some advice that I've been turning over in my mind ever since.

19. 'What's it going to be then, eh?'

20. Who is John Galt?

Answers to Quiz 182: Pot Luck

1. Proxima centauri
2. Danish
3. INXS
4. Water
5. Richard II
6. Light intensity
7. A metre
8. Norway
9. Steven Soderbergh
10. Bruce Springsteen
11. Gateshead
12. Mayo
13. 8 minutes
14. Brechin City
15. 33/1
16. 814 miles
17. Triathlon
18. Sandwich, Dover, Hythe, Romney and Hastings
19. Plaster
20. If by Telly Savalas

DIFFICULT

Quiz 184: Pot Luck

1. Which planet has the longest day?

2. St Thomas Aquinas was born on which Mediterranean island?

3. The Rolling Stones took their name from a song by which blues legend?

4. A horse called Comanche was the only survivor from which battle?

5. Madison is the capital of which US state?

6. Who was governor of the Bahamas during World War Two?

7. At 226,612 miles, which country has the longest railway network in the world?

8. What is the sum of the internal angles in a pentagon?

9. In which city would you find Jorge Chavez Airport?

10. Queen Margerethe II is the head of which European state?

11. Discovered by William Ramsay, which chemical element takes its name from the Greek word for hidden?

12. Christiania is the former name of which European capital?

13. Prince William gained a 2:1 university degree in what subject?

14. What is the southernmost county in the Irish Republic?

15. What is the least densely populated country in the world?

16. Which Scottish football team is nicknamed the Gable Endies?

17. Which fictional character rode a horse called Shadowfax?

18. Which former World Heavyweight Boxing Champion later went on to lecture on Shakespeare at Yale University?

19. An epithalamium is a poem written specifically for what ceremony?
    a) baptism
    b) funeral
    c) wedding

20. What is the most common occupation of holders of the US Presidency?
    a) lawyer
    b) soldier
    c) teacher

Answers to Quiz 183: Opening Lines

1. The Da Vinci Code by Dan Brown
2. Charlie and the Chocolate Factory by Roald Dahl
3. Ulysses by James Joyce
4. Tinker, Tailor, Soldier, Spy by John Le Carré
5. Lady Chatterley's Lover by DH Lawrence
6. Harry Potter and the Philosopher's Stone by JK Rowling
7. Fear and Loathing in Las Vegas by Hunter S Thompson
8. The Curious Incident of the Dog in the Night-Time by Mark Haddon
9. The Bell Jar by Sylvia Plath
10. Eat, Pray, Love by Elizabeth Gilbert
11. Room by Emma Donoghue
12. The Satanic Verses by Salman Rushdie
13. Rebecca by Daphne du Maurier
14. The Princess Bride by William Goldman
15. Frankenstein by Mary Shelley
16. The Sun Also Rises by Ernest Hemingway
17. Metamorphosis by Franz Kafka
18. The Great Gatsby by F Scott Fitzgerald
19. A Clockwork Orange by Anthony Burgess
20. Atlas Shrugged by Ayn Rand

DIFFICULT

Quiz 185: Closing Lines

Identify the books from the following closing lines:

1. He turned out the light and went into Jem's room. He would be there all night, and he would be there when Jem waked up in the morning.

2. The old man was dreaming about the lions.

3. Very few castaways can claim to have survived so long at sea as Mr. Patel, and none in the company of an adult Bengal tiger.

4. He is coming, and I am here.

5. There was some open space between what he knew and what he tried to believe, but nothing could be done about it, and if you can't fix it, you've got to stand it.

6. A LAST NOTE FROM YOUR NARRATOR. I am haunted by humans.

7. And then, while the pretty brunette girl finished singing her verse, he buzzed me through like I was someone who mattered.

8. And presently, like a circling typhoon, the sounds of battle began to return.

9. He turned away to give them time to pull themselves together; and waited, allowing his eyes to rest on the trim cruiser in the distance.

10. She looked up and across the barn, and her lips came together and smiled mysteriously.

11. And then we continued blissfully into this small but perfect piece of our forever.

12. Because it is written that you reap what you sow, and the boy had sown good corn.

13. One bird said to Billy Pilgrim, 'Poo-tee-weet?'

14. An excellent year's progress.

15. Old father, old artificer, stand me now and ever in good stead.

16. 'God's in his heaven, all's right with the world,' whispered Anne softly.

17. Again and again I called out for Midori from the dead centre of this place that was no place.

18. But this is how Paris was in the early days when we were very poor and very happy.

19. The knife came down, missing him by inches, and he took off.

20. It was the devious-cruising Rachel, that in her retracing search after her missing children, only found another orphan.

Answers to Quiz 184: Pot Luck

1. Venus
2. Sicily
3. Muddy Waters
4. Little Bighorn
5. Wisconsin
6. The Duke of Windsor (formerly King Edward VIII)
7. USA
8. 540 degrees
9. Lima, Peru
10. Denmark
11. Krypton
12. Oslo
13. Geography
14. Cork
15. Mongolia
16. Montrose
17. Gandalf
18. Gene Tunney
19. Wedding
20. Lawyer

DIFFICULT

Quiz 186: Pot Luck

1. Which astronomer discovered Jupiter's moons Io, Europa, Ganymede and Callisto?

2. In 2012, Joyce Banda became the president of which African country?

3. Which English philosopher was known as Doctor Mirabilis?

4. Which indie rock group take their name from a member of Charles Manson's 'family'?

5. What is the smallest US state by area?

6. Which future monarch took part in the Wimbledon Tennis Championships in 1926?

7. What is the name of the luxurious train service that operates between Cape Town and Pretoria in South Africa?

8. Africa's first female elected head of state is from which country?

9. Dennis Franz played Detective Sipowicz in which American cop show?

10. In 2002, Prince Harry left Eton College with A Levels in which two subjects?

11. What was the first city in Asia to host the Commonwealth Games?

12. Which 18th century author wrote, 'All intellectual improvement arises from leisure'?

13. Which amendment of the the US Constitution gives the right to bear arms?

14. What was the homosexual slang common in London in the 1950s and 1960s?

15. Where would you find commonly find Decus Et Tutamen written?

16. Who wrote the Booker Prize-nominated novel Pigeon English?

17. Which country won the first football World Cup?

18. What is the largest country in the Balkans?

19. Priapus was the Greek god of what?
a) fertility b) fire c) flowers?

20. What was the maiden name of astronaut Buzz Aldrin's mother?
a) Sun b) Moon c) Star

Answers to Quiz 185: Closing Lines

1. To Kill a Mockingbird by Harper Lee
2. The Old Man and the Sea by Ernest Hemingway
3. Life of Pi by Yann Martell
4. The Time Traveller's Wife by Audrey Niffenegger
5. Brokeback Mountain by Annie Proulx
6. The Book Thief by Markus Zusak
7. The Devil Wears Prada by Lauren Weisberger
8. Vile Bodies by Evelyn Waugh
9. Lord of the Flies by William Golding
10. The Grapes of Wrath by John Steinbeck
11. Breaking Dawn by Stephanie Meyer
12. Alone In Berlin by Hans Fallada
13. Slaughterhouse Five by Kurt Vonnegut
14. Bridget Jones's Diary by Helen Fielding
15. A Portrait of the Artist as a Young Man by James Joyce
16. Anne of Green Gables by Lucy Maud Montgomery
17. Norwegian Wood by Haruki Murukami
18. A Moveable Feast by Ernest Hemingway
19. Catch-22 by Joseph Heller
20. Moby Dick by Herman Melville

DIFFICULT

Quiz 187: Crime and Punishment

1. In 1981, Mehmet Ali Agca attempted to assassinate which world leader?

2. Who is the central character in Dostoevsky's Crime and Punishment?

3. Who, in 2009, was convicted of the murder of actress Lana Clarkson?

4. Which Pakistani politician was murdered by Al Qaeda terrorists while leaving a political rally in Rawalpindi in 2007?

5. Who lived at Flat 23 Cranley Gardens, Muswell Hill?

6. How many American presidents have been assassinated?

7. On The Inside was the theme tune to which TV show?

8. Who was the last woman to be hanged in Britain?

9. Who murdered Bobby Kennedy in 1968?

10. In 1972, Delaware became the last state in America to outlaw what form of punishment?

11. Which three Pakistani cricketers were jailed in 2011 for their part in a spot fixing scandal?

12. Who, in 1981, survived an assassination attempt by John Hinckley?

13. In 1782 David Tyrie was the last man in England to suffer what punishment?

14. In the 18th century, Jane Wenham, Mary Hickes and her nine-year-old daughter Elizabeth were all found guilty of what?

15. In 1881, which US president was shot dead by Charles Guiteau?

16. The life of fraudster Frank William Abagnale Jr was turned into a film. What was it called?

17. What is a dactylogram more commonly known as?

18. Which criminal duo opened a club called The Double R?

19. High security hospital Broadmoor is in which English county?
    a) Devon
    b) Dorset
    c) Berkshire

20. Which of the following was a torture device from the Middle Ages?
    a) Scavenger's Daughter
    b) Scavenger's Mother
    c) Scavenger's Sister

Answers to Quiz 186: Pot Luck

1. Galileo
2. Malawi
3. Roger Bacon
4. Kasabian
5. Rhode Island
6. King George VI
7. Blue Train
8. Liberia
9. NYPD Blue
10. Art and Geography
11. Kuala Lumpur
12. Dr Samuel Johnson
13. Second
14. Polari
15. On a £1 coin
16. Stephen Kelman
17. Uruguay
18. Romania
19. Fertility
20. Moon

DIFFICULT

Quiz 188: Pot Luck

1. Manama is the capital city of which country?

2. The most notable work of which Roman philosopher was the hexameter poem De Rerum Natura?

3. Isabella Rossellini is the daughter of which actress?

4. The song Mad About the Boy was written by which English actor and playwright?

5. Which band took its name from a slang term for a German brothel?

6. Stretching some 5,777 miles, what is the longest continuous rail line in the world?

7. What was the former name of JFK Airport?

8. In 1901, Hubert Cecil Booth invented what labour-saving device?

9. Since ascending to the throne in 1952, the Queen has met every US president bar one. Which one?

10. Which leading jockey is nicknamed Choc?

11. Who wrote The Devil's Dictionary?

12. What is the first event on the second day of a decathlon?

13. Who was the first Secretary General of the United Nations?

14. Lateral epicondylitis is the medical name for which common condition?

15. Uroxicide is the killing of what relative?

16. Philematephobia is the fear of which amorous activity?

17. What are the two female-only sports in the Olympic Games?

18. Drek, nosh and oi are words originating from which language?

19. Which actress appeared in the most Carry On films?
    a) Joan Sims
    b) Barbara Windsor
    c) Hattie Jacques

20. Which singer's real name is William Broad?
    a) Billy Fury
    b) Billy Idol
    c) Billy Paul

Answers to Quiz 187: Crime and Punishment

1. Pope John Paul II
2. Rodion Romanoyich Raskalov
3. Phil Spector
4. Benazir Bhutto
5. Serial killer Dennis Nilsen
6. Four
7. Prisoner Cell Block H
8. Ruth Ellis
9. Sirhan Sirhan
10. Flogging
11. Salman Butt, Mohammad Amir, and Mohammad Asif
12. Ronald Reagan
13. He was hanged, drawn and quartered
14. Witchcraft
15. James A Garfield
16. Catch Me If You Can
17. A fingerprint
18. The Kray Twins
19. Berkshire
20. Scavenger's Daughter

DIFFICULT

Quiz 189: Britain

1. Which island in the Bristol Channel takes its name from the Old Norse word for puffin?

2. The National Library of Wales is in which town?

3. Which chalk cliff's name derives from the French 'beau chef' meaning beautiful headland?

4. Forward is the motto of which English city?

5. The National Railway Museum is in which city?

6. Which London tube station was the first to install escalators?

7. What is Scotland's fourth largest city?

8. What was the first garden city built in England?

9. The Roman road Fosse Way ran from Lincoln to which city?

10. The most easterly point of London is in which borough?

11. Which English county shares borders with Devon, Somerset, Wiltshire and Hampshire?

12. Which city in England is spelt using the fewest letters?

13. Which four English counties share a border with Wales?

14. Which two Scottish administrative areas have a border with England?

15. What is the county town of Rutland?

16. The Goose Fair is held every October in which English city?

17. The headquarters to the Open University are in which town?

18. Mull is part of which island group?

19. Walt Disney World is twinned with which English town?
    a) Oxford
    b) Reading
    c) Swindon

20. Which of the following places hasn't hosted Eurovision?
    a) Harrogate
    b) Manchester
    c) Brighton

Answers to Quiz 188: Pot Luck

1. Bahrain
2. Lucretius
3. Ingrid Bergman
4. Noel Coward
5. Joy Division
6. Trans-Siberian Express
7. Idlewild
8. Vacuum cleaner
9. Lyndon B Johnson
10. Robert Thornton
11. Ambrose Bierce
12. 110m hurdles
13. Trygve Lie
14. Tennis elbow
15. Wife
16. Kissing
17. Synchronised Swimming and Rhythmic Gymnastics
18. Yiddish
19. Joan Sims
20. Billy Idol

DIFFICULT

Quiz 190: Pot Luck

1. San Jose is the capital city of which country?

2. In Greek mythology, who was the daughter of Oedious and Jocasta?

3. The song Don't Rain On My Parade first appeared in which musical and film?

4. Which US state has the second smallest population?

5. Who wrote the Tom Thorne crime novels?

6. Which 15-year-old topped the charts in July 1998 with Because We Want To?

7. 'A lot can happen in the middle of nowhere' is the tagline to which Coen Brothers film?

8. Who is sixth in line to the British throne?

9. Former prime minister Gordon Brown is a fan of which football club?

10. Which flamboyant singer launched a youth foundation in 2012 called Born This Way?

11. The then Princess Elizabeth found out that she had become queen while on a visit to which country?

12. Which daily newspaper was founded by C Arthur Pearson in 1900?

13. Who directed the 2007 film Looking For Eric?

14. Nadsat is a fictional language used by teenagers in which novel?

15. Who was the last unmarried Prime Minister of Britain?

16. 'Who's there?' is the first line of which play by Shakespeare?

17. And Another Thing... by Eoin Colfer is the sequel to which classic sci-fi novel?

18. Which number one hit doesn't include the title in the lyrics but contains part of the title of the song that replaced it at number one?

19. Which cartoon character appeared first?
    a) Batman
    b) Superman
    c) Spiderman

20. In 1929, the blind Swedish scientist Gustaf Dalen invented what?
    a) microwave oven
    b) Aga
    c) electric hob cooker

Answers to Quiz 189: Britain

1. Lundy
2. Aberystwyth
3. Beachy Head
4. Birmingham
5. York
6. Earl's Court
7. Dundee
8. Letchworth
9. Exeter
10. Havering
11. Dorset
12. Ely
13. Cheshire, Shropshire, Herefordshire and Gloucestershire
14. Dumfries and Galloway and Borders
15. Oakham
16. Nottingham
17. Milton Keynes
18. Inner Hebrides
19. Swindon
20. Manchester

DIFFICULT

Quiz 191: British Politics

1. Which Liberal Democrat resigned as Chief Secretary to the Treasury, in 2010, after admitting claiming expenses to pay rent to his partner?

2. Who lives at 12 Downing Street?

3. Which comedian was David Cameron's childhood musical hero?

4. In 2011, Dr Alasdair McDonnell MP succeeded Mark Durkan as the leader of which party?

5. Former Prime Minister Harold Wilson supported which football club?

6. Who was described by Winston Churchill as 'a modest little man with a great deal to be modest about'?

7. Denis Healey likened being attacked by Geoffrey Howe to being 'savaged by a dead' what?

8. Which prime minister wrote the novels Sybil and Coningsby?

9. What connects Lord Hanningfield, David Chaytor, Lord Taylor of Warwick and Jim Devine?

10. Who was the prime minister at the start of the 20th century?

11. Which 20th-century Prime Minister was born in Canada, in office for only seven months and is buried in Westminster Abbey?

12. Who killed Spencer Perceval?

13. Following his retirement from politics, John Major became president of which cricket club?

14. Who is Britain's longest-serving Chancellor of the Exchequer?

15. Derry Irvine, Charles Falconer, Jack Straw and Kenneth Clarke have all held which office?

16. The slave trade was abolished under which British Prime Minister?

17. Jacqui Smith, Geoff Hoon, Nick Brown. What name comes next?

18. John Prescott was famously snapped playing croquet at which grace and favour house?

19. How old was William Pitt the Younger when he took the office of Prime Minister?
a) 24 b) 30 c) 36

20. What is the name of the cat that lives at 10 Downing St?
a) Barry b) Harry c) Larry

Answers to Quiz 190: Pot Luck

1. Costa Rica
2. Antigone
3. Funny Girl
4. Vermont
5. Mark Billingham
6. Billie Piper
7. Fargo
8. Princess Eugenie
9. Raith Rovers
10. Lady Gaga
11. Kenya
12. Daily Express
13. Ken Loach
14. A Clockwork Orange
15. Ted Heath
16. Hamlet
17. The Hitchhiker's Guide To The Galaxy
18. Bohemian Rhapsody (followed by Mamma Mia)
19. Superman (in 1938)
20. Aga

DIFFICULT

Quiz 192: Pot Luck

1. Dili is the capital city of which Asian country?

2. In Greek mythology, who is the son of King Laius and Queen Jocasta?

3. Which singer had a hit with The Laughing Gnome?

4. Which three US states are officially known as commonwealths?

5. Which British monarch was known as the Sailor King?

6. Which Aussie rockers have had 19 UK top 40 hits but have never troubled the top 10?

7. Which poet wrote Sailing To Byzantium and The Lake Isle of Innisfree?

8. In Italy, which Disney character is known as Topolino?

9. What is the only Football League club from Somerset?

10. Charles Dickens was born in which town?

11. What are the two official languages of Macau?

12. Which English poet's works included Ode To A Nightingale and To Autumn?

13. Goscinny and Uderzo were the creators of which set of comic-strip books?

14. Scarlett is the official sequel to which 1930s novel?

15. Vince Clarke had top five hits with which four acts?

16. Who sent a Native American to refuse his Best Actor Oscar in 1972?

17. Who resigned as Foreign Secretary in 1982 after the invasion of the Falkland Islands?

18. What film 'Does for rock and roll what the Sound of Music did for hills'?

19. In the 2004 film Napoleon Dynamite, people are urged to vote for
    a) Pedro
    b) Javier
    c) Luis

20. In what year was capital punishment permanently abolished in the UK?
    a) 1959
    b) 1969
    c) 1979

Answers to Quiz 191: British Politics

1. David Laws
2. The government Chief Whip
3. Benny Hill
4. The SDLP
5. Huddersfield Town
6. Clement Attlee
7. Sheep
8. Benjamin Disraeli
9. They were all jailed for expenses fraud
10. Marquis of Salisbury
11. Andrew Bonar Law
12. John Bellingham
13. Surrey
14. Gordon Brown
15. Lord Chancellor
16. William Wyndham Grenville
17. Patrick McLoughlin (Government chief whips)
18. Dorneywood
19. 24
20. Larry

DIFFICULT

Quiz 193: Natural World part 1

1. What era came between the priscoan and proterozoic?

2. French physicist Henri Becquerel discovered what?

3. What is the oldest known mineral on earth?

4. To the nearest thousand, what is the circumference of the earth at the equator in miles?

5. What is the most common mineral found in the earth's crust?

6. Measuring some 383m tall, the biggest sand dunes in the world are found in which African country?

7. Plants of the Aizoaceae family resemble what?

8. Pantanal, the world's largest area of wetlands is largely in which country?

9. Which area of grassland translates into English as 'endless plains'?

10. In which African country would you find the White Desert?

11. Jostedalsbreen, the largest glacier in continental Europe, is in which country?

12. What is measured in Sverdrup?

13. Lake Baikal, the deepest on earth, is in which country?

14. What is dendrochronology?

15. In what country is the volcano Pinatubo?

16. Sagarmatha and Chomolungma are alternative names for which mountain?

17. Found in Yellowstone National Park, what is Old Faithful?

18. Norwegian Vilhelm Bjerknes was a pioneer in in what field?

19. On average, what percentage of sea water is made up of salt?
    a) 3.5%
    b) 5.5%
    c) 7.5%

20. Where on earth would you find Black Smokers?
    a) on a volcano
    b) at the bottom of the ocean
    c) in a desert

Answers to Quiz 192: Pot Luck

1. East Timor
2. Oedipus
3. David Bowie
4. Massachusetts, Virginia and Kentucky
5. William IV
6. AC/DC
7. WB Yeats
8. Mickey Mouse
9. Yeovil Town
10. Portsmouth
11. Chinese and Portuguese
12. John Keats
13. Asterix
14. Gone With The Wind
15. The Assembly, Depeche Mode, Yazoo and Erasure
16. Marlon Brando
17. Lord Carrington
18. This Is Spinal Tap
19. Pedro
20. 1969

DIFFICULT

Quiz 194: Pot Luck

1. What Are We Gonna Get 'Er Indoors was a hit for which TV duo?

2. What are the six states that make up New England?

3. Who was the first British monarch to live at Buckingham Palace?

4. The Duchess of Kent Challenge Cup is awarded to the winners of which event at Wimbledon?

5. The fictional ship HMS Compass Rose appeared in which classic war film?

6. The Giant's Causeway is in which Irish county?

7. Who wrote Sinead O'Connor's number one hit Nothing Compares 2 U?

8. A utopian socialist settlement called New Australia was established in 1893 in which South American country?

9. Which comic actor wrote the novels Shopgirl and The Pleasure of My Company?

10. The films Donnie Darko, Sexy Beast and Harvey all feature which animal?

11. Serial killer Patrick Bateman appears in which novel-turned film?

12. Yowie is a mythical creature said to live in which country?

13. Who won the 2012 BDO World Darts Championship in Frimley Green?

14. What is a shtreimel?

15. In what year was the first Apple iPod released?

16. The RBSA Gallery is in which English city?

17. In TV drama New Tricks, the retired policemen work for UCOS but what does UCOS stand for?

18. Science and Faith was a bestselling album by which Irish rock band?

19. How many strings does a harp have?
    a) 28
    b) 38
    c) 48

20. The Polish currency the zloty is divided into 100 what?
    a) groszy
    b) bani
    c) stotinki

Answers to Quiz 193: Natural World part 1

1. Archean
2. Radioactivity
3. Zircon
4. 24,901
5. Quartz
6. Namibia
7. Pebbles or stones
8. Brazil
9. Serengeti
10. Egypt
11. Norway
12. Ocean currents
13. Russia
14. A method of dating based on the analysis of patterns of tree rings
15. Philippines
16. Mount Everest
17. A geyser
18. Meteorology
19. 3.5%
20. At the bottom of the ocean

DIFFICULT

Quiz 195: Awards and Prizes

1. The Nobel Prize is awarded in which six fields?

2. Who comes next in this list? Aravind Adaga, Hilary Mantel, Howard Jacobson...

3. Who, in 1934, became the first Briton to win an Oscar for his role in Private Life of Henry VIII?

4. Rachel Johnson, Jonathan Littell and Rowan Somerville have all won which unwanted literary award?

5. The Gordon Bennett Cup is contested by users of what form of transport?

6. Barbara Windsor won the first in 1976. Carol Vorderman and Anton du Beke won it in 2011. What did they win?

7. What organisation won the Nobel Peace Prize in 1917, 1944 and 1963?

8. The Golden Lion is the top prize at which film festival?

9. The members of which organisation vote for the Golden Globe awards?

10. With the exception of the Peace Prize, the Nobel Prize award ceremony takes place in which city?

11. The actresses who played Janine Butcher, Sadie King and Tracy Barlow have all won which category in the Inside Soap Awards?

12. Who won the BBC Sports Personality of the Year Award 35 years after her mother won it?

13. The Lance Todd Trophy is awarded to the man of the match in which sporting event?

14. In 1984, which alliterative artist won the inaugural Turner Prize?

15. 1999's Race for the Prize was the first top 40 hit for which group, led by Wayne Coyne?

16. Harold Wilson, David Bryant, Rod Hull and Stephen Fry have all won what award?

17. The Eisner Awards are given in which field of literature?

18. Which literary award is sometimes known as the Bookie prize?

19. Who are eligible to win a Dickin Medal?
    a) animals b) politicians c) women

20. The Pritzker Prize is awarded in which field
    a) architecture b) literature c) science

Answers to Quiz 194: Pot Luck

1. Dennis Waterman and George Cole
2. Connecticut, Maine, Massachusetts, New Hampshire, Rhode Island and Vermont
3. Queen Victoria
4. Ladies' Doubles Championship
5. The Cruel Sea
6. Antrim
7. Prince
8. Paraguay
9. Steve Martin
10. Rabbits
11. American Psycho
12. Australia
13. Christian Kist
14. A hat worn by Orthodox Jews
15. 2001
16. Birmingham
17. Unsolved Crime and Open Case Squad
18. The Script
19. 48
20. Groszy

Quiz 196: Pot Luck

1. Which English rugby player's award-winning autobiography was called Beware of the Dog?

2. What birthday did the BBC World Service celebrate in 2012?

3. The Queen is the Head of State in how many countries?

4. Caprica was the prequel to which science fiction series?

5. Which Hollywood star's first name comes from the Hawaiian for 'cool breeze over the mountains'?

6. What is the second largest city in the Irish Republic?

7. Roderick Jaynes is a pseudonym of which film-making brothers?

8. Which writer created the character Adrian Mole?

9. On display in Dublin, what book is also known as the Book of Columba?

10. 'Even a hitman deserves a second shot' is the tag line to which film starring John Cusack?

11. Which Scottish singer won the second, and last series of Pop Idol?

12. Which Hollywood icon died during the shooting of Something's Got To Give?

13. What is the sixth largest country in the world by area?

14. Which comedian wrote the book How I Escaped My Certain Fate?

15. What nautically inspired celebration takes place annually on 19th September?

16. The oldest university in the world is in which Italian city?

17. Which group asked fans to pay what they liked for their 2007 album Rainbows?

18. The volcano Paricutin is in which country?

19. Iorwerth is the Welsh equivalent of which name?

20. Which Monty Python film came first?
    a) The Meaning of Life
    b) The Life of Brian
    c) The Holy Grail

21. Complete the title of the 2005 book: Stuart: A Life...?
    a) Backwards
    b) Forwards
    c) Sideways

Answers to Quiz 195: Awards and Prizes

1. Peace, Literature, Medicine, Physics, Chemistry, Economics
2. Julian Barnes (Booker Prize winners)
3. Charles Laughton
4. The Bad Sex In Fiction Award
5. Hot Air Balloon
6. Rear of the Year
7. The Red Cross
8. The Venice Film Festival
9. Hollywood Foreign Press Association
10. Stockholm
11. Best Bitch
12. Zara Phillips
13. Rugby league Challenge Cup Final
14. Malcolm Morley
15. The Flaming Lips
16. Pipe Smoker of the Year
17. Comic books
18. William Hill Sports Book of the Year
19. Animals
20. Architecture

DIFFICULT

Quiz 197: Geography part 2

1. What is the second largest desert in the world?

2. What is the highest waterfall in the world?

3. Which country has the longest land border in the world?

4. What is the only South American country that has English as an official language?

5. Which Shipping Forecast Area was formerly known as Finisterre?

6. The Monte Desert is in which country?

7. Sudeley Castle is in which English county?

8. Yellowstone National Park lies in which three American states?

9. Regina is the capital city of which Canadian Province?

10. Bechuanaland was the former name of which African country?

11. What is the only country in the Pacific ruled by a monarchy?

12. Which city did the Romans call Mediolanum?

13. What is the least densely populated country in Europe?

14. Which geographical feature takes its name from the Latin word for abandoned?

15. What is the smallest independent nation in South America?

16. Which river forms the border between the US states of Maryland and Washington DC?

17. What country shares borders with more countries than any other?

18. Which West African country was founded by freed American slaves?

19. The T-Bana railways serves which European capital city?
    a) Copenhagen
    b) Oslo
    c) Stockholm

20. What is the capital of the US State of Pennsylvania?
    a) Frankfort
    b) Harrisburg
    c) Pierre

Answers to Quiz 196: Pot Luck

1. Brian Moore
2. 80th
3. 16
4. Battlestar Galactica
5. Keanu Reeves
6. Cork
7. The Coen Brothers
8. Sue Townsend
9. The Book of Kells
10. Grosse Point Blank
11. Michelle McManus
12. Marilyn Monroe
13. Australia
14. Stewart Lee
15. International Talk Like a Pirate Day
16. Bologna
17. Radiohead
18. Mexico
19. Edward
20. The Holy Grail
21. Backwards

DIFFICULT

Quiz 198: Pot Luck

1. Will Somers was the Court Jester of which English monarch?

2. Which author's novels include What A Carve Up and The Rotters' Club?

3. What is the largest of the Greek islands?

4. In Midsomer Murders, how are Tom and John Barnaby related?

5. Art collector Charles Saatchi was born in which city?

6. Britt Reid is the real name of which comic book superhero?

7. What newspaper is mentioned in The Beatles song Paperback Writer?

8. The extremely dangerous funnel web spider is native to which country?

9. A statue of which silent movie star can be seen in London's Leicester Square?

10. Hangul is the name of the alphabet used in which language?

11. What was The Beatles' last number one hit single?

12. How many players are in a Gaelic football team?

13. Which comedy duo reached number two in the UK singles chart in December 1975 with Trail of the Lonesome Pine?

14. Who was the first British prime minister to serve under Queen Elizabeth II?

15. Castlebar is the biggest town in which Irish county?

16. What was the name of the American woman cleared of the murder of flatmate Meredith Kercher?

17. Detective drama Monk is set in which American city?

18. The soundtrack to which film holds the record for the most weeks at the top of the UK album chart?

19. What metal gave David Guetta a 2012 Top 10 hit?
    a) Gold
    b) Silver
    c) Titanium

20. Oswald Cobblepot is the real name of which cartoon villain?
    a) The Joker
    b) The Penguin
    c) The Riddler

Answers to Quiz 197: Geography part 2

1. The Arabian Desert
2. Angel Falls
3. China
4. Guyana
5. FitzRoy
6. Argentina
7. Gloucestershire
8. Wyoming, Montana and Idaho
9. Saskatchewan
10. Botswana
11. Tonga
12. Milan
13. Iceland
14. Desert
15. Suriname
16. Potomac
17. Russia
18. Liberia
19. Stockholm
20. Harrisburg

DIFFICULT

Quiz 199: Natural World part 2

1. The volcano Mount Tarawera is in which country?

2. What mineral is the main source of aluminium?

3. Lambert-Fisher, Novaya Zemlya and Nimrod-Lennox-King are examples of which natural phenomenon?

4. An aiulurophile is a lover of what type of animal?

5. In which country would you find the Thal desert?

6. Solanine is a poison found in which common food?

7. What poisonous plant is also known as belladonna?

8. The Maine Coon is a breed of what type of animal?

9. The Lion's mane is the largest variety of which fish?

10. What are blusher, morel and Satan's boletus?

11. An ostentation is a collective noun given to a group of what animal?

12. What is the main shaft of a feather called?

13. The sea wasp is another name for which dangerous sea creature?

14. The sea parrot is another name for which animal?

15. What name is given to a wind at force 11 on the Beaufort Scale?

16. A coleopterist is interested in what type of creatures?

17. What creature has the biggest eyes in the animal kingdom?

18. What is the only bird that can fly backwards?

Answers – page 405

19. In the geolithic timescale what came after the Triassic period?
    a) Jurassic
    b) Cretaceous
    c) Palaeocene

20. Vredefort, Chicxulub and Manicougan are examples of what?
    a) lakes
    b) meteorite craters
    c) islands

Answers to Quiz 198: Pot Luck

1. Henry VIII
2. Jonathan Coe
3. Crete
4. They're cousins
5. Baghdad
6. The Green Hornet
7. Daily Mail
8. Australia
9. Charlie Chaplin
10. Korean
11. The Ballad of John and Yoko
12. 15
13. Laurel and Hardy
14. Winston Churchill
15. Mayo
16. Amanda Knox
17. San Francisco
18. South Pacific
19. Titanium
20. The Penguin

DIFFICULT

Quiz 200: Pot Luck

1. Which singer had a backing band called The Famous Flames?

2. The world's largest bull ring is in which city?

3. Which Irish-born poet wrote mystery stories under the pseudonym Nicholas Blake?

4. Food writer Jay Rayner, cricketer Andrew Flintoff and Archbishop of Canterbury Rowan Williams have all won which award?

5. Which poet was born in St Louis, USA in 1888?

6. Proesch and Passmore are the surnames of which artistic duo?

7. Malaga is in which autonomous region of Spain?

8. John Ravenscroft was the real name of which broadcaster?

9. Which crooner represented the UK in the 2012 Eurovision Song Contest?

10. The Four Year Plan was a film documentary about which football club?

11. In which French city will you find the house of artist Henri Matisse and the Musee Marc Chagall?

12. In 1999, which Scotsman became the Secretary General of NATO?

13. Monte Cervino is the Italian name for which Alpine mountain?

14. Gus Hansen, Daniel Negreanu and Phil Ivey are top professionals in which game?

15. Which two English football teams take part in the A420 derby?

16. According to the nursery rhyme, on what day did Solomon Grundy take ill?

17. Which English painter's last words were reportedly 'The sun is God'?

18. The words admiral and alcove derive from which language?

19. David Lloyd George was born in which British city?
    a) Cardiff
    b) Glasgow
    c) Manchester

20. The highest honour in Denmark is the Order of the
    a) Elephant
    b) Bear
    c) Eagle

Answers to Quiz 199: Natural World part 2

1. New Zealand
2. Bauxite
3. Glacier
4. Cat
5. Pakistan
6. Potato
7. Deadly nightshade
8. Cat
9. Jellyfish
10. Types of fungi
11. Peacock
12. Rachis
13. Box jellyfish
14. Puffin
15. Violent Storm
16. Beetles
17. Giant squid
18. Hummingbird
19. Jurassic
20. Meteorite craters

DIFFICULT

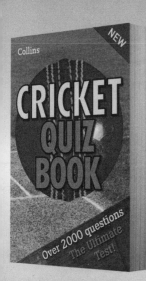  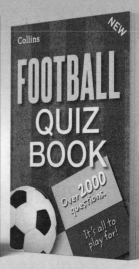